Paradoxes of Prosperity

About TEXERE

TEXERE seeks to become the most progressive and authoritative voice in business publishing by cultivating and enchancing ideas that will illuminate the global business landscape. Our name defines the spirit of our vision: TEXERE is the ancient Latin verb "to weave." In an increasingly global business community, we seek to create an intersection where authors and readers can share the best thinking and the latest ideas. We want to leverage the expertise and insights of leading thinkers by weaving them with TEXERE's capability to deliver them to the marketplace.

To learn more and become a part of our community visit us at:

www.etexere.com

and

www.etexere.co.uk

About the Typeface

This book was set in 11.25/15 Electra LH Regular

Paradoxes

of

Prosperity

WHY THE NEW CAPITALISM
BENEFITS ALL

DIANE COYLE

TEXERE

NEW YORK • LONDON

Published by
TEXERE
55 East 52nd Street
New York, NY 10055
Tel: 212.317.5106
Fax: 212.317.5178
www.etexere.com

In the UK:
TEXERE Publishing Ltd.
71-77 Leadenhall Street
London, EC3A 3DE
Tel: 20 7204 3644
Fax: 20 7208 6701
www.etexere.co.uk

This publication is designed to provide accurate and authoritative information in regard to the subject manner covered. It is sold with the understanding that the publisher is not engaged in rendering legal, accounting, or other professional services. If legal advice or other expert assistance is required, the services of a competent professional person should be sought.

Designed by Elliott Beard

Library of Congress Cataloging-in-Publication Data has been applied for.

ISBN 1-58799-082-2

Printed on acid-free paper.

Printed in the United States of America

10 9 8 7 6 5 4 3 2 1

Contents

Acknowledgments

There could scarcely be more interesting times in which to be an author writing about the global economy and technology. But writing a book is fueled not only by the material but also by a strong web of love and support—above all from Rory, Adam, and Rufus.

I am especially grateful to my colleagues at the Centre for Economic Performance at the London School of Economics, notably Richard Freeman, Richard Layard, Danny Quah and Tony Venables, and my former colleagues at *The Independent*, including Ian Birrell, Matt Hoffman, David Lister, Hamish McRae, Philip Thornton, and Jeremy Warner. Ed Mayo and Andrew Simms at the New Economics Foundation have also had a tremendous influence on my thinking.

Many other people have contributed their time generously to discuss ideas, provide information and read drafts, and I must thank Charles Bean, Steven Bell, Jagdish Bhagwhati, Michael Blastland, Martin Brookes, Alison Cottrell, Nick Crafts, Ed Glaeser, Mervyn King, John Llewellyn, Bethan and Richard Marshall, Richard Portes, Julia Rowntree, Peter Sinclair, Raj Thamotheram, Romesh Vaitilingam, Stephen Yeo, and a number of officials who might not welcome being singled out in print, but know who they are.

Finally, the book would not have happened without the faith of my agent, Sara Menguc, my publisher, Myles Thompson, and the editing skills of Jena Pincott. The responsibility for any errors and omissions is mine.

Introduction

You say you want a revolution
Well you know
We all want to change the world.

JOHN LENNON/PAUL MCCARTNEY

I have ever been of the opinion that revolutions
are not to be evaded.

BENJAMIN DISRAELI

Revolutionary technologies have revolutionary consequences. That is precisely why the wave of new technologies, the Internet, and genomics that developed commercially from the early 1990s triggered the hope that a New Economy was emerging, one offering the prospect of improved productivity, faster growth, and full employment. However, the dream of an economic nirvana has obscured the fact that such fundamental economic change would go hand in hand with political upheaval, as it always has in the past. The political consequences of a new technological framework, which is undermining existing power bases just as surely as the original Industrial Revolution undermined the traditional landed aristocracy, will nevertheless become impossible to ignore. There's no halting this revolution midway.

The premise that there is something fundamentally new about the economy is still widely challenged, especially now that it has become clear that the old-fashioned business cycle is not dead after all; so the political consequences have gone pretty much unnoticed. Yet there are already plenty of signs of tension and transformation.

Capitalism and the existing political and corporate structures are under attack. For the first time in nearly forty years young people and workers have been taking part in mass street protests against capitalism, in the anti-globalization riots in Seattle, Washington, Melbourne, and Prague. Local people in countries such as India, Nigeria, and Turkey have slowed or halted projects planned by multinational companies in some of the most effective efforts so far to force executives and governments to consult those most affected by new dams or oil pipelines. Broken windows and clouds of tear gas mean it is impossible to miss the sense that there is some public appetite for change. Less dramatically, teenage computer programmers running Napster have undermined the stranglehold a multimillion-dollar industry has had over the distribution of music. In order to protect online commerce, businesses are able to use methods of encryption that even a decade ago would have been kept secret by government agencies and the military. Voters in Western democracies are quietly turning their backs on conventional party politics, and when they vote are doing so in ways that overturn conventional wisdom about what wins elections.

The desire for a changed political order is partly a result of the late 1990s boom, as affluence brings people the confidence to protest. Thus the first "paradox of prosperity": our very prosperity seems to have brought great anxiety and insecurity with it, and the sense of unease will only increase if there is a short-term economic downturn. These sentiments mean that the good news about the new technologies and the consequent economic change is too often overlooked. And it is good news, big time. Great leaps forward in technology do translate into faster growth and big improvements in human well-being; who would really want to turn the clock back and live in 1950 or 1900? There is such a thing as economic progress, and most people's lives are getting better, not worse. The time has come to rediscover the unfashionable idea of progress.

The folly of many of the demonstrators and activists today is that they believe in the need for worldwide economic change but reject capitalism as the engine for doing so. Unfortunately, many of the critics of modern capitalism are failing to grab a once-in-a-lifetime opportunity to bring about radical political change, frittering away the chance to build a fairer and better society. They think of the underlying economic transformation now taking place as more of the same, instead of understanding its revolutionary nature. By insisting that the New Capitalism is business as usual except more so — simply more free market, more big business, the same old capitalism gone turbo or manic — they back themselves into conclusions that may well be the exact opposite of the truth and fall victim to their own myths.

For example, critics might claim that inequality in America or Britain is as bad now as it was in the late nineteenth century. This is formally true on some measures of the relative gap between rich and poor. But it is also profoundly false, because in no deprived pockets of the Western democracies are living standards as bad as they were in the 1890s. Or they conclude that growth is bad for the vast majority of citizens, that globalization is harming the poor, and that genetic technology will damage people; in fact, economic growth is what reduces mortality rates and improves health, engagement in the global economy is essential for development, and biotechnology holds out the first genuine hope for the treatment and cure of a number of terrible diseases.

The myths embraced by those critical of the current economic and political order in part reflect a long-standing fear of technological change. It's a familiar scene from a grainy old black-and-white movie seen one wet Sunday afternoon: thunder, lightning, torrential rain, the wrath of all the elements. A glimpse of a vile half-human creature, which turns briefly with a chilling leer at its pursuers before vanishing into the turbulent night. Ever since Mary Shelley created the obsessed scientist Victor Frankenstein and his ghastly, tragic monster in 1818, we have felt uneasy about the power of technology and our potential to create inhuman intelligence. Frankenstein confesses: "It was already one in the morning; the rain pattered dismally against the panes, and my candle was nearly burnt out, when, by the glimmer of the half extinguished light, I saw the dull yellow eye of the creature open. . . . Now that I had finished, the beauty of my dream vanished, and breathless horror and disgust filled my heart." The literary tradition of techno-phobia has continued unbroken, even amongst enthusiasts. Isaac Asimov devised rules that forbade the construction of robots that might harm their creators. Arthur C. Clarke created HAL, the monstrous plotting computer, in his novel *2001*. Robocop gets out of hand. And so on. Such creations crystallize a deep-seated fear that technology teeters on the edge of our control.

The gothic tradition, and its cyberpunk incarnation, is a far cry from the alternative, breathlessly optimistic approach to today's new technologies. Whether it's sequencing the human genome, the latest teeny brushed-silver MP3 player or digital camera, or the remote future prospects for teleportation, technophiles are relentlessly chirpy abut the possibilities. And it is this cheery approach that has characterized much comment on the New Capitalism. But the monsters are creeping back out of the shadows. The "tech wreck" on the world's stock markets when share prices in high-tech companies started plummeting from their unprecedented peaks in the spring of 2000, and the subsequent downturn in the economic cycle after a decade-long American boom that had come to feel like normality, would be enough in themselves to raise some doubts about any shiny new high-tech future. But these events have also opened the way to posing deeper questions about the underlying economic trends, just as the 1997–98 financial market crisis gave rise to the anti-globalization protest movement.

When the Internet boom was in full swing, it was hard to dent the dominant mood of euphoria. Frequent warnings about stock market bubbles being bound to burst were swamped by the sheer enthusiasm of investors, of new entrepreneurs, of media commentators and market pundits. For a full twelve months the sun shone perpetually in America, the Millennium Bug stayed away from the New Year 2000 celebrations, share prices rose and rose, sparkling productivity gains were chalked up, jobs were plentiful, and consumers indulged in an orgy of spending.

At the same time, though, a growing number of people started feeling deep unease with the unprecedented prosperity, a sentiment voiced by many commentators. There are dozens of recent books critical of modern capitalism. Richard Sennett wrote: "Our affluence in its present form is becoming an intolerable weight to those who supposedly enjoy it." Marshall Berman argued there was an abundance of critical ideas and added: "Maybe only violent economic collapse will shake Americans out of their narcolepsy. This would put the left in the creepy position (where it has been before) of longing for horrible catastrophe. On the other hand, it may be, as it was forty years ago, that it will create imaginative space where people can begin to think about a better life than this."

He wrote that comment when Internet fever was at its height, the long U.S. economic boom just starting to lose steam. The uneasy transition to more awkward and anxious times does not mean, however, that the New Economy was a brief collective hallucination. This book argues that the economy is indeed changing in a fundamental way, and that society and politics are changing with it. It will, beyond the downs and ups of the business cycle, lay the foundations for huge increases in our future prosperity and transformations of our way of life, like earlier waves of technology-based growth. Just as earlier generations saw electric light, antibiotics, the automobile bring unimaginable changes to their way of life, we and our children will live through an extraordinary transformation.

Building on those basic foundations will depend on understanding the links between technology, economy, and society; on using them to overturn vested interests in order to redistribute power and wealth; and on recognizing the radical potential today's new technologies contain. For they depend on a resource we are all blessed with: humanity. Economic success in the future will depend not on scarce land, nor on capital, which is now if anything in overabundant supply, but instead on intelligence, creativity, empathy, and other characteristics economists describe as "human capital." What sort of distribution of power this will actually deliver in the societies of tomorrow is still open to question. Industrial revolutions are not revolutionary by chance, but rather only because innovations are put to revolutionary uses, and these are as much political and social as economic.

Left-wing intellectuals are mostly still very hostile to the notion that free-market capitalism can be good. Many prefer the social market variety that can be found in Germany or Japan to the untrammeled English and American version. But as Ronald Dore noted in his book exploring the contrasts between the two versions, the latter is certainly driving out the former, the scope of markets is expanding (unfortunately, in his view) at the expense of institutions like the works council or the business combine. He adds, regretfully: "And outcomes are not just in the hands of elite decision makers. People are voting with their feet." This is hardly surprising. The Japanese economy has remained stagnant for a full decade. Germany has an unemployment rate that had barely fallen below double digits after three years of growth. Although it is a commonplace amongst some critics of "turbo-capitalism" that countries like Japan and Germany have a more successful industrial policy toward their traditional manufacturing industries, both the UK and the United States had slightly expanded the number of jobs in manufacturing between 1992 and 1999 despite increasing imports of goods from overseas—whereas Japan and the social market economies in Continental Europe lost 15–20 percent of their workforce in manufacturing.

Conventional rhetoric cannot hide such dismal realities. Nobody in their right mind would claim any country has yet built the New Jerusalem, but certainly the countries that offer the most extreme examples of bureaucratic management of the economy are in trouble, and their governments and voters know it. Since the dusk of the Cold War and the dawn of the Internet, there has been only one game in town.

It's New, But Is It True?

But to begin at the beginning, the first question that must be addressed is whether the formerly overhyped and currently underplayed New Economy really exists. The vagueness of the term doesn't help. I take the New Economy to mean a lot more than the stock market bubble and the "new paradigm" whereby shares in high-tech companies were believed, for a while anyway, to justify valuations vastly in excess of past levels. This is a contrast to some authors who have concentrated on the stock market phenomenon and, not surprisingly, tend to be skeptics about whether anything fundamental in the world has changed. The lesson of past investment booms is that unusually high profits, which might justify valuations higher than previously experienced, almost always get competed away. The great beauty of competitive markets is that consumers are the ultimate beneficiary of innovation and growth. The share of national output going to profits, and hence company shareholders, has been relatively stable over long periods.

Instead of concentrating on the high-tech bubble, the first chapter of this book looks in detail at the empirical research on patterns of growth and how recent developments compare with very long-term trends. In a nutshell, there is convincing evidence that the long American boom marked a genuine departure from the dismal growth and productivity performance that characterized the mid-1970s to mid-1990s. In the sense that potential output could grow faster than it had in the recent past, the U.S. economy had returned to an earlier golden age. However sharp the current downturn proves to be, the long boom will remain exceptional. And if this economic slowdown is less severe than past ones, despite the possibility of tumult in financial markets, that will be exceptional too. Outside the United States, there is as yet little evidence of a departure from past patterns in the other developed economies. The American experience has been exceptional, although there is no reason to believe that exceptionalism is inevitable.

The reason for that is spelled out in the second chapter, which looks at the possible causes of the American boom in the "general purpose" nature of technologies like the microprocessor and in the wave of new innovations aside from computers and the Internet. The main impact of this great wave is to make the economy increasingly weightless. As my previous book, *The Weightless World*, showed, the creation of value in modern economies depends on the immaterial qualities of physical goods, such as design, creativity, and marketing, and on the quality of service. While we still want more physical things, we do not value them for the metal or plastic but for weightless characteristics that are embodied in the stuff.

Making the adjustment from a heavy industrial age economy to a weightless information age one requires a lot more than the invention of some new technologies. These have to be implemented by investment in new equipment, the reorganization of companies and work, and complementary investment in new infrastructure, training, legal frameworks, and so on. In short, it is misleading to think of general-purpose technologies as new gizmos. Rather, they are an entire system. The electrification of the economy involved investment in power stations and power lines, new transmission mechanisms in the factories and in turn new factories, electric lightbulbs and appliances, new technical skills in the workforce, including universal basic literacy, and so on. The economic potential of the internal combustion engine was not realized until there was a road network and logistical system.

It is in fact extremely easy to see why a technology that obviously has very wide applications does not make any apparent difference to economic growth for a very long time. It might even impose large transitional costs before it starts contributing to the economy. The so-called "productivity paradox," summed up by Robert Solow as "You can see evidence of the computer revolution everywhere apart from the productivity figures," is relatively easily explained. A growing body of economic research focuses on the adjustments being made by individual companies in order to exploit computer and communications technologies. Outside the United States, though, little of the needed complementary investment is yet in place.

The absence of any clear evidence of a changed economy elsewhere makes interpretation of globalization and the New Capitalism seem a question of passing judgment on the American model. Although this will not last, it is a complication. For fear and loathing of the American model is a habit clouding many radicals' judgment. If it is happening in the United States and boosting corporate profits, it must be bad, is the reflex. Even without any real alternatives, since the collapse of Communism in 1989, the long-standing suspicion of capitalism remains. Surely, surely it must carry the seeds of its own destruction?

There are certainly internal contradictions. The middle section of this book looks at a number of paradoxes in the changes now taking place. The paradoxes help explain why well-meaning people are getting into a muddle about what it will take to make the world a better place. For the New Economy contains seeds that could germinate into a fairer and more prosperous society. It will do so by making it possible to usurp established elites, to by-pass corrupt or simply incompetent governments, and to take advantage of new opportunities. Anti-globalization campaigners fail completely to understand the radical possibilities of capitalism. Yet there is no better time to exploit them for the benefit of this world's have-nots than now, a time when capitalism has triumphed. This is the best of times to ensure it delivers what it promises. The most basic promise is that high technology makes people more, not less, important. In an age of increasingly intelligent machines it is human skills that are in short supply. Moreover, the specifics of history and place matter more than ever in the modern global economy, how we got here and where here is. The high-tech economy is a high-trust economy. It is based on the exchange of ideas, on reputations, on personal qualities. For markets do not exist in a vacuum, and a free-market economy is not some kind of abstract force. On the contrary, the more marketized the economy, the more important the social framework and institutions that support the markets.

There are two compelling reasons why twenty-first-century capitalism, the "New Capitalism," could be fairer than its twentieth-century beta version, and they stem from the nature of the technologies that are underpinning future prosperity, which depend on the exchange of ideas. That means people engaging with other people.

The first reason is that diversity has a big economic payoff when growth is based on complex problem solving and innovation. People who all think alike, no matter how brilliant and educated they are, will solve problems or generate ideas less easily than people who are different. As established economic elites are self-selecting and all think alike, this opens the door to newcomers—as we have seen over and over again in the computer industry. What happened there first will spread economy-wide.

A second, crucial point is that the more complex the technological basis of the economy, the more complicated and subtle the society needed to operate it. The weightless economy requires a stronger social infrastructure than ever to work well. Countries will need to build their social capital to grow. They will need to be fairer places with an even more highly educated workforce. They will have to have vigorous legal and political institutions. Healthy economies do not exist where social capital has been depleted by war, or bad government or extreme inequality and poverty or widespread corruption.

It used to be possible to imagine that economic growth could occur in authoritarian countries. This was a presumption of the "Asian model," whereby a number of Southeast Asian countries achieved economic modernization without a transition to democracy, at least as understood in the West. Some commentators argued economic development was actually easier without having to worry about voters or unions. This is no longer true. It is not going to be possible to build a vigorous modern economy without building a fair society. That poses as great a challenge to the Western democracies as to countries still aspiring to join their club.

The final section of the book looks at some of the implications of this argument, particularly for today's elites. For them, it is not good news. Like the courtiers of the Sun King, officials, politicians, and corporate executives are oblivious to the sound of the tumbrils rattling toward them over the cobbles. The centralized, bureaucratic economy in place since the 1920s is as corrupt as any ancient regime and on its way to the guillotine.

1

The Growth Revolution

Why is it that so many people are so pessimistic and angry about the state of the world at a time when new technologies hold out the promise of tremendous increases in prosperity and human well-being? Since the collapse of Communism in 1989 and the subsequent early 1990s recession, a number of countries have enjoyed the taste of a New Capitalism boom. A technological revolution is under way, one that has not abolished the business cycle or created a perpetual bull market in share prices, but nevertheless a revolution that has enormously boosted the potential for economic growth. During the last century everyday living standards were utterly transformed by new technologies, and the recent U.S. experience suggests that the twenty-first century has the same potential. However, the dominant mood is far from being one of optimism, even allowing for the downs that follow the ups of the economic cycle. On the contrary, one of the fastest-growing and highest-profile public movements in the Western democracies best poised to benefit from the New Capitalism is the backlash against capitalism.

Some of the critics engaged in this movement often argue that the New Capitalism is nothing more than hype, and would even take a backhanded pleasure from a serious global downturn. Those who do accept there is some reality to the deep structural changes taking place in the advanced economies would claim instead that the information revolution and the process of globalization it triggered are benefiting the rich few at the expense of the impoverished many. The financial market crises that scarred the 1990s in Mexico, Southeast Asia, and Russia, the debt crisis still affecting much of Africa, and the environmental degradation of many poor countries form their stockpile of critical ammunition.

There is no arguing with the fact that about 1.2 billion human beings live on less than one dollar a day, that the process of reducing poverty is pitifully slow, or that gross inequality is unacceptable when those at the bottom of the income scale are ill, hungry, or lack basic shelter. While the symptoms are not in dispute, though, the critics' diagnosis is fundamentally wrong. The world's economic problems stem from too little capitalism, not too much. Those turbo-charged free markets could well prove the best vehicle for spreading the New Economy potential of technological progress as widely and fairly as possible.

A lot of the campaigners will have stopped reading by now. One of the dominant characteristics of the protest movement that has evolved since the December 1999 meeting of the World Trade Organization in Seattle is absolute certainty. The bulk of its membership consists of the children of affluence: young people who have gained more than almost anybody else on the planet, give or take a few computer moguls and investment bankers, from the triumph of capitalism. Despite their personal experience, probably in rebellion against it in a classic intergenerational conflict, they have developed an intense hatred for the capitalist system unparalleled since the late 1960s. The radical Canadian author Naomi Klein is a good figurehead, evolving from a teenage mall rat to an impassioned critic of consumerism.

The other part of the protest movement consists of intellectuals from developing countries. Their anger is easier to understand. Many live in countries whose politicians and bureaucrats, generally in favor of becoming more like the developed countries, are often corrupt and authoritarian. Leading spokespeople such as Martin Khor from Malaysia's Third World Network or the Indian environmentalist and feminist Vandana Shiva are absolutely right to point out that in the past, capitalism on the terms set by rich countries has promised vastly more than it has delivered to the poor. As Mike Moore, the director general of the beleaguered World Trade Organization, has admitted, speaking from behind the razor wire barricades protecting the rich and powerful at the World Economic Forum in Davos in January 2001: "The playing field is no more level than the earth is flat." Although his critics from developing countries, like any representatives, vary in their degree of closeness to the very poor people they speak for, they make many valid and compelling criticisms about world trade rules, debt terms, and the behavior of some multinational corporations and international organizations. They have an awful lot of very genuine grievances.

Nevertheless, I believe they are wrong, too, and in danger of closing their minds to any analysis that does not consist of outright opposition to capitalism and globalization. While the ability to buy yet another pair of shoes with a designer logo might seem trivial, the technology-driven capitalist economy is the only reason any of us has a comfortable home, plentiful food, longer life expectancy than our parents and grandparents, and children who have a good chance of surviving infancy. It has given us personal freedoms and opportunities the common people of earlier generations could not have imagined: the ability to travel and meet people from other cultures, the time to read or listen to music, the energy to engage in politics or volunteer in the community. These were not so long ago the privileges of the elite. Most of us in the West take them for granted. Any of us will turn out to have surprising depths, from the opera-loving executive to the busy mother who joins a book circle to an exhausted

The technology-driven capitalist economy is the only reason any of us has a comfortable home, plentiful food, longer life expectancy than our parents and grandparents, and children who have a good chance of surviving infancy.

cleaner who still loves to play in a band during the weekends. We also almost all have heating or air conditioning, refrigerators, TVs, and other creature comforts. Now, thanks to the forces of globalization, it is possible to imagine these opportunities being available to all.

Such goods and freedoms that we in the affluent West now take for granted as the basics of a civilized society have of course been shaped by political struggles and class conflicts. But it was the dynamic of the capitalist economy that created anything worth struggling over, and that is what the anti-globalization movement is in danger of denying to billions of people around the world.

It is an important time to make this unfashionable argument precisely because the New Capitalism, based on the new technologies, means there is a lot at stake. For one thing, there are always more opportunities to share the benefits of economic growth fairly when there is more economic growth. More important, however, is the fact that existing concentrations of wealth and power are being thoroughly shaken up by the New Capitalism. The restructuring of an economy is destabilizing, anyway, as the landed aristocracy of Europe discovered in the eighteenth and nineteenth centuries. The economist Joseph Schumpeter famously characterized capitalism as the process of waves of "creative destruction," one of which is building up right now. It is a process that, as the disintegration of the planned economies demonstrated dramatically, can only occur through free markets. Markets are not an abstraction; they operate in specific institutional and historical contexts and can have many failings. Their operation can often be improved, especially when distorted by powerful players or special interests. But they are far and away the best way of coordinating the economic activity of millions of individuals, especially at a time of rapid change. They are the most effective expression of ordinary human needs and wants, and freedom in markets is as desirable as freedom in other aspects of life.

The information-based nature of new technologies gives them an even greater radical potential than past waves of change. They demand a creative and thoughtful workforce. They reduce barriers to entry in many businesses. They undermine hierarchies. Anybody who claims to have a shred of radicalism in their fiber ought to be embracing this potential rather than condemning it, and trying with all her might to shape a capitalism for all. This book starts, therefore, with growth and the New Capitalism.

> The information-based nature of new technologies gives them an even greater radical potential than past waves of change. They demand a creative and thoughtful workforce. They reduce barriers to entry in many businesses. They undermine hierarchies.

So many questions. Is the New Economy, the New Capitalism, hype or reality? Does it matter if the dot.com bubble—if it is a bubble—bursts? If something really is changing, then what is it? Where do we look for evidence that anything unusual is happening to the economy? Can the Internet possibly be important enough to be causing everything claimed for it?

Answers are in short supply, and those there are tend to address much narrower issues, which presents any author with both an opportunity and a challenge. There is clearly a lot to be said, but not many hard facts.

For an economist in particular, the New Capitalism is unconquered territory both in theory and empirical research. Indeed, most professional economists find it hard to see any scope for newness in either theory or practice and therefore incline heavily toward skepticism about the suggestion that a new industrial revolution is taking place right under their noses. So what if the Internet reduces transactions costs and improves the matching between buyers and sellers?

There is no fresh analytical insight needed to understand this. Economic theory can easily handle such changes, which can be measured, and at best the New Economy therefore calls for some new data and econometric testing. Or perhaps there are indeed network effects and scale economies in the new technologies that create monopolies for the first or biggest business in each market. But this is a well-known phenomenon that has applied to many technical innovations during their infancy, when technical standards are still being set. The less dusty textbooks already spell that out.

Of course, economists are not the only dismal doubters. Many investment analysts were convinced the prices of technology stocks were overvalued right through their rise and fall, from beginning to end. These bears rub their paws with glee every time a high-profile dot.com goes bust. They are pretty confident that the surge in tech stocks was just a fad, reflecting no underlying reality. In fact, there seems to be a basic law of financial punditry declaring that every New Capitalism enthusiast should have an equal and opposite New Economy skeptic.

Rather than settle into one of these well-defined camps, I take a different approach in this book. I do believe something fundamental is changing in the economy, something related to new technologies. For if the hunch that something on the scale of the first or second Industrial Revolutions is now under way is correct, the implications for business, for governments, for all of us individually, and even for the face of the planet are profound indeed. Industrialization gave us richer, healthier, longer lives. It also ultimately created an urbanized and bureaucratic society out of a rural and decentralized one. The steam engine and later the electric motor were ancestors

> If the hunch that something on the scale of the first or second Industrial Revolutions is now under way is correct, the implications for business, for governments, for all of us individually, and even for the face of the planet are profound indeed.

to the assembly line, the industrial workforce, and the welfare state. A new industrial revolution could work out wonderfully well for humankind, but it might not. Which way it goes, however, will depend on us understanding what is happening today in order to shape the future.

The first chapters of the book look at what we do know about today's economy, which turns out to be not as much as might have been hoped nearly a quarter of a millennium after the founding father of economics, Adam Smith, published *Wealth of Nations*. In particular I survey economic growth: how much there has been, in which countries, and why. In a sense this is the most fundamental question of all: what is it that increases human prosperity?

Since technological progress seems to be the answer, this first section goes on to look at the available evidence on whether some technologies make a difference to long-run growth, at whether today's new technologies are of this kind, and at how much of a growth dividend they have already delivered or might yet deliver. It is only fair to warn right at the start that there is not very much available evidence. New Capitalism is just too new, and there are huge statistical problems involved. For this reason the history of earlier industrial revolutions can seem to offer as much help as the latest economic statistics. If we can't be sure yet what is happening now, there may be much insight to be gained from parallels in the past.

Yet, although direct evidence that computer and communications technologies and the Internet are reshaping the economy is still sparse, there is some telling indirect evidence, covered in the final chapter of this section. Other all-too-apparent economic developments are consistent with a big technical step forward. These include, for example, another important clue that the New Capitalism is real, is the manifestation of globalization itself, and specific patterns of inequality between and within nations. So, for example, the rewards of skill have increased, benefiting hugely both the individuals and the countries with the biggest reserves of brainpower and technological expertise.

If a new industrial revolution is taking place, holding out the promise of greater future prosperity, then realizing that promise might not be easy. . . . Yet unless we accept the reality of these fundamental changes, it will be impossible to use them to shape a fairer and more prosperous future for all. Hence the paradox of my title.

The richest countries and richest people have been pulling further and further ahead. Simply to mention these makes it immediately apparent that if a new industrial revolution is taking place, holding out the promise of greater future prosperity, then realizing that promise might not be easy. On the contrary it could well be bitterly resisted. Yet unless we accept the reality of that fundamental change, it will be impossible to use it to shape a fairer and more prosperous future for all. Hence the paradox of my title. The economy of the future is still in the making, and this is an absolutely crucial time in its formation.

But first—is there evidence of a new industrial revolution? Is there a New Capitalism?

A Century and More of Growth

There is a sense in which the history of the world economy does not begin at all until the late eighteenth century. Before then there was almost no growth that was not due simply to population increase. Real GDP (Gross Domestic Product, or national output) per head, to use the modern term, had not advanced more than fractionally for many centuries. Other indicators of prosperity such as average life expectancy at birth or mortality rates were also static. Even from about 1780 to 1830 there was very little economic growth. "Indeed, the experience of Industrial Revolution in Britain, while representing a major breakthrough from the past in terms of technological advance and resulting in extremely rapid industrialization and urbanization, is also remarkable, viewed through a modern lens, for what it reveals about the limits to growth in a leading economy of the mid-19th century," writes the economic historian Nicholas Crafts in his survey. Real per capita GDP in the British economy expanded at up to 0.4 percent a year for those first fifty years of industrialization.

It was not until the last century that growth as we know it started to occur, at least in some parts of the world. And for much of the twentieth century and for most countries rates of 1–2 percent have been common. Higher growth than that is truly exceptional, and there are only two episodes that stand out. One is the postwar period, 1950–75 in the OECD countries, the then-planned economies of Central and Eastern Europe, and much of East Asia and Latin America. For the first group in particular these stand out as a golden age of growth. Incomes per head grew by more than 2 percent a year in most cases and as much as 8 percent a year in Japan. The years since the mid-1970s have seen a marked slowdown from these extraordinarily high rates. Explaining this growth slowdown has been a major preoccupation on the part of economists.

The American experience is, not surprisingly, exceptional. Like the rest of the world, the United States grew very slowly indeed in the nineteenth century, significantly faster throughout the whole period 1913–73 but especially during the 1920s, and more slowly again since then. One economist has characterized America's experience as "one big wave," and says the real issue is not why growth has slowed in the past thirty years but why it was so fast for so much of the twentieth century. Yet despite recording high growth through most of the twentieth century, not just the postwar era, the U.S. economy also suffered a post-1973 slowdown.

The second really striking episode is the "Asian Miracle" from the mid-1970s up to 1997, when per capita GDP growth of around 5 or 6 percent was common. The global financial crisis of 1997-98 put a halt to that; it is too soon to tell whether the subsequent rebound will mark a return to the earlier pattern. The reasons for Asia's take-off during the 1970s when the developed economies were slowing has also been endlessly and inconclusively debated.

The other feature that really stands out from the historical record is the dismal performance, by comparison with other parts of the world, of South Asia and Africa. India, along with the rest of Asia, saw GDP per head decline from 1913 to 1950. India's growth rate has since improved but lags far behind the so-called Tiger economies like Hong Kong, Singapore, South Korea, and Malaysia. Growth in Africa has lagged since the early nineteenth century, which is as far back as GDP figures are available, and has been negative for the past quarter century.

One implication of this divergence is that inequality between countries has risen significantly. Essentially, America had established a big lead by the mid-twentieth century, Europe and Japan had nearly caught up by the mid-1970s, and East Asia made great strides toward catching up in the later decades of the twentieth century. But the gap between richest and poorest countries has become ever wider. For example, in 1900, average income per head in the richest country was about fifteen times that in the poorest. By 1990, it had pulled away to a level more than fifty times higher. Countries seem to have converged on either a high or a low standard of living, and transitions from one "club" to the other are unusual. Explanations of why economies grow have to account for this divergence, which is something we will return to in a later chapter. The explanations are also important, of course, in order to work out how the gap can be narrowed again in the future, how the developing nations in the poverty club can graduate to the wealth club.

Of course, real GDP per head—the output of the nation as conventionally measured, adjusted for inflation and divided by the population—is not an ideal measure of prosperity, although it is the only type of statistic easily available for many countries over very many years. Economists are well aware that, especially over long periods, it can drift away from the commonsense understanding of living standards.

In fact, it seriously understates improvements in the standard of living. For example, advances in medical science and public health have brought spectacular improvements in health and longevity even in countries that remain very poor. Nowhere in 1870, not even in the UK or United States, did people attain the levels of life expectancy now reached in many African or Asian countries. The highest life expectancy amongst the leading economies was 49.3 years, now exceeded almost everywhere. In his magisterial history of the world economy, David Landes recalls the death of Nathan Meyer Rothschild. The banker was the richest man in the world when he died in 1836 in Paris, succumbing to a burst abscess. A five-dollar dose of antibiotic would have cured him, had it been invented then, but an expensive team of the best doctors in the world could not do so at the time.

The hit television series *The 1900 House* provides many down-to-earth examples of this phenomenon whereby well-being increases at a faster rate than GDP thanks to new inventions. An ordinary family agreed in 1999 to live the lives their counterparts would have enjoyed at the turn of the previous century, in every detail. For women in particular it was an eye-opener. The wife returned to a life of domestic drudgery in order to keep her family fed, clothed, and warm. Staying clean as well was a real luxury—one of the problems that drove her to tears was the unavailability of a modern shampoo that would keep her hair free of grease. And one of the few late-twentieth-century intrusions allowed was a modification of the coal-fired range in order to heat up enough water for baths.

A less obvious but related problem is that conventional price indices, used to turn dollar or nominal levels of GDP to "real" measures, have a strong upward bias, giving real GDP a strong downward bias. The reason is that they tend to ignore improving quality or new goods. This is an issue that came to prominence in the 1998 report of the Boskin Commission in the United States. The report argued that the measured inflation rate could be overstated by around 1 percent due to the tardy inclusion of new items such as laptop computers, whose prices were falling rapidly, and due to insufficient adjustments for the improved quality of goods. A thousand-dollar computer today is a far more powerful beast than one costing about the same just a couple of years ago, so price per unit of computer power (measured by millions of instructions per second) has fallen substantially. Most national statistical offices make some adjustment for this, but not enough.

To understand why an apparently small statistical problem with inflation matters, consider the usual figures for GDP per worker in the United States. These show average economic growth since the end of the Civil War has been 1.6 percent a year, implying that output per worker has doubled every forty-four years and the average U.S. worker today could produce the same output as a mid-nineteenth-century equivalent in one eighth of the time. Or to look at it another way, an American living 133 years ago would have needed eight times the average income of the day to be as well off as the average earner of today. However, if the Boskin Commission's estimate of the bias in the inflation figures is correct, meaning the conventional figures for growth in real output per worker have been underestimated to the same extent, productivity would have doubled every twenty-seven years, not every forty-four years. And today's Mr. or Ms. Average would be producing thirty-two times, not eight times, more than their mid-nineteenth-century counterparts.

> The figures we have simply do not capture the reality. They do not—and perhaps cannot—take account of the transformations of modern life. . . .

The point can be made even more dramatically by thinking about what goods and services a typical citizen in one of the most advanced economies can easily afford now. Most solid middle-class citizens might curse themselves for leaving a light on at home when they go away for the weekend, but perhaps more for the unnecessary contribution to global warming than the addition to their electricity bill. It would have been unthinkable for their counterparts in the 1900s to have done the same thing. Few households had electric lighting before 1920, and the use of electricity was eked out carefully. Electric power is the next best thing to free now, by comparison. Research looking at the price of illumination over a long period (rather than an item like a lightbulb) shows that traditional figures fail to capture the sharp drops in price—or equivalent jumps in productivity—whenever one technology of lighting succeeds another.

There are other reasons why, generally speaking, the statistics we have massively underestimate increases in living standards. An obvious one is that the hours of work put into reaching a certain level of national output have been on a firm downward trend. For example, in the UK average hours worked per person has dropped from 1,251 a year in 1870 to 764 in 1996, and in France from 1,364 to 600. Only the United States is exceptional, with a decline from 1,089 hours in 1870 to 859 hours in 1950 being partially reversed to 931 hours in 1996.

The argument that we underestimate growth hugely might seem surprising because, after all, we more often hear about the extent to which conventional economics overestimates living standards. There are competing measures to GDP that reduce it by taking account of important considerations such as pollution, depletion of nonrenewable resources, and, more controversially, factors such as levels of crime, poverty, or inequality. These are obviously important to our well-being in a broad sense. Still, the advocates of these alternatives overstate their case. The scale of the downward adjustment to GDP proposed by measures like these is dwarfed by the upward adjustment that would be needed to take account of step improvements over time. Even indices of national economic attainment like the United Nations Human Development Index that do incorporate indicators of poverty make the point that there has been astonishing growth. The pace of human development has outstripped conventionally measured economic growth, and by a greater margin in the second half of the twentieth century.

The figures we have simply do not capture the reality. They do not—and perhaps cannot—take account of the transformations of modern life, from clean water and central heating to television, bowling alleys, mass transportation, and cheap paperbacks. As the economic historian Brad De Long puts it: "Modern growth is so fast it's off the scale." And what takes it off the scale seems to be technology.

Accounting for Growth

The role of technology is plain enough in the long sweep of history. Economists estimate it using a method prosaically known as "growth accounting." This splits growth in output between growth in the inputs used—the important ones being physical capital and labor—and additional growth in the total productivity of those inputs, or in other words in the extra output per combined unit of input. The calculation can look at the contribution of different types of capital, identifying the contribution of investment in computers separately, for example. It can also be expressed in terms of labor productivity alone, or in other words output per worker hour, in which case more workers, more capital, and more capital per worker can all contribute to labor productivity improvements. Either way there is a residual "technical progress" term, usually known as "total factor productivity," taken as a measure of technical progress. This has to be treated with some caution. If anything is mis-measured or left out, it will turn up in the calculation of this residual item. Most experts, though not all, accept that the method is more likely to underestimate than overestimate the contribution of technology, however.

Investment in new physical capital like machine tools, forklift trucks, or computers certainly matters. So does population growth, which boosts the size of the available workforce and also investment in labor, or human capital, through better education. In the case of the United States the biggest contribution to growth from rising investment in physical capital came in the nineteenth century, whereas in other OECD countries it was delivered by the postwar investment boom of their economic golden age. The United States has seen a bigger contribution than other countries from labor growth, mainly because of more rapid increases in its population. Hours worked have also shrunk outside the States during the past century.

What surprised economists when growth accounting calculations were first developed in the 1950s was the fact that growth in labor and capital inputs accounted for so little of the recorded growth. Depending on the adjustments made, between half and two-thirds of the increase in the American economy's real output during the course of the twentieth century was due to this "technical progress" term. This finding has been repeated for other countries and other time scales. In a famous 1956 paper, Moses Abramovitz observed: "Since we know so little about the causes of productivity increase, the indicated importance of this element may be taken to be some sort of measure of our ignorance about the causes of economic growth."

It is all the harder to understand the causes as the contribution to the average annual growth rate from "total factor productivity" has been highly variable. It reached 3.6 percent in Japan and 3.3 percent in Germany in the years 1950–73, with both countries apparently able to make great strides in catching up to American technological attainments. Other high contributions from technological change were seen in some Southeast Asian countries after 1960. Of particular interest is a productivity surge in the United States between the two world wars, which probably reflects the electrification of the economy. This is an episode to which many people look for a parallel with what might be happening now. But economists are even less able to explain variations in this source of growth than to account for its overall importance.

In particular, broadly speaking, technical progress on this measure rose from the late nineteenth century to the mid-1970s and has slowed sharply since. Why did technology-linked growth slow just as the use of computers started to become widespread, along with microelectronics, lasers and fiber optics, composites and biotechnology? And has the pace of technical change actually picked up in very recent years, with any implications for future living standards?

Computers and the "Productivity Paradox"

Robert Solow, the Nobel Prize–winning economist, voiced this well-known paradox as long ago as 1987. Many people continue to be persuaded by his observation: "You can see evidence of the computer revolution everywhere apart from the productivity figures."

At that time it seemed obvious enough to many people that computers were not going to offer anything in terms of productivity. Erik Davis, describing the craze for Dungeons and Dragons that spread like wildfire throughout university research labs when these were first connected in an early network in the mid-1970s, observes: "All work ceased throughout the entire country at these research sites. It was almost like an infection." A few years later rudimentary computer games like Pac-Man had the same effect in offices throughout the Western world. It might be different in industry, where computer-aided design and manufacturing and the use of robots started to spread, but as desktop computers multiplied throughout offices worldwide, it was clear that workers were spending a lot of time playing games. Email and the Internet have taken this to a new level, cynics point out. A bored desk-bound employee can spend a lot of time circulating jokes around the world and surfing the Web, and there is so much of it going on that employers are starting to monitor exactly what staff are getting up to at their screens.

The figures showing the spread of computer power and the decline in price of computing and telecommunications do coincide rather strikingly with the slowdown in productivity growth in all Western economies after 1973, at least up to the recent past. For example, in the UK our measure of the contribution of technical progress to growth slid from 1.2 percent in 1950–73 to 0.7 percent in 1973–92. In the United States there was a more marked decline still from 1.6 percent to 0.2 percent. And in Germany the contribution to growth dropped from 3.3 percent in the earlier period to 1.5 percent.

Yet at the same time as productivity growth more than halved, computer power became staggeringly cheap and absolutely ubiquitous. In the United States, which can be taken as a benchmark, the price of PCs and peripheral equipment fell by nine-tenths between the early and late 1990s and more than halved between October 1997 and October 1999. According to the annual report on the Digital Economy from the Department of Commerce, prices are falling at an accelerating rate. And while America was well in the lead, other countries were becoming more wired at the same time. For example, by mid-1999 Finland (impressively advanced technologically despite its tiny size) and the United States each had more than 120 Internet hosts per 1,000 inhabitants, but Sweden and Norway were close behind with 100 per 1,000. Of the world's 201 million estimated Internet users in September 1999, 55.9 percent were in the United States and Canada, and 23.5 percent in Europe. Worldwide, there were 3 million people on the Internet by the end of 1994, and 300 million by early 2000, when an estimated 3 million new pages a day were being added to the World Wide Web.

> Why did technology-linked growth slow just as the use of computers started to become widespread?

Was this just an unfortunate coincidence, or, as the skeptics have argued, is it clear evidence that technical advance in information technology has nothing to offer the economy in terms of growth?

Debate about the productivity paradox has been raging for some years. In its first stage, believers in the New Economy relied on two main arguments. One was that the productivity improvements resulting from a major innovation take a long time to emerge. Another was the possibility that increases in output and productivity were not being measured properly. It is worth spending a little time on these initial defenses before going on to the current state of the debate.

Measuring and Understanding

This chapter has already touched on the fact that the staggering pace of growth over the course of the past two centuries has not been captured by mainstream economic statistics. In fact, even measuring GDP itself on the conventional definition has become steadily harder in the advanced economies as they switch progressively from manufacturing goods to delivering services. The output of service industries is just much harder to get a grip on. Statisticians can count turnover of service sector companies in nominal dollars or pounds. They can count the number of employees. But price is harder to figure out because it is not obvious what a "unit of service" is in many cases. Real, inflation-adjusted output is most often measured by the number of employees, so productivity per worker is defined to be zero whatever happens.

It has been known for some time that adjustments made by U.S. statisticians actually ended up showing declining productivity in some "hard-to-measure" services during the 1970s and 1980s. These include financial services and business services. The result simply is not plausible; it is overturned by experience.

In addition, as the U.S. Commerce Department noted in its report "The Digital Economy 2000," including for the first time business spending on software in the definition of investment in the national statistics (in October 1999), gave a huge impetus to the currency of the idea that a New Capitalism was emerging. After all, this spending had ballooned from $28 billion in 1987 to $149 billion in 1999. "This had a catalytic effect on economists' perceptions," the report observes. Yet software is only one kind of intangible investment. It would be just as reasonable to count others, such as spending on training or workplace reorganization. This would tie in with research that strongly suggests this kind of spending complements companies' investment in information technology. Those businesses that do not spend on training and business reorganization do not appear to reap any productivity benefits from their spending on computers and software.

Statisticians are well aware of some special additional problems resulting from the information-technology revolution. While it is fairly straightforward to measure the amount spent on the products or services of a company or group of companies, it is much harder to keep track of unit prices. Particularly in the case of computers themselves, prices have been falling extremely rapidly—19 percent a year over the whole period 1958–92, and a staggering 30 percent a year during the late 1990s. At the same time, the quality of the products has risen sharply, so price per unit of equivalent computer power (it would be price per safe and comfortable passenger mile, say, in the case of a car) has fallen much faster than list prices. This is the result of the well-known Moore's Law, which says computer power doubles every eighteen months, a regularity experts believe could continue for another two or three decades. This means computers in 2015 will be 1,000 times more powerful than computers in 2000, for the same price, and approximately ten to the tenth power times more powerful than a 1976 computer.

In addition, there is more diversity and consumer choice, and a rapid rate of introduction of altogether new technology products, such as mobile phones, electronic organizers, wide-screen TVs, and so on. None of these difficulties for the official statisticians is entirely new conceptually, but they have become more intense. The index number used to calculate the price level in the economy has always combined apples and pears; now it is a bit like calculating the average height of humans and giraffes. You can work out the number but it is not clear what it means. As we saw, such considerations are why in the United States the Boskin Commission said the upward bias in inflation conventionally measured by the consumer price index could amount to as much as 1 percent a year. And why step changes in price and quality are never captured in price indices. If prices are overestimated, measures of "real" output, or in other words money values adjusted for inflation, will be underestimates.

While this point about measurement is uncontroversial, some economists would argue that it has always been true, and is not more true now than in the past. So any miscalculation of growth should not be any worse in degree than it was before. I disagree, not least because of the increasing diversity of the economy.

There is, however, an even deeper problem with economic statistics and measuring today's increasingly weightless economy at all. The more products and services consist of intangible elements, and the more of an experience or performance every purchase becomes, the more difficult is the notion of a standardized unit of real output. There might well be more output in the economy but it is not the same kind of "more" that we are used to. Rather, it is diversity or choice, something whose value is increasingly personal to each consumer.

Already there is an unmissable trend toward ever greater choice. Between the early 1970s and the late 1990s, the number of types of running-shoe styles had exploded from five to 285. There were seventeen varieties of Colgate toothpaste alone, rather than two. The United States saw the publication of nearly 80,000 new book titles a year, up from 41,000. And the Ford motorcar came in forty-six possible colors, not just black. Dell Computer famously does not start assembling a PC until it has received the customer's order. Indeed, with the most obviously weightless products such as software or music, producers are able to tailor both the product and the price to specific groups of consumers. Our existing statistics have no way of addressing this diversity.

> The more products and services consist of intangible elements, and the more of an experience or performance every purchase becomes, the more difficult is the notion of a standardized unit of real output.

As the economist Paul David put it, in a discussion of why measured productivity had not increased as much as might have been expected: "A substantial degree of uniqueness and context-dependence inheres in the very nature of information products. The intuitive and conventionalized association of the notion of 'productivity' with the engineering concept of standardized task efficiency thus is being increasingly challenged by the increasing intangibility and mutability of 'outputs' and 'inputs.'"

Alan Greenspan, the chairman of the U.S. Federal Reserve, has made similar comments about trying to measure productivity. In one speech he said: "Only when the data are disaggregated can we reasonably hope to tie productivity performance directly to business practices in our offices, on our plant floors, and through our distribution channels." In another he went further, calling for "a major shift in the process of how one evaluates what we're producing."

It should not come as a surprise that statistics have not kept up with the economy at a time of rapid change. The framework of national accounting that gives us Gross Domestic Product, the conventional indicator of an economy's size and health, dates back to the Second World War. They reflect the mass-production economy in full bloom, following the Fordist transformation of manufacturing in the 1920s and 1930s and the unprecedented planning and control of economic production during wartime. The system of national accounts was launched in conditions that were never more suited to their conceptual framework. GDP is the measure of an economy based on mass production. It counts the contribution to the economy of a hundred copies of this book as equivalent to copies of a hundred different books. It will count the production of one of tomorrow's personalized anticancer drugs as equivalent to one of today's profoundly less powerful drugs. Half a century on from the development of the framework of national accounts, the economy has changed beyond recognition and the old clothes no longer suit.

It was inevitable measurement should find it hard to keep up. Paul David concludes: "It is not surprising that a statistical system designed to record productivity in mass production and distribution should be challenged when the business systems in this model change as a result of innovation and the use of information and communication technologies." It is even hard to collect raw data on sales and jobs from existing business surveys when a relatively small number of large companies no longer account for the same high share of the economy, and when new and small companies are being formed at a rapid rate.

Reimagining the Economy

The same kind of conceptual delay occurred in an earlier era of change. After all, history represents a massive investment, financial, cultural, and emotional. For example, there were almost no factories in England in the 1820s, but they were obviously going to become exceedingly important. That was already twenty years after the visionary William Blake had written of dark satanic mills. Yet it was not until the second half of the nineteenth century that we at least got around to counting the number of mills. A statistical abstract for the UK for 1871 to 1885 shows there were 7,465 textile mills, with 773,704 power looms and employing just over 1 million people, by the end of that period.

However, nearly three generations on from Blake's Jerusalem, the number of factories and their employees were amongst the only statistics in the volume to track manufacturing in the world's foremost industrial economy. We also counted the number of miles of rail track laid and numbers working in mines. Some manufactures were classified in exports, but the categorization reveals how much the collection of statistics did not understand industrialization the way we do now. For example, woolen manufactures are a subcategory of wool. Metals are lumped together next to musical instruments. There are lots more, decreasingly interesting, figures for agricultural production. This gives scant hint that the economy had been transformed from predominantly rural to only 20 percent agricultural in the space of a century.

The measurement problem might seem a bit of a diversion, something of interest only to statistical nerds, but it matters for several reasons. Most obviously, it is harder for policy makers to know how to steer interest rates when they do not know how much spare capacity there is in the economy or how fast productive capacity is growing. Resolving this problem will not be straightforward, however.

Take another example of the emerging shape of the economy. Family doctors often feel their heart sink when a patient turns up with a sheaf of printouts of information they have collected from the Internet. If somebody has incorrectly diagnosed herself and thinks she has the solution, too, the doctor has to work twice as hard, first persuading the patient she is wrong and then finding the correct diagnosis. However, the Internet offers huge scope for improving the quality of medical treatment. Patients correctly diagnosed have every incentive—far more than their hard-pressed family practitioner and even their specialist—to discover the latest medical evidence on their illness and its treatment. Like busy professionals in any field, doctors have no time to keep abreast of the frontiers of research once they have ended their studies. It is not hard to foresee a time when patients filter out the information for their doctors and pass it on to them. This is an unexpected and radically new channel for a big improvement in quality, one driven by consumers, not producers. But it is a quality improvement we would never measure with today's framework of statistics.

There is a mountain to climb before we get to a better measurement of the New Economy. We do not have a good understanding of the information technology infrastructure, of the way businesses are being organized, of the extent of ecommerce, or of prices. The conventional boundaries of industrial structure and geographical place are being eroded. The new framework we will need depends on how we come to understand the economy—what "more" is it that we are interested in measuring?—and this is a question I will return to later. For just as two-dimensional maps represent the three-dimensional world in a way that necessarily reflects their makers' mental geographies, so statistics must represent the economy they measure differently in each era.

The Delay Defense

So the measurement problem is real, but perhaps it seems a slender reed on which to base the belief that the economy is switching to a new paradigm. Despite these difficulties you might still have expected to see some hint of a productivity upturn in the kinds of figures that are available. A second important weapon in the armor of New Capitalism advocates is therefore the likelihood that radical new technologies are implemented slowly, so their effects can take many decades to emerge.

Indeed, it is quite easy to think of potential explanations for an initial slowdown in productivity growth after the adoption of a new technology. The people working with it need to learn new skills. Businesses might need to restructure their operations. Installing new equipment can be costly in terms of disruption and might even require new buildings. A detailed study by Paul David of the electric dynamo gave much weight to the idea of lengthy delays due to such adjustments.

> An important weapon in the armor of New Capitalism advocates is therefore the likelihood that radical new technologies are implemented slowly, so their effects can take many decades to emerge.

He emphasizes the fact that technologies do not exist in splendid abstraction. In the real world they operate in an entire economic, social, and political structure, and the path switching an economy from one technological regime to another is strewn with historical accidents and interdependency with other, parallel changes. David argues that overlooking this complexity means we suffer from "technological presbyopia," a condition whereby technological advance prompts huge overenthusiasm about the fantastic improvements likely to result from it, followed swiftly by commensurate disappointment about the slow and contingent progress that actually occurs.

Certainly we have these symptoms of hyping and debunking

now. The detailed example of the diffusion of the electric dynamo and electrification of America's factories and homes offers a thought-provoking parallel to the process of computerization and networking under way in recent years. As the Yankees' Yogi Berra famously put it, it's a case of "déjà vu all over again."

The initial innovations in electricity generation came in the years 1856–1870, with the magneto and the dynamo permitting enough energy efficiency in electricity generation to make it commercially viable. Yet in 1900 under 5 percent of factories and households had electricity, and the 50-percent mark was not passed until around 1920. Initial delay occurred because old manufacturing plants were very durable. Electrification therefore occurred fastest in industries that were expanding very rapidly, building new plants. These included tobacco, fabricated metals transportation equipment, and electrical machinery itself. In addition, electrification first took the form of adding electric motors to existing equipment. Plants tended to keep their existing system of overhead belts and shafts, which had been run by steam, running groups of machines from one new electric motor instead. Another decade passed before engineering opinion swung over in favor of the "unit drive" alternative whereby each machine got its own motor. When this started to happen, it became apparent that factory layouts could become more flexible; machines did not need to be positioned around a single driveshaft. Ultimately, removing the overhead driveshafts permitted the building of much lighter single-story factories (tall factories had reduced the power losses that would have been involved in turning very long driveshafts). This in turn improved the handling of materials and configuration of machines along an assembly line. New factories built "horizontally" rather than "vertically" involved relocation to green-field sites outside the old urban centers, and that required road-building and transportation systems.

Thus it was that the big surge in productivity growth occurred in the 1920s, some half century after the primary innovations and after a good deal of investment in new equipment and infrastructure.

Electrification also made possible the development of important innovations in chemicals and energy industries such as petroleum refining around the same time, including the introduction of automatic process control. And, to hammer home the point about undermeasurement, the figures will never reveal benefits like the improvement in working conditions in lighter factories with greater fire safety.

David's argument that there was a gap of as much as fifty years between innovation and productivity surge is now widely accepted. In a lesson for countries hoping for a step forward in prosperity now, it emphasizes the importance of investment spending that embodies the new technologies; but it also holds out the hope of being able to leapfrog the extended learning process the leading economies have had to go through by following their example directly. The historical record suggests that the peak productivity improvement seems to come only after a new technology has passed the 70-percent mark in diffusing amongst its user population. But it alone would not have won the debate about the productivity paradox, either. For that, we have the stunning performance of the American economy in the late 1990s to thank.

The U.S. Productivity Upturn

In February 2000 the U.S. economy broke all records. The level of GDP had increased for thirty-six quarters in succession, the longest unbroken period of growth since the mid-nineteenth century, which is as far back as any figures go. Not surprisingly, unemployment was low, but so too was inflation. The favorable combination of rapid growth and low inflation appeared to be due to a big improvement in productivity growth.

Certainly labor productivity, easy to measure as GDP divided by the number of hours worked, was growing astonishingly fast. It reached an annualized rate of 7 percent at the end of 1999. And study after study found that the wider measure—total factor productivity growth, taken as an indicator of the contribution of technology—had also picked up markedly.

One of the most optimistic assessments came from two researchers at the U.S. Federal Reserve Board. In an earlier paper, they had concluded there was a nascent upturn in productivity growth but that it was small in 1995 because despite their appearance of being "everywhere," computers still represented a tiny proportion of the enormous stock of physical capital in the American economy. Nobody should have expected them to be making a big contribution to growth at that stage. However, business investment in computers and peripheral equipment had multiplied fourfold, measured in real, price-adjusted terms, between 1995 and 1999. Redoing their growth accounting calculations, and dividing the capital stock into computers and semiconductors on the one hand and everything else on the other, their latest result is that the combination of investment in computers, software, networks infrastructure, and so on—with massive efficiency gains in the manufacture of computer equipment and semiconductors—accounted for about two-thirds of the U.S. acceleration in productivity growth in the late 1990s.

To put it another way, the improvement came mainly from greater use of information technology and greater efficiency in its production. Average U.S. growth climbed from 2.75 percent in 1991–95 to 4.82 percent in 1996–99. Of this two-point improvement, 0.5 point came from growth in the input of information-technology capital, 0.9 from other capital and labor input, and 0.6 from increased growth in total factor productivity. The contribution to growth from this measure of technical progress shot up from 0.48 percent a year in the early 1990s to 1.16 percent in the second half of the decade.

This basic result for the American economy is essentially confirmed by other researchers, with caveats. The productivity paradox is resolved by the passage of time and the late-1990s surge in investment in the American economy.

The Gordon Critique

Or is it? One of the most formidable skeptics about the proposition that something akin to a new industrial revolution is taking place is Robert Gordon, economics professor at Northwestern University and one of the titans of modern empirical macroeconomics. In one paper he too went through the conventional growth accounting procedure using the most recent data for the United States—and partly recanted.

"The data for 1995–99 are consistent with the beginning of a new age of productivity growth," he wrote. Even accounting for the massive investment boom, raising the contribution of capital to growth, there was also evidence of a large rise in the growth of total factor productivity.

But his was an incomplete conversion. For he argues that the increased productivity growth has been confined to a small part of the economy, accounting for just 18 percent of total output. This consists of the computer (hardware) industry itself and other industries manufacturing durable goods. Outside the computer and durables sectors, he found no evidence of accelerating technical progress. "The New Economy is alive and well, but only within computer manufacturing and the remainder of the manufacturing durable sector," he wrote. "How could there be such a low payoff to computer investment in most of the economy where the vast majority of computers are located? In this sense Solow's paradox survives intact."

Paul David's arguments suggest it is not surprising to find productivity growth improving first in the most rapidly expanding industries, including the one at the heart of the innovation. Other economists have challenged Professor Gordon's figures, particularly the way he adjusts his results downward for the normal way productivity growth picks up in a business cycle. The objection is that, as this is no normal business cycle, that approach is bound to be flawed. The Federal Reserve Board's alternative calculations also look at the effects of computers plus semiconductors and not surprisingly find a bigger impact, and one throughout the economy.

This debate over empirical detail is bound to continue for some time. More interesting, perhaps, is Robert Gordon's eloquent denunciation of the very idea that computers and the Internet can have a fundamental large and lasting effect on the economy. He puts forward two arguments. One is that information and communications technologies are not remotely as important or beneficial to human welfare as a set of five huge technological leaps forward that took place from 1860 to 1913, a period sometimes known as the Second Industrial Revolution.

You only have to list these to see this is a powerful argument. They were: electric light and motors (1879 on); the internal combustion engine (1870); petroleum extraction, petrochemicals and pharmaceuticals (modern chemistry dates from the discovery of synthetic dye in 1856); entertainment and communications including the telegraph (1844) and telephone (1876); and running water and indoor plumbing (1880s on). In line with the now-accepted delays before an innovation has its full economic impact, he reckons these combined delivered the big wave of growth in the United States from 1913 to 1973 (although not elsewhere until after 1945).

Looking at the communications advances alone, the closest parallel to the Internet revolution, the increase in speed of communication and reduction in cost made possible by the telegraph between the mid-1840s and mid-1850s have not been bettered. Time per word delivered fell by a factor of 3,000 while costs fell hundredfold during that decade. And the network expanded from forty miles in 1846 to more than 23,000 miles in 1852.

I will argue later that the Internet is not all there is to the technical advances underpinning the New Economy and the possibility of another long wave of growth. Shopping online and sending email is not the limit of it, and looking back from 2100 it will be possible to list a similarly impressive array of technological innovations. But I want to postpone that discussion until the next chapter. To get back to the very existence of the New Capitalism, Professor Gordon's other argument is that it is not conceptually possible for computers to trigger an economy-wide acceleration in growth. Think about those dramatic declines in prices. The U.S. price index for computer hardware and peripherals, quality adjusted, has been declining at an average 19.4 percent a year, and the rate has been faster since 1995. He suggests this demonstrates the law of diminishing returns in a big way: we get less and less benefit from each additional increase in available computer power.

After all, computers don't do much unless there are humans using them, and there is a natural limit of twenty-four hours to the human day. The professor notes that the really big improvement in his own productivity came with his first word processor in 1983. Subsequent upgrades only made, at best, marginal improvements in the number and quality of academic papers he could write. What's more, computers cannot substitute for all jobs done by people. They can count checks but they can't wait a table in a restaurant or take a patient's temperature or develop an economic theory. This is a point made elsewhere by other instinctive skeptics in the economics profession. If computers and microchips are plentiful, what will be in short supply is human attention and care. It is hard to see how a revolution in computing will increase productivity in cleaning and waitressing, nursing, gardening, and hairdressing.

And Why He's Wrong

There is a bit more professorial ranting about the overhyping of the Internet, which Gordon sees as essentially a form of entertainment that people indulge in at the office when they should be working. But what about this point that the returns to investment in computers must be diminishing? And that the machines need people to work with them, so there is a limit to how much they could boost growth? He writes: "Set against this exponential increase in computer capability is a fixed endowment of time and a limited endowment of human brainpower, creating diminishing returns at a rate never seen before in economic history. . . . The speed at which diminishing returns have taken hold makes it likely that the greatest benefits of computers lie a decade or more in the past, not in the future."

Try substituting another technology into this statement. Steampower, perhaps, instead of computer capability, and muscle for brainpower. Or electrical power. The invention of the lightbulb made it possible to extend the working day, but there were even then just twenty-four hours in the day, so there was a limit to the process and a point at which diminishing returns had to set in. The gain from the first reliable oil lamps was probably far greater than the gain from switching from oil to electricity for lighting at night, and the benefit from the first candle greater still.

Other technologies have also seen extremely rapid declines in price as they became widely adopted. The telegraph was one, but so was the cost per mile driven or the cost of travel per passenger air mile. Yet the internal combustion engine was indeed a transforming technology. There is something wrong with the Gordon critique, and I believe it lies in a narrowness of focus. If you interpret the computer and Internet revolution as being a technical step that allows the same people to do the same things they always did—write research papers, buy groceries—then the diminishing returns will set in.

However, the great transforming technologies end up changing what people do, and which of them do it, with all sorts of unpredictable knock-on effects. Leaps in computer processing power certainly seem to do this, enabling entirely new uses and capabilities. Without cheap computer power, nobody would have formulated the ambition of sequencing the human genome, for instance. The possibility of such a broad transformation in activity is precisely why eventually the evidence of a trend upturn in economy-wide productivity growth will be needed.

> The great transforming technologies end up changing what people do, and which of them do it, with all sorts of unpredictable knock-on effects.

In fact, the current pattern of productivity gains in the United States starting in a modest way in just one sector of the economy is a repetition of those resulting from earlier innovations. Despite the invention of steampower, the railroad, mule spinning, the blast furnace, and so on in the First Industrial Revolution, productivity growth and overall economic growth in Britain remained low throughout the nineteenth century. One reason was the small size of the relevant capital stock, just as the Fed economists argue. In 1800 only about 35,000 horsepower were in use, compared with 2,000,000 in 1870. In addition, the impact was uneven, with scarcely any advance in productivity in the service sector in the UK, already 40 percent of the economy.

Furthermore, long-run productivity growth depends on the existence of a virtuous circle running between technical progress and the social and market conditions in which innovation has to take place. So a strong patent system, the existence of a big market for the products, the skill base of the workforce, the availability of finance, and so on are crucial. The social and institutional framework required for faster growth was built up throughout the nineteenth century. To take just one example, the idea of a limited liability company got its first legal reality in 1856, making equity finance possible. Expanding economic capacity requires alongside it increased social and political capacity, too.

There is support for this line of argument in the timing of recent technological developments. The productivity slowdown in the United States and other OECD countries had certainly started by the mid-1970s and perhaps as early as the mid-1960s. Yet computer use started to spread only from 1980 with the advent of the desktop machine. Earlier, computing was essentially confined to universities and a few very research-intensive companies. Paul David argues: "It is possible that the productivity slowdown and the computer productivity paradox are different and mutually reinforcing features of the same set of phenomena." Both, in other words, reflect a social and institutional transformation as well as a purely technical one.

Nobody would now argue that the First Industrial Revolution

didn't amount to a hill of beans because there was no significant upturn in productivity growth outside the mining and manufacturing sector. As Nicholas Crafts points out, the innovations allowed the economy to escape for the first time in history the "Malthusian trap" whereby rising population matched or exceeded growth, keeping per capita living standards flat at a miserable level. Secondly, the face of the British workforce and landscape changed forever. The number of people working in agriculture halved to 22.7 percent between 1780 and 1870 (whereas the proportion of Germans working on the land was still that high in 1950), and the country rapidly became urbanized and industrialized.

> Long-run productivity growth depends on the existence of a virtuous circle running between technical progress and the social and market conditions in which innovation has to take place.

Of course the Industrial Revolution brought with it the infamous misery and squalor of Victorian Britain's cities, inspiring not just Karl Marx and Friedrich Engels but also some of the best novels in English literature by authors including Charles Dickens, George Gissing, and Elizabeth Gaskell. But it should not be forgotten that the degree of poverty was exceeded by the earlier rural squalor. Industrialization did not destroy an Arcadian way of life, even though it took decades of passionate campaigning and political engagement to ensure that the potential for raising living standards for the masses became a reality.

So for these reasons I believe the Gordon critique is misdirected. The question to pose is not "Why do the measured gains only show up in a small part of the economy?" but rather, "What will it take to turn this now-evident technical progress into widespread improvements in the standards of living—what institutions and policies do we need?" Similarly, the question is not why is the information revolution only making the rich richer, but rather how can we make sure it benefits the poor, too.

Nobody should ever knock intelligent skepticism, a quality generally in pitifully short supply. The doubts raised by such renowned economists would be a positively useful counterweight to lots of silly hype if only there were not a strong self-fulfilling element to the New Economy. It is an insight dating back at least to Keynes's emphasis on the importance of "animal spirits" in investment, and updated by modern theorists writing about "endogenous growth," that there is an important self-perpetuating element in building the future by investing today. New technologies are going to be used, thus boosting growth and living standards, only if businesses and consumers invest in them, embodying the technical advances in new pieces of equipment. They are not going to invest in them if they believe the whole thing is mostly hype. It seems reasonable to suppose there is more evidence of a significant pickup in productivity growth in the United States than elsewhere partly because many Americans were so swiftly and firmly persuaded that something new and exciting was happening, and therefore flung capital confidently at the new technologies. The contrast between American and European attitudes during the late 1990s was accurately reflected in the diverging economic performances on either side of the Atlantic.

> The question to pose is not "Why do the measured gains only show up in a small part of the economy?" but rather, "What will it take to turn this now-evident technical progress into widespread improvements in the standards of living—what institutions and policies do we need?"

A Verdict on the New Economy Elsewhere

Painstaking recent research on the statistics by the Organization for Economic Co-operation and Development (OECD), which has tried to assemble figures on a comparable basis for different countries, has concluded that there is indeed evidence of a significant upturn in growth in the Unites States compared with the post-1973 slowdown—but no comparable evidence for any other country. Collecting all the data was a nontrivial part of the exercise, as countries use different definitions—again, measurement is a serious issue. With that caveat, the study confirms the finding of greater contributions to growth in America from investment in information and communications technology and from total factor productivity growth, mainly in the industries producing that technology but also in other industries.

For other countries, however, the evidence is just not there. The OECD tentatively concludes that Sweden and Finland might be at the start of a growth pickup, as might Canada and Australia. The UK shows no signs at all of a productivity improvement, but is one of only three countries, along with the United States and Canada, to have seen an accelerated rate of investment in information technology in the second half of the 1990s. In Asia, Japan has shown scant sign of growth for more than a decade. Despite its advanced technological base and highly educated workforce, it will not benefit from any New Economy investment surge without addressing its broader economic problems, like the need to reform the banking and financial sector. Outside the OECD club, India, China, and Taiwan could be poised to benefit from the investment and expertise in high-technology industries by their large expatriate communities and overseas investors, but it has not happened yet. All would need to expand their skilled workforces and in the cases of India and China address other problems typical of developing countries, such as inadequate infrastructure and the need to deregulate the economy.

Even so, that no other countries have shared the American experience is another puzzle. After all, there is nothing secret about America's New Economy and almost no restrictions on the export and use of the technology in the post–Cold War era. Even if other countries can't innovate in the same way, they should be able to imitate. It is a very effective strategy, as Japan and many European countries found in the quarter century after 1945. If they are imitating the New Capitalism with a lag of a few years, it is reasonable to wait a bit longer for evidence. Part of the explanation for the puzzling absence of a productivity improvement outside the United States must be the lack of investment in the new information and communication technologies elsewhere. Each step forward has to be embodied in the equipment companies install and the products consumers buy and the infrastructure provided by the public sector. Outside Scandinavia, America is way ahead of most of the rest of the world on most measures of the installation and use of the technology, a legacy that will survive an economic downturn.

For example, by late 1997, the United States had more PCs per hundred white-collar workers than any other country except Sweden, and vastly more PCs per hundred households than anywhere else. It had the second highest density of Internet hosts, after Finland. It had thirty-six of the fifty biggest IT companies (ranked by revenues). And throughout the 1990s it had had consistently the highest spending on information and communication technologies both relative to GDP and in absolute terms.

One exception is mobile telephony, where the early establishment of a common European standard helped jump-start the market. Many European countries, along with others such as Korea and Australia, had more subscribers to mobile services than the United States by 1998, with only one in five Americans using a cell phone compared to three in five in Finland, world leader in that technology. Europe and Japan are not so far behind in all new technologies, either; for instance, there is a bit less of a lag in biotechnology.

Still, it seems there is good reason for a bit of American triumphalism. It is not simply a question of the amount of investment or the number of computers bought for use at home. For one thing, investment needs financing, and high-technology investment is risky. The United States has a bigger venture-capital industry and far more extensive individual share holding. In the EU a lot more investment is financed by banks and pension funds, not institutions known for either their appetite for risk or their judgment when they do take it on. Europe's equity markets are smaller than America's, and its venture-capital markets just fledglings by comparison.

New technologies also need different skills in the workforce. The U.S. job market might have the right kind of flexibility to make possible large-scale switches from one kind of occupation to another. And while parts of the American education system are crumbling, its leading universities are magnets for the best scientific brains on the planet. These issues are aspects of the organizational and social change that are both caused by the New Economy and also needed to create it. In other words, the current transformation of the economy by the latest wave of new technologies is not just about technology and not just about the economy. It is this feedback between economics and politics, in its broadest sense, that makes coping with profound change so controversial and unsettling. If there is a New Economy, there is going to have to be a New Society and a New Politics, too.

If there is a New Economy, there is going to have to be a New Society and a New Politics, too.

Economists do not believe in Kondratiev waves—the theory that there is a regular fifty-year economic cycle of growth picking up and slowing down—because it is not possible to identify them in long-run growth data unless you are really looking for them. The waves are beyond the reach of rigorous econometrics as there are too few data points for statistical confidence. Yet one tantalizing observation by long-wave theorists is that the upswings are always, counterintuitively, times of war and political struggle. For instance, the early years of the twentieth century brought the Russian Revolution and revolutionary movements throughout the other advanced economies of the time. Another long upswing came from 1950 to the mid-1970s, roughly the postwar golden era. For many readers of a certain age the sixties, the decade of the Great Society and Woodstock, of *les évènements* of 1968, of the Prague spring, plumb in the middle of these years, will always send a frisson of excitement down the spine.

It isn't necessary to believe in these unverifiable waves, however, to appreciate the scale of social change and uncertainty that lie ahead of us. Sociologists, such as Manuel Castells and Francis Fukuyama, have been swifter than economists to grasp this. In his latest book, the latter writes: "Social norms that work for one historical period are disrupted by the advance of technology and the economy; and society has to play catch-up." The contribution of economics, and particularly recent growth theory, has been the observation that technology and the economy are also always adjusting to society.

First, though, the next chapter puts in place some more building blocks. It asks why this is all happening, and looks at what these fantastic new technologies offer us exactly.

2

The Technological Recipe

The scene: a large, brightly lit seminar room with picture windows on two sides, looking down over the River Thames and the London skyline, the mighty dome of St. Paul's Cathedral in view on the opposite bank. It is gloomy and pouring rain outside, making the room feel like an ark, a haven of warmth and cheer. Rows of chairs are arranged in a horseshoe around a central table; at the side, trays of canapés and wine.

Dramatis personae: a group of about twenty-five artists and actors, theatre administrators and business executives. The tribes are easily distinguished by their dress, the businessmen (and most are men) in their uniform gray suits, the theatre folk (mainly women) in bright linen and silk.

Enter stage left, a bearded and bespectacled man wearing a suit, but with jacket off and shirt sleeves rolled. The floor is held by Bill Sharpe, a former Hewlett Packard scientist now running The Appliance Studio, a design and technology consultancy.

BILL SHARPE: Absolutely everything is going to be an information-technology product. What businesses do will no longer be defined by technological capacity, because that capacity will be there. It's not in question.

AN EXECUTIVE: In that case how will I define what it is that my business does?

BILL SHARPE: That's the big issue. What values do organizations stand for and how will they embody them? I predict that in ten years' time you will see a list of credits on the products you buy. Producing anything will become a performance. The idea of a performance delivered by a troupe is natural for technology-based innovation. The most important part of any product is its design and the service it provides to customers. This will not be just a table in the future [*he thumps the standard conference room table by his side*] but a whole table experience.

The event was a meeting of the business-arts forum organized by the biennial London International Festival of Theatre. The forum offers executives a space to think creatively about their business, with the creativity injected by contact with the wide range of international performers attending the festival. The highly successful forum answers an appetite amongst a growing number of people in business to address a question so vague that few can spell it out. Julia Rowntree, its organizer, describes this as a search for meaning in an economy that many have a hunch is changing profoundly. What is it that produces value—both in the sense of what customers will pay for and in the deeper moral sense?

Bill Sharpe went on to give the example of Apple's extremely successful iMac as a computer experience rather than a boringly functional computer. Here was the first desktop computer you could really covet for its own sake and even love. Within a short time of its launch, the iMac was appearing in the background of fashion shoots for glossy magazines, colonizing ad agencies and design studios. It even conquered the desktops of France's Ministry of Finance in what must have been intended as a signal of the bureaucrats' commitment to economic modernization. It is hard now to understand why no computer company before then had thought of producing a desktop machine that was anything other than a clunky beige box, of offering any beauty alongside the functionalism. Perhaps even more surprising is that the reaction of most other manufacturers has been simply to mimic the iMac's basic design idea—translucency and bright color; curves, not corners—rather than to imagine other possible desktop computer experiences.[1]

Yet the personal computer is neither the first nor the only product to embody more value in its design and marketing than in the metal and plastic that give it physical existence. Cars, the very symbol of the assembly line and mass production, which Henry Ford famously only made in black, have become the weightless product par excellence. The value of the creativity in its design, the intelligence in its electrical wiring and engineering, the imagination in its marketing and quality of personal attention in its sale and follow-up service make up the vast bulk of the cost of an automobile.

This characteristic of modern economies was the focus of my earlier book, *The Weightless World*. Economists are very familiar with the trend in all developed countries for services to account for a growing proportion of national output. In the most extreme case, the United States, services accounted for 70 percent of 1999 GDP and total employment, manufacturing for just 18 percent. Services took more than a two-thirds share in all the OECD countries. What was new to me in 1996 was the insight that value in manufacturing, as well as the rest of the economy, was being increasingly created by specifically human contributions rather than raw materials. It is the design or marketing, creativity and flair, that add value, not the physical molding of stuff into a different shape.

This point was flagged by Alan Greenspan in a number of speeches. He pointed out that GDP weighed about the same near the end of the twentieth century as it had at the beginning, despite being twenty times larger in real terms. And once you start thinking about it, it is easy to see how this can be true. Cars are made of aluminum and plastic, not steel, and are smaller. Miniaturization is widespread in consumer electronics. Even commercial buildings are made of glass rather than marble or stone. And while a pair of sunglasses bought today must weigh about the same as a pair dating from the 1970s or 1950s, chances are that a much higher proportion of today's price reflects the designer label or the cachet provided by the marketing campaign rather than the actual cost of making the glasses. It costs around $3 billion to produce a new aircraft engine, but the cost of the second is just $50–100 million, so great are the costs of design relative to physical production. As Greenspan has more recently described it, "The share of output that is conceptual rather than physical continues to grow."[2]

In this increasingly weightless economy, old ways of understanding measures of output—what it is that is being produced—are defunct. Take the conventional split between "manufacturing" and "services" that characterizes every nation's economic statistics. There have always been aberrations simply because the boundary between industrial categories is arbitrary. UK national statistics counted me, as a journalist, as a manufacturing worker because newspapers are included in the sector "printing and publishing." True, there is a physical product, but my work was a world away from any assembly-line job in a factory. Another peculiarity is that when companies in manufacturing outsource functions like payroll or cleaning, the same work is immediately redefined from manufacturing to services. Nothing real has changed, but outsourcing has certainly made the shrinking of the measured manufacturing sector in the United States and UK look more pronounced than it "really" is. More fundamentally, when the value in manufacturing consists of the services provided by designers, engineers, managers, marketers, and so on, and it is increasingly industrial robots that do the making, there seems little sense in continuing with the conventional distinction.

It's the Technology, Stupid

Weightlessness is one way of characterizing the changes transforming our economy, but there are many others in use. You could describe it instead, less precisely, as the New Capitalism or the Knowledge Economy. Fundamental to all of these descriptions of the New Capitalism, however, is the notion that the increased capacities of machines are making the contribution of humans more, not less, important. Economic progress is being driven by tremendous technological advance. The previous chapter documented the evidence that long-term growth does depend on technology and that technology is now fueling a new surge in potential growth.

Further evidence of the growing reliance of the economy on brain, not brawn, can be found directly in figures for spending on research and development. Across the OECD, the club of rich nations, spending on R&D—which is just one part of total spending on innovation—surged during the 1990s to reach $700 billion in 1997, or more than 2.2 percent of GDP. Preliminary figures indicate it has grown more since. A growing share of the total is accounted for by civilian, as opposed to military, and by business, as opposed to government, expenditure. The trend has been most pronounced in the United States and also a number of smaller countries such as Australia, Denmark, Finland, and Ireland. They were correspondingly disappointing in some other big economies like France and Japan, but all of the former group have enjoyed a significant upturn in the growth of total factor productivity, as we saw. Other indicators include surging spending on software, and a soaring number of applications for patents, particularly in the same list of countries. Just taking the number of applications for U.S. patents, these grew at an annual compound rate of 12.5 percent between 1995 and 1998, a pace of increase well in excess of the upturns in patenting in the early decades of the twentieth century and the postwar golden age of growth.[3]

Yet there is technical change all the time—it is one of the con-

stants of capitalism—and despite such evidence many skeptics simply do not buy the argument that there is anything new or special
going on. So the next step is to establish that today's technologies are
the right kind to have a large and general impact on the economy.
Are they what economists term "general-purpose technologies"? If
so, the implications are radical for both developed and developing
economies.

In an address to the American Economic Association in 1998,
Arnold Harberger divided technological effects into two categories,
"yeast" and "mushrooms." The latter consist of advances that boost
the productivity of specific processes or industries. The effect can
be dramatic but it is narrowly confined. Mushroom-like upsurges
in productivity are very localized, independent of each other and
unlikely to generate any important spillovers of knowledge or efficiencies from one industry to another. In his empirical research on
earlier U.S. growth, he found productivity gains were confined to
less than half, and often much less, of the manufacturing sector.
Technical progress in the 1970s and 1980s, he concluded, was
mushroom-like.

Yeast-like advances, on the other hand, cause gains to spread
widely over the economy, like a loaf rising as it proves in a warm
place. Repeating Harberger's calculations for the 1920s, Paul David
and Gavin Wright found the results for that era were emphatically
yeast-like. Virtually every branch of industry saw a surge in productivity growth.[4] Even so, it was the most rapidly expanding industries
that enjoyed the earliest and biggest gains. The reason is that it was
easier to embody improved production layouts and management
methods in new, electrified plants. It took new buildings, single story
and laid out in modules, to capture the productivity improvements
promised by electrification. And often, as we saw earlier, building on
green-field remote sites often required also new suburbs and roads.
There were simply more new plants in the fastest-growing industries,
which were metals, transportation equipment, and electrical ma-

chinery itself. In industries that were expanding more slowly, there was no hurry to replace steam-driven plants that were still profitable. So in these cases the productivity gains came later.

Certainly, the evidence that the computer industry itself has enjoyed the most dramatic improvement in productivity seems to support a mushroom interpretation of the latest episode of U.S. growth. But the reason could be the ultra-fast growth in that industry and others closely linked to it, meaning they have just got there first.

> Yeast-like advances . . . cause gains to spread widely over the economy, like a loaf rising as it proves in a warm place.

So let's look more closely at the notion of general purpose or yeast-like technologies. They obviously need to have a wide range or generality of use, and to be applicable across a lot of the economy. If they complement other technologies they are more likely to have the yeast-like effect, as there will be spillovers between advances in one industry and others. In addition, if they have scope for big improvements when they are first introduced, that will mean there is the potential for a considerable boost to productivity growth extended over time. These four characteristics constitute a widely accepted definition of general-purpose technologies.[5]

There are many examples of them in history. Steam and electricity are two of the most recent and obvious. Writing (first developed around 3500 B.C.) and printing (1452) are two older ones that might offer parallels to the information technology revolution. In transportation, examples are the railways and the motor vehicle. The internal combustion engine lay behind multiple industrial uses and air transport as well as cars, one of the first uses for engines. The development of new materials can also constitute a general-purpose technology—bronze is one example, plastics another.

Such technologies are often interrelated. To take one example, a cluster of mid-nineteenth-century technologies, the railroad, the iron steamship, the telegraph, and refrigeration, would have been important individually, anyway. But together they combined to form a radical new transportation system that globalized the market for many foodstuffs and other commodities. The possibility of importing food from across the world made urbanization possible, revolution-ized nutritional standards amongst the working population, and transformed home agricultural production. General-purpose tech-nologies are often grouped together in technology systems in this way. The way they mutually reinforce each other is part of the ex-planation for their radical and dramatic effects. Indeed, the social and institutional changes they both trigger and require should also be counted as part of the broad technological paradigm.

There is a complex structure both responding to and facilitating every technology-driven transformation of the economy. It includes investment in new capital, the acquisition of new skills, a reorgani-zation of production, changes in managerial and financial organi-zation, changes to the infrastructure of the economy, and a chang-ing geographical location of activity and industrial concentration. Part of the skill of science-fiction writers lies in their ability to de-velop a complete vision—often profoundly dystopian, as it hap-pens—of a society utterly transformed by technology. Authors like William Gibson and Neal Stephenson can certainly do this for com-puters and the Internet. They understood that the virtual reality of cyberspace would change the "meatspace" that had created it—in their imaginations what emerged was an ultra-urban society pitting the ingenuity of individual rebels against remote and monolithic power structures.

So what technologies might now be contributing to a revolu-tionary new social and economic order the world over? Information and communication technologies are the most obvious. Before the next two decades are out, computers will be so cheap and small that they will be disposable. We will have scrap computers that we can throw away, like scrap paper. They will also be liberated from cables by wireless technology. That means computers will be ubiquitous, and used for many tedious and easily forgotten tasks. Hence the refrigerators that will be able to reorder your groceries, the cars that can navigate for themselves, the electronic books downloaded from the Internet, and all those other consumer goodies imagined by enthusiasts like the Media Lab at the Massachusetts Institute of Technology. Many are currently under development by the leading manufacturers of consumer goods. These clever products might still sound like fantasy to most of us, but in fact they are well on their way to market.

Embedding microchips in products is, however, only a tiny part of the computer and Internet revolution. The process of manufacturing has already started to change. Complex products can be designed and tested on the computer before any machine tool is switched on, cutting costs to an astonishing extent. "Mass customization" of products is possible, whereby any good can be tailored to a customer's own specifications because it is so easy to reconfigure a computerized production line. Links to suppliers and customers mean companies have shrunk their inventories of both materials and finished goods, because they have so much better an idea of what they will need and when.

Apart from also reducing costs and improving customer service, this has almost certainly made the business cycle less volatile. In many countries GDP growth has been much less volatile than normal since the early 1990s. In the past variations in economic growth were amplified by huge swings in levels of stocks, which companies had to hold as a cushion of safety against changes in their market, but these are being steadily eliminated. The ratio of stocks to GDP has fallen steadily over many years in most advanced economies. In the United States manufacturers reduced inventories as a share of sales by a quarter between 1989 and 1999. With swings in levels of inventory responsible for up to two-fifths of the variability in GDP over the course of a business cycle, it is not surprising that lower stock-to-output ratios in many businesses have already contributed to more stable growth.

Alan Greenspan has referred in several speeches to the greater ease of doing business when information technology has dissipated some of the old uncertainties. As he put it in one speech: "Large remnants of information void, of course, still persist, and forecasts of future events on which all business decisions ultimately depend are still unavoidably uncertain. But the remarkable surge in the availability of more timely information in recent years has enabled business management to remove large swaths of inventory safety stocks and worker redundancies."[6] Innovations such as the electronic links between store shelves, retail checkout, and factory floor, or the satellite positioning of delivery trucks, had dramatically reduced delivery times and inventory requirements, he noted. "Fewer goods and worker hours are caught up in activities that, while perceived as necessary insurance to sustain valued output, in the end produce nothing of value."

Throughout the production chain, lead times and uncertainty have diminished. Design times are much shorter, for example. Many decisions to buy expensive capital equipment are no longer so hampered by the need to invest for a wide range of eventualities in the distant future. As the Fed chairman put it: "In short, information technology raises output per hour in the total economy principally by reducing hours worked on activities needed to guard productive processes against the unknown and the unanticipated."

Information and communication technologies hold the seeds of many future changes, too. In the last chapter I gave an example of how this might improve medical treatment, as the people with the greatest incentives to track down the latest expertise—the patients—can now do so. The empowerment of customers relative to producers thanks to better information will occur in many walks of life, however. Professions built on the supposed superiority of expertise on the part of their practitioners will be in the forefront of improvements in the quality of service as the information monopoly is breached.

Other Technologies

It is not all about computers and telecommunications, however. Far less attention is paid to other revolutionary technological advances, partly facilitated by cheap computer processing power. One is the development of new materials, tailor-made for specific applications. No longer are materials developed in an evolutionary way out of natural materials and earlier products. Rather, they are created purposefully for a given function. New materials are fundamental in a wide range of industries including microelectronics, transportation, architecture and construction, energy, aerospace, and medicine.

Biotechnology is another, one that at last came to the fore with announcements around the turn of the millennium that scientists could clone mammals and also had published the map of life, with the sequencing of the human genome. Selective breeding has been a widely used technique since Neolithic times. However, the biotech revolution dates back to 1953 and the discovery of the structure of DNA. The breathtaking practical applications of biotechnology are now beginning to take shape.

Medical applications will make perhaps the biggest impact on the quality of human life. Thousands of disorders are due to defective genes. Genetic therapies will facilitate treatments and vaccines for ancient and modern scourges like cystic fibrosis, cancers, AIDS, asthma, rheumatoid arthritis, multiple sclerosis, and many others. It will be possible to tailor-make drugs for, say, personalized treatments for certain cancers. It is impossible to foresee the detailed changes the next thirty years will bring in medicine, but it will be utterly transformed. Ours might well be the last generation whose genetic inheritance is its inescapable destiny. It goes without saying that the ethical and social implications are staggering and, to many, very alarming.

Biotechnology will have equally profound agricultural applications, already causing concern with the launch of genetically modified crops. Genetic engineering is not brand-new in agriculture. One high-profile example is the "Green Revolution" of the 1970s.

Still the new applications are causing serious public concern because of the capacity to insert genes from one organism into others. Nevertheless, the potential exists to engineer plants and animals for specific characteristics, such as disease- and pest-resistance, increased yield, faster growth, tolerance to freezing, and so on. For instance, one benign application, "golden rice," has vitamin A added to increase its nutritional value.

Such applications hold out huge potential hope for the poorest developing countries, where life expectancy at birth is fifty years, compared to an average of seventy-seven years in the richest countries, and where 169 out of every 100,000 under-fives will die from disease or hunger. Medical and public-health advances have been the biggest contributors to past gains in prosperity. One of the biggest policy challenges is ensuring that globalization works for the poor in this specific dimension, and campaigners are rightly critical of, for example, the fact that the world pharmaceutical industry and intellectual property rights are overwhelmingly geared toward the needs of the rich. The United Nations Development Program is pressing for the recognition of "global public goods" such as an HIV/AIDS vaccine, goods whose social benefit exceeds the likely private profit they will generate, and which therefore tend to be under-provided if left to private companies. Biotechnology advances such as new seeds are equally controversial. For instance, Monsanto has been heavily criticized for preventing farmers replanting seed to grow next year's crop. It wants them to buy new seed in order to profit from its intellectual property in the new varieties it has developed. But tradition and cost make the idea of buying new seed each year nonsense to farmers in developing countries. These are difficult issues that will need to be resolved if the fruits of the new general-purpose technologies are to translate into a great leap forward in prosperity for all. There were equally difficult issues in the past, for example in the electrification of rural areas or access to health care. This is why the New Economy is inextricably political and now on the challenging global, not national, scale.

Genetic engineering has potential uses in mining. Microbes and algae can be developed to clean up oil spills and contaminated sites. They can extract metal from crushed rock, or potentially even from the rock itself, without any need to mine it. Other possibilities down the road include using engineered enzymes and microbes in industrial processes—cleaning machinery, processing medicines, food, or cosmetics. Bugs might be the machines of the future.

Scientists point to two other potentially revolutionary technologies, currently far less advanced than the new materials and biotech revolutions. One is the development of new fuels in place of fossil fuels. Solar energy is growing more efficient and is much closer to commercial realization than ever before, and nuclear fission might be harnessed finally some time this century.

The other is nanotechnology, the production of goods by building them up from individual atoms and molecules—just like the replicators on *Star Trek*. Nanotechnology is no longer entirely science fiction. Although its applications remain in the imaginations of engineers, it works in the research lab. The power to manufacture anything by rearranging molecules has mind-blowing implications for economic growth. Goods could be produced at far lower cost than now. The ability to manipulate every atom into a precise place will also revolutionize quality. Early applications are likely to be medical, as nanotechnology is already being used to develop pioneering noninvasive surgery. New nano-engineered materials can be expected.

The future of computing itself might also lie in nanotechnology when silicon-based computing reaches its physical limits around 2020. While fiber optics will take computing past the bottlenecks created by transmission through copper wires, permitting the transfer of information at up to light speed, microprocessors will hit another barrier—the physical impossibility of creating chips with light beams smaller than 0.1 micron (compared with the beams of wavelength between 0.3 and 0.4 micron used to build the most powerful chips available as I write)—within another twenty years. Beyond the limit set by the wavelength of light beams, the development of molecular computers could be the next step.

In just the past year or so molecular electronics has made revolutionary strides. As long ago as July 1999 researchers at Hewlett-Packard and UCLA announced they had successfully built an electronic switch consisting of a layer of some millions of molecules of an organic substance. Linking several of these allowed them to perform some of the basic logic operations of digital computing. Other groups followed with similar developments in subsequent months, including a molecular memory device. Researchers from one of these, writing in *Scientific American*, said: "The inexorable drive to produce smaller devices may leave technologists no choice but to migrate to a new form of electronics in which specially designed individual molecules replace the transistors of today's circuits."[7] Fantasy? Already microelectronic mechanical systems—not true molecular machines, but nevertheless miniature sensors and motors about the size of a speck of dust—exist in prototype. Their commercial development is under way. Within two decades these are expected to form the basis of a several-billion-dollar industry.

A remoter possibility is the first revolution in housework since the invention of the washing machine and vacuum cleaner: nano-scale dirt-eating machines are a possibility. So are airborne, molecule-sized machines with substantial computing power that could obey any command—"Bring me a beer from the fridge!" or "Answer the door!" Is it any wonder some scientists see nanotechnology as a development likely to be as radical in human history as the replacement of stone by bronze, or electrification?

Breathless lists of possibilities like these—microscopic servants, self-service genetic engineering, or even something pretty down-to-earth like wearable computers—can easily sound a bit silly. After all, futurologists are notorious for getting it wrong. Even realistic technologies can fail in the marketplace because they do not meet genuine consumer demands. Remember the excitement about the hovercraft? These boats borne on a cushion of air just above the waves were supposed to revolutionize sea travel, but they never made a profit and were finally mothballed early in 2000. Supersonic air travel did a bit better with Concorde flying a couple of regular routes, but most passengers have continued to make do with subsonic speeds. Nuclear power was supposed to eliminate energy shortages forever, according to 1960s hype, but Germany has now become the first country to announce it will close all its nuclear plants, and others might follow suit. Very serious technologies full of promise can end up being not at all revolutionary.

In the case of computers, however, the consistent pattern has been to underestimate their scope. Thomas Watson, chairman of IBM in 1943, predicted there would be a market for five computers. Of course, they did cost tens of thousands of dollars and weigh tonnes at the time, so perhaps he can be forgiven. Ken Olsen, the president of Digital Equipment Corporation, made an even bigger howler in 1977, saying: "There is no reason anyone would want a computer in their home." Their mistake was to overlook the power of Moore's Law, generalized by Ray Kurzweil into the "Exponential Law of Computing." Taking the succession of computing technology, from Charles Babbage's mechanical "Analytical Engine" at the end of the nineteenth century through electromechanical then vacuum tube–based computers, like Colossus in 1943 and ENIAC in 1946, on to transistor-based computers and today's integrated circuits, one can see an extraordinary empirical regularity in the increase in computing power over time. The speed of computation doubled every three years at the start of the twentieth century, and every year by its end. As Kurzweil puts it: "If the automobile industry had made as much progress in the past fifty years, a car today would cost one hundredth of a cent and go faster than the speed of light."[8]

It would take a brave pundit to downplay the role of computers now, especially if small, disposable microchips are included in the definition. After all, the new networked and mobile applications are compelling. As long ago as 1901 one journal article predicted a rosy future incorporating, along with widespread use of the automobile

It would take a brave
pundit to downplay the
role of computers now.

and electricity, the mobile telephone. The author wrote of: "pocket telegraphy by means of which a man may carry his own apparatus in his pocket and receive messages even from people who do not know where he is. [He] takes his small receiver with him when he goes out to lunch, and places it beside him on the restaurant table."[9]

The moral is that some of the predicted technical developments will definitely turn out to be silly, but others will prove visionary. The one thing absolutely nobody can predict is exactly which is which.

Is It Yeast?

Getting the fine detail right is not essential. But what is important is to assess whether the list of exciting possibilities adds up to yeast-like or merely mushroom-like technical progress. How do the information and communications technologies stack up against the list of characteristics that define general-purpose technologies?

Wide range of uses: Processing information is a generic description that includes a multitude of uses, from writing books, broadcasting movies, and other media functions to designing cars or creating scans of a human body. The ubiquity of microchips now puts their generality of use beyond doubt. Where there used to be one computer per hundred humans, the ratio will soon be a hundred computers per human. As well as the one on your desk and in your mobile telephone, there will be one in each of your domestic appliances and several in your car, not to mention the one in every musical greeting card you send.

Apply across a lot of industries: Can you think of an industry that does not use any computer power? Or even one that doesn't use the Internet, less than a decade after Net access first became commercially available? Pretty much every industry has already set up or is currently establishing an online business-to-business supply chain, with predictions of the likely cost savings typically 15–25 percent.[10]

Complement other technologies: Computer technology goes hand in hand with the other new technologies listed here. None of the others could have progressed without the availability of cheap and extensive information processing power, or indeed cheap communications that allowed geographically separated researchers to collaborate. In turn, developments in biotechnology and nanotechnology are likely to contribute the next step in computer technology.

Scope for big improvements: Computing has come a long way already in the past twenty years, but there is plenty more scope for improvements in speed, power, user-friendliness, and so on. You only have to think about the real prospect of voice-activated computers to appreciate the potential. And the potential of other complementary technologies is so much greater that it lies still beyond our imaginations.

It is therefore beyond doubt that today's new technologies are indeed general-purpose yeast, and will work their magic and proliferate through the whole economy. While it might have been possible to imagine a world without computers as recently as around 1975, that is no longer true. Why, after all, were some people so worried about the Y2K bug that they stockpiled drinking water and canned food as 1999 drew to a close? Fears of Armageddon might always have been overdone, but the prospect of serious economic upheaval that would have resulted if a lot of the world's computers had malfunctioned at midnight on December 31, 1999, is clear testament to the fundamental economic importance of the microchip.

Governments and businesses around the world thought it a danger that warranted their spending some billions of dollars in total to

It is therefore beyond doubt that today's new technologies are indeed general-purpose yeast, and will work their magic and proliferate through the whole economy.

make their computers Y2K compliant. That suggests the potential economic losses were at least as great. Of course, even billions of dollars make up only a small fraction of world GDP, but then the risk of total computer malfunction was always understood by most sensible people to be very small one. If it had been greater, the amount of preventive investment would no doubt have been huge.

Many skeptics about the New Capitalism and its new technologies have their eyes closed to the scope and potential of their use. If social science academics, then they imagine computers are used mainly for word processing, so perhaps it should not come as a surprise if they think a technology that generates more economics and sociology articles is at best a mixed blessing for the world. What we are doing, the debunker says, is producing nicer graphs in the same old reports in free moments between downloading pornography.

More generally, it is easy to think about the way computers contribute to what we already do and form an opinion about how much that might boost productivity in a particular task. But it is much harder to appreciate the way they make new things possible. This blinkered vision is normal with new technologies. After the invention of the telephone it was widely expected it would be used as a broadcasting device, for example allowing a subscriber to dial up a (live) orchestra and hear a concert in comfort at home, rather than traveling to a distant concert hall. Nobody imagined people would use the telephone for talking to each other directly, and certainly not just for idle chat.

Some of the most wildly misplaced skepticism in the past has actually concerned communications technologies. Take Harry M. Warner, founder of Warner Brothers, who said in 1927: "Who the hell wants to hear actors talk?" Some people could not imagine any use for wireless broadcasts—who would pay for messages broadcast over the ether to no one in particular? No doubt printing had its de-bunkers, too, asking what on earth the peasantry would want books for. The killer application in printing turned out to be the Bible. On the other hand the telegraph and telephone pretty much lived up to most of the wild hype of the day. I have not been able to find equally silly predictions at the other extreme because many of the techno-enthusiasts' wildest dreams came true. The moral is that it is unwise to underestimate the impact of information technology, the vehicle for the fundamental human passion for communication.

Slowing Down to Leap Ahead

It will come as a consolation to fervent believers in the New Capi-talism that the most important general-purpose technologies, and their associated structural changes, have in the past been followed by a productivity slowdown. The early stages of the factory system in the late eighteenth century had this effect, and so did early-stage elec-trification in the late nineteenth century.

One obvious parallel between the early stages of those previous industrial revolutions and today's is the still rather vague and diffuse nature of the potential efficiencies and productivity improvements. To a skeptic this could be another way of saying computers actually don't hold out a lot of promise for the economy. But rather, the rea-son it is hard to see the promise is that the computer hardware and software we have, although much improved on the past in terms of price and performance, are not at all well-tailored to specific tasks. It might well be necessary to refine both hardware and software—per-haps mobile or wearable, networked devices will work better for some types of business, virtual reality systems for others, whereas all most businesses have at this stage is a network of desktop machines running a handful of generic software applications. Other patterns of computer use are only just rolling out through our economies.

It cannot be emphasized too much that a new general-purpose technology also requires a great deal of additional investment of various sorts before it results in a yeast-like upsurge in productivity. The economists Elhanan Helpman and Manuel Trachtenberg note in one of the key texts on these technologies: "It seems that complementary investments play a critical role, which has been largely overlooked."[11] The induced complementary investments can include investment in education, in infrastructure, and in organizational or managerial change.

For example, many researchers have noted the importance of the spread of high school education in the early decades of the twentieth century. The emerging factory system of mass production required a lot of standardized workers. They needed to have a minimum level of numeracy and literacy, a capacity to perform various routines of work. Completing high school signaled enough skill to be trained in most factory tasks with sufficient consistency of performance. General worker quality, not the traditional highly specialized set of craft skills, was needed by the new set of technologies in the 1920s. The expanded public school system rose to the challenge, drawing young people from rural to urban areas and giving them a basic education rather than elite academic training as a preparation for university.

> It cannot be emphasized too much that a new general-purpose technology also requires a great deal of additional investment of various sorts before it results in a yeast-like upsurge in productivity. . . . The induced complementary investments can include investment in education, in infrastructure, and in organizational or managerial change.

If a step change in the educational preparation of the IT generation is going to be needed, then we are still a long way from seeing the full fruits of new technology. Entire books have been written about the elite of today's workforce, those on the coal-face of the computer revolution. Robert Reich described them as "symbolic analysts," those whose job day in, day out involves the highest abstract cognitive skills.[12] They are the executives, consultants, and programmers familiar with airport terminals and five-star hotels the globe over, cosmopolitans engaged in a global rather than a local economy. They earn large salaries, topped with generous stock-option schemes, putting them in a different league to most workers. They are in a class of their own.

However, for the vast majority of people, even in the advanced economies, there has been no change in their educational preparation. It is no exaggeration to say every country believes its education system to be in crisis. Crisis is a fair description of the situation of the centralized, state-dominated educational assembly lines through which our children are still being processed. A later chapter explores in detail just how inappropriate an education we are currently offering the next generation. The implication is that a huge investment needs to be made in redesigning education, and even if reform starts right now it could take another decade or two before our societies have made an adequate investment.

In fact, there has been inadequate change in many areas that fall within the remit of government as opposed to the private sector, although this varies between countries. For example, the U.S. economy has almost certainly benefited from early deregulation of its telecommunications industry, from the light-touch labor regulation so strongly opposed by many Europeans, and by an absence of red tape that makes it easy to start a new business on that side of the Atlantic. Many other countries continue to struggle with the dilemmas posed by the apparent clash between political preferences and economic imperatives. It is not only the French who resist the idea that traditional values and culture apparently need to be ditched in order to guarantee future economic success. The "Asian model" of capitalism has also been widely seen as one of the victims of the 1990s financial crisis and America's subsequent New Capitalism triumphs, having been relabeled "crony capitalism." The overwhelming success of the American model and the backlash against it is one of the most salient features of the global economy at present, although it will become increasingly apparent that successful capitalism does

The overwhelming success of the American model and the backlash against it is one of the most salient features of the global economy at present, although it will become increasingly apparent that successful capitalism does not come in just the one flavor and is consistent with a variety of political choices.

not come in just the one flavor and is consistent with a variety of political choices.

Necessary changes in business organization and managerial competence are probably much further advanced in all OECD countries. Some companies, and business schools, have been experimenting with new structures for years now. Corporations have delayered, thinning out their inherited hierarchies. The use of information technology has allowed more decentralization of decision making. There is a lot more diversity in the practice of management. The size of firms has shrunk on average. For the first time it has become possible to organize production on a genuinely global scale, so even small firms are multinationals, and few companies anymore have no export market.

Looking Forward to a Great Leap Forward

I will look in detail at the emerging institutional structure of the weightless economy in the final part of this book, at exactly what political and social as well as financial investments will be needed to ensure technological change translates into higher productivity and living standards. The point I want to drive home here is that such investments will indeed be needed. The economist Richard Lipsey argues that the information-technology revolution is at about the same stage as that in electricity in the late 1930s. "Much has been worked out, and the full potential of the computer is foreseen but not yet realized. Many of the structural adjustments in the organization of offices and plants, design and information control, as well as the infrastructure of the information highway, are already in place, at least in embryo form."[14] He predicts that if the past is a good guide, we can expect a long economic boom from around now into the 2020s or 2030s.

Many of the changes in the physical infrastructure, the nature of human capital, or skills, the organization of production and work, management practices, geographical location of businesses, and so on are already foreshadowed in current developments. Yet there is a strange reluctance to project obvious results from well-established trends. This is partly because the world will become a very different place, and we are more comfortable with the familiar. But it is also partly because change brings the prospect of conflict.

One dimension of this is the potential for conflicts of interest between rich and poor countries. The technical and political changes that unleashed globalization have already led to a huge industrial restructuring across national borders. Although most cross-border investment still takes place among the OECD countries, the amount invested by multinationals in poor countries has soared. Indirect investment flows through bank loans and stock markets had reached record levels before the 1997–98 Asian financial crisis but has since fallen sharply. On the other hand direct investment by Western companies in factories and offices in the developing world has continued to grow. It reached an estimated $128 billion in 2000, the second highest on record, after $145 billion in 1999. The flow was expected to increase again in 2001, according to the Institute for International Finance. Much of this investment represents the outsourcing of traditional manufacturing. Thus, notoriously, Nike does not manufacture any running shoes but subcontracts the work to factories in countries such as Indonesia. But it is unfair to single out Nike. Dell makes no computers and Ericsson no mobile-phone handsets. In the clothing and footwear industries, semiconductors and computers, and other consumer electronics, a huge amount of the low value-added work is now carried out in low wage cost countries.

In the grand scheme of things this is a massive mutual benefit. The jobs created in the rich countries are more highly skilled, less boring, and more highly paid. There is nothing intrinsically attractive about factory jobs. At the same time, the work is often—excepting the factories run by unscrupulous exploiters—better paid and more skilled than the alternatives available in poorer countries. A job in a factory with a contract to supply a multinational is often the only escape from grinding rural poverty and traditional oppressive attitudes for young women from villages in countries like China or Thailand, and certainly better than prostitution in the sleazy bars of Bangkok. Even in middle-income countries like Mexico such transplant jobs are giving women new freedoms. Like so many arrangements in the global economy, it is genuinely a win-win pattern. Less directly, developing countries also gain technical know-how and management expertise from foreign investors. Somebody who works as a foreman in one of their plants is soon equipped to set up his own business instead.

To blue-collar workers in the United States, Europe, or Japan, however, it looks like a zero-sum game where cheap labor in the third world is "stealing" their jobs. What's more, there is nothing to stop developing countries from investing in new technologies and very rapidly progressing from traditional manufacturing to weightless activities. The Indian software industry is a good example. Its revenues have grown from just over half a billion dollars in 1993 to an estimated six billion plus last year, still a small share of the $500 billion world software market but very rapidly growing. While India has not proved yet to be a software innovator, it is estimated that more than a hundred of the Fortune 500 companies have outsourced programming work to India. Indian companies such as Wipro and Tata Infotech are certainly gaining a higher global profile. The attraction of outsourcing routine programming to India is the combination of high quality and low cost. Although wages are rising in India, even a highly qualified network administrator will earn under $20,000 a year, less than half of their American counterparts. In programming, software development, and support the gap is bigger. And software is not the only example. Other services like call centers, back-office settlement in banking, and so on can, thanks to technology, can be transferred to countries where workers are cheap and plentiful.

Developing countries will themselves have to make huge investments in order to capture the benefits of the new general-purpose technologies. Their task is harder because of the scale of the complementary investments they need to make, from the education system to the communications infrastructure, not to mention regulatory reform, civil-service modernization, financial liberalization, and a whole host of other policies likely to prove at least difficult and probably highly contentious. As the next section spells out, the quality of human contact and institutions, which add up to what economists and sociologists term "social capital," is more important than ever for economic success. In businesses using sophisticated and complex technologies and dependent on people's creativity and the quality of their communication with one another, the social context is more, not less, important. So, contrary to the impression given by many current critics of capitalism, the free-market, globalized New Capitalism is one in which the nature of society and political institutions are crucially important. This gives the Western liberal democracies, with their efficient legal systems, institutions for mediating conflict peacefully, mass media, and so on, a huge advantage. For all the scope, poor countries have to catch up economically thanks to the technological leap forward, crystallizing those gains will not be easy.

As one recent publication from the OECD 15, generally very enthusiastic about the potential for a long boom, notes: "Even though this tapestry has been rewoven on numerous occasions

> Developing countries will have to make huge investments in order to capture the benefits of the new general-purpose technologies.

as the world economy has moved through different phases, it has so far never been done without very high costs." It continues: "Profound transitions in how and where people live and work as well as what they produce and consume do not come easily." Periods of transition are often ridden through with conflict.

The deindustrialization of the richest economies demonstrates this vividly. It is a process that started as long ago as the early 1970s, when the OPEC oil-price shock sent the world economy reeling into recession and gave a coincidental boost to new technologies, cleaner, increasingly weightless ones, even as it started to destroy old industries. Industries such as steel, shipbuilding, and textiles never regained that zenith. To recover and thrive, manufacturing had to become an altogether higher value, higher skill affair.

The remaking of the car industry thanks to Japanese management know-how and green-field investment is a perfect example of this up-skilling. In the process, one involving enormous upheaval, cars were steadily transformed into the beautifully designed (and oil-efficient) computers on wheels we drive today. However, for many years it would have been hard to persuade, say, a General Motors employee from Flint, Michigan, that there was any silver lining to the clouds of unemployment and loss of hope inflicted during the transition.

Other technologically sophisticated industries like electrical and optical engineering or pharmaceuticals have taken their place in the vanguard of productivity and output growth. The high-technology revolutionaries have toppled the old aristocracy of labor. Before many more years pass, there will be hardly any miners, or textile workers, or assembly-line fodder in the developed world. Either poor laborers in the developing world or, more likely, machines will do their work. They are redundant, in the truest sense of that ominous word.

Yet while the deindustrialization of the Western economies, especially the United States and UK, has turned out to be a blessing in disguise, clearing the ground for the New Capitalism, the human cost was appalling. Entire cities were almost fatally damaged by the progressive disappearance of industries that had given birth to them a century earlier—thriving Victorian municipalities like Liverpool and Glasgow, powerhouses like Detroit and Pittsburgh. Earlier geographic advantages such as location on a major waterway for shipbuilding, or plentiful soft water in the case of textiles, became irrelevant. There was nothing obvious to anchor economic activity in these rust-belt regions anymore.

In families that had had three generations of shipbuilders or weavers, the decline of traditional industries had a catastrophic effect. Men—it was mainly men—in the prime of life who had held the most respected and sought-after jobs, with high pay and high status in the community, suffered a blow from which they never fully recovered. Many never worked again. Families broke up. The social costs are still with us, in the stubborn problems of unemployment, underachievement, ill health, violence, drugs, and crime in many urban sink areas. For a generation of young people with the misfortune to be born when and where they were, this was their only inheritance. And while there are some writers and artists who have managed to convey this desperation, it is largely a class as voiceless as it is powerless.

The political legacy of deindustrialization lived on, too, in the decline of the traditional working-class support base for the mass center-left parties, internecine conflict on the left, and many years of right-wing government. Thatcherism was one of the most striking examples of the political fallout from the crisis of capitalism of the 1970s and 1980s. With such examples, it is no wonder economic change breeds at least as much bitterness as optimism.

More than a quarter of a century on from the first oil shock, however, it might seem easier to be optimistic. The worst pain of economic restructuring is long past, and most of the payoff lies ahead of us. Some groups, unfortunately, still stand to lose out from this process. The reasons lie in the very nature of the new technologies.

3

The Gathering Clouds

Prague, the ancient capital of the Czech Republic, is one of the world's most beautiful cities. Wenceslas Square, a long, narrow open space right in the center of this jewel of human civilization, saw those huge, peaceful demonstrations that above all gave the collapse of Communism in 1989 its name, the Velvet Revolution. Hundreds of thousands of citizens gathered in calm vigil night after bitter cold night as 1989 drew to a close, the power of their presence at last enough, after just a few skirmishes with the police, to force the discredited old regime to step aside. It was a rare moment of hope, a turning point deserving the clichéd description of a new dawn, before traditional fin-de-siècle doubts set in during the 1990s. The first time I went to the Czech capital was February 1991, when tourism and commercialization were starting to take firm hold, and crowds of backpackers crammed the hot spots like the Charles Bridge and Old Town Square. But my abiding memory is one of quiet streets dusted with snow, music at every corner, and history in each shadow.

Those exhilarating weeks at the end of 1989 certainly did not mark the first time Prague had been the scene of a decisive confrontation between freedom and tyranny. But in the earlier demonstrations of in the spring of 1968 the wrong side had won, and government reformers were ousted violently, thanks to the firepower of Russian tanks. The march of history does not always proceed in the desired direction.

In Prague in September 2000 it was perhaps not at all obvious what direction would be the most desirable. The occasion for this latest clash on its narrow streets—not between hated regime and its own oppressed citizens this time, but between the Czech police and crowds of radical activists from many other countries—was the annual meeting of the International Monetary Fund and World Bank. The anti-globalization bandwagon had rolled into town. There were fewer people on the streets than in 1989 but more violence than it had taken to overthrow Communism. Despite a huge security operation that had included turning back a whole trainload of Italian anarchists at the Czech border and throwing a police blockade around the convention center, groups of determined demonstrators provoked the security forces into using tear gas and water cannon to try and keep the way in to the meeting open for the official delegates. That proved impossible for a few hours—at least at street level. The protestors forced the bankers, officials, and politicians to abandon their limousines and descend to the metro if they wanted to travel to and fro.

Still, despite the noisy riot and plentiful minor injuries, there was also something of a carnival, an odd sense of feverish excitement, in the atmosphere, aided by the cavalcade of television cameras on the lookout for the good images a bit of trouble would bring. Any baby boomer for whom the 1968 uprisings and demonstrations in Prague and elsewhere—Paris and London as well as the United States—still strike a chord of thrilling rebelliousness could not help but have some sympathy for the environmentalists, the development campaigners, and the anarchists on the march now against globalization, against the power of multinational corporations, against the marginalization of the poor. There is after all no shortage of injustices to protest against.

But the activists out on the streets in London, Seattle, Washington, and Prague since mid-1999 have a problem. They are articulating a wholly admirable set of values—justice, fairness, freedom— against a rapidly shifting background, which makes it very hard to be sure how these values would be best served. It is certainly not obvious that global capitalism works against these values. On the contrary, the evidence points firmly the other way. Thirty-odd years ago it seemed pretty clear to most radicals that capitalism was bad, socialism (at least in a form unperverted by Soviet influence) good.

Since 1968, however, capitalism has chalked up one success after another. The Soviet Union not only lost the Cold War, it destroyed the economies of half of Europe and many other countries in the process. Central planning represents perhaps the biggest mistake anywhere, ever, in economic policy. The Iron Curtain lifted to reveal unhealthier, unhappier, and poorer peoples eager to embrace the market economy. The Yugoslav writer Slavenka Drakulic brought home most tellingly for me the human costs of a drab half century of central planning. Capitalism meant being able to buy lipstick, and lipstick matters. "In the five-year central plans, made by men, of course there was no place for such trivia as cosmetics," she wrote in 1988. She went on to explain how much effort it took to avoid the uniformity of wearing the same blue eyeshadow and red hair dye that every other women had also had to buy, involving home manufacture of beauty products and black-market hustling. She added that the effort had a cost: "To be yourself, to cultivate individualism, to perceive yourself as an individual in a mass society is dangerous. You might become living proof the system is failing. Make-up and fashion are crucial because they are political."[1]

> The protesters are articulating a wholly admirable set of values— justice, fairness, freedom—against a rapidly shifting background, which makes it very hard to be sure how these values would be best served. It is certainly not obvious that global capitalism works against these values. On the contrary.

The Principle of Openness

The freedom built into a market economy is itself an aspect of economic development, beyond the material goods it delivers, as Amartya Sen has so persuasively argued. A liberal economic regime is a good thing in itself. However, it is also beyond dispute that global free-market capitalism has brought extraordinary material gains. The growth of trade and cross-border investment boosts living standards, in all the countries engaged in the global economy, and for people at all points on the scale of income distribution.

The evidence that trade and cross-border investment raise overall economic growth is robust. Estimates of the size of the impact do vary. Even so, there is a consistent result, known as the "twin peaks" finding. Open economies have higher growth, and the poorer ones amongst them catch up with the leaders, converging on a high income "peak." Closed economies instead converge relentlessly on a low "peak."[2] Those countries excluded from the postwar process of economic liberalization and trade, many of them with centrally-planned economies, have plainly fared less well than those engaged in the global market economy. Just compare East and West Germany, for example. The most desperately poor countries today are those the most isolated from the world economy by conflict or atrocious government, such as Afghanistan, Albania, and Sierra Leone.

> It is beyond dispute that global free-market capitalism has brought extraordinary material gains. The growth of trade and cross-border investment boosts living standards, in all the countries engaged in the global economy, and for people at all points on the scale of income distribution.

Openness is becoming even more important as economies grow more dependent on the flow of ideas and on new technologies. It is more important because the ideas and technologies are so much more complex. New technologies also cause industrial restructuring, which can only go ahead, delivering the growth benefits, if existing vested interests cannot lobby successfully against change. As the economist Mancur Olson argued so convincingly, freer trade and inward investment provide the best way to prevent vested interests from getting their own way at the expense of wider economic gains. "If foreign or multinational firms are welcome to enter a country to produce and compete on an equal basis with local firms, they will not only bring new ideas with them but also make the local market more competitive. . . . That is one reason they are usually so unpopular," he wrote.[3] Besides, good ideas always come from somewhere else, just as an oyster needs a piece of foreign grit before it can form a pearl. The principle of openness holds just as much for countries as for individuals and companies. It holds most true for those that have a lot of catching up to do.

Jeffrey Sachs, the eminent development economist from Harvard, has emphasized the importance of reaching a critical mass of ideas and technology, noting that new ideas come from "recombinations" of existing ideas. In poor countries, he says, the fruitful interaction among universities, governments, and industry that typically drives innovation is "unheard of." But without it, the developing countries will never catch up with the developed ones, for "innovation shows increasing returns to scale, meaning that regions with advanced technologies are best placed to innovate further." His prescription is rethinking development policies in order to overcome the forces that will tend to widen the gap between rich and poor countries.[4]

Clearly generalizations about the paths taken by different countries should all be treated with caution, and openness is certainly not the only explanation for differences in economic performance; but it is intellectually dishonest to make the opposite case that openness to trade and investment is in general bad for living standards.

Nor is it true, as some anti-globalizers still claim, that growth resulting from trade is good on average but bad for the poorest people in poor countries. Openness to foreign trade benefits those on low incomes as well as the rich. The growth resulting from globalization in no way impoverishes the poor, but on the contrary makes them better off. However, one recent World Bank study establishing this result caused absolute outrage amongst even moderate campaigners.[5] One key conclusion was that: "Openness to international trade raises incomes of the poor by raising overall incomes. The effect on the distribution of income is tiny and not significantly different from zero."

I believe this is a conclusion many of those concerned about the poorest people in the world today are unable to accept, and hence the outrage. For it is widely perceived that inequality is increasing dramatically. It is also impossible to ignore the phenomenon of globalization. I think many observers find it equally impossible to avoid the conclusion that the globalization is causing greater inequality, whereas in fact both are the consequences of deep and revolutionary technical change in the world economy.

An Unequal Globe

On the face of it the inequality figures look pretty obscene. Average living standards as compared between the very richest and very poorest countries diverged remarkably over the course of the twentieth century. Whereas the club of rich countries has got richer and richer, there has been virtually no growth in sub-Saharan Africa for half a century. So per capita GDP in the richest country is now about fifty times higher than in the poorest, while it was only about fifteen times higher in 1900.

The overall picture is not quite so bleak. A group of Southeast Asian countries experienced rapid development that took them a long way toward the living standards of the OECD. India and China have begun to record significant improvements since about 1980. The divergence between the very poorest and the rest means 1.3 billion people live on the equivalent of less than one dollar a day, while the average income in the OECD as a whole is nearly fifty times greater, and in wealthy Switzerland about seventy times greater.

Even more breathtaking are the contrasts between the expanding ranks of the superrich, the wealthy businessmen feted in *Forbes* magazine's annual "rich list," and the poor or even the typical human being. The annual turnover of big corporations such as General Motors, WalMart, or Shell exceeds the GDP of many small and medium-sized countries like Thailand, Norway, and Israel. The net worth of the world's richest 200 people passed the $1 trillion mark in 1998, while that of the three richest exceeded the combined GNP of the forty-eight least developed countries.[6] True, this compares a stock of wealth with annual flows of output, but it is still a telling comparison. It is perhaps a sly comfort to the rest of us that a big chunk of such fortunes could evaporate in a serious stock market crash.

Income inequality has also risen within certain countries as well as between some of them. The contrasts between rich and poor are biggest by a long way in Latin America and sub-Saharan Africa. But there have been increases in inequality, after decades of stability in the income distribution, in a number of developed countries, notably the UK, United States, and New Zealand. In the United States for several years during the 1990s there were even absolute declines in inflation-adjusted incomes amongst some groups of low-paid workers, as well as a deterioration in their relative position. Other countries, notably in Continental Europe, have seen inequality remain unchanged or even diminish, although some would argue that very high levels of unemployment over many years in these countries were simply a different manifestation of inequality.[7] Again, the picture should not be overexaggerated. All rich countries have about the same dispersion of incomes, which is pretty even compared to the distribution in Latin America or Africa. Nevertheless, there is now a great deal of political sensitivity to inequality even if it overlooks some factual nuances.

No economist can claim to have a rock-solid explanation for growing income inequality. We don't fully understand, partly because different countries' experiences have been diverse due to the wide variety of government policies and social norms. But some ex-

planations can be ruled out. Inequality has not grown just because
tax systems are less progressive than they used to be. Reductions in
the highest rates of income and capital gains taxes in many countries
are blamed by many for making the rich so much richer. This stum-
bles against the fact that where inequality has risen, it has been on
such a scale that it dwarfs the impact of tax cuts. It also clashes with
evidence that the highest earners are paying a larger share of total
taxes than before.[8] Even though governments have backed away
from active policies of redistribution by "squeezing the rich until the
pips squeak" (in the memorable phrase of Denis Healey, one of
Britain's former Chancellors of the Exchequer, who had precisely
this aim in mind), the tax burden on the richest fifth of the population has risen in the United States and UK.

One of the two most popular overarching explanations for inequality in the rich countries is that it is the effect of competition with
cheap labor countries and therefore globalization is to blame. But
that cannot be right, either. Paul Krugman argues persuasively that
the pattern of wage and employment changes is not consistent with
this explanation, and instead suggests that within each industry demand for skilled workers has risen relative to unskilled workers for
reasons other than trade.[9] What's more, the United States and UK
simply import too little from developing countries for this trade to
be able to explain the big change in the distribution of wages. Most
developed countries still do the vast majority of their trade with
each other even if imports from developing countries are increasing
rapidly.

Is Technology to Blame?

That leaves technological change as the other big explanation for
growing inequality,which may be boosting demand for skilled workers without there being any matching increase in supply. The evidence in support of this explanation is building up as economists test
the hypothesis for different countries and industries. It is found in

patterns of employment growth, with jobs expanding fastest in the high-technology sectors in most OECD countries.[10] There is support from history, too, with vast inequalities developing in the late nineteenth century until the spread of public schooling created an enhanced supply of appropriately skilled labor. Technology created a demand for certain workplace skills that were in short supply, depressing the incomes of those left behind relative to the lucky few who could forge ahead. But thanks in large part to schooling the supply caught up, creating subsequent generations that could reap the technological harvest as more productive, better-paid workers and also as consumers. In the short term it proved a disruptive force, altering patterns of employment and the earnings potential of different groups before delivering, in the long term, greater prosperity to all.

This ties in with what has become a commonplace view, that the skills of the workforce need upgrading—as Tony Blair said in Britain's 1997 election campaign, what mattered above all was "education, education, and education." He was right, as Robert Reich had been, making the same point when he was U.S. Secretary of Labor in the first Clinton administration. A later chapter will look at the kind of education system needed as the technological basis of the economy changes. The lag between the demand for appropriate skills and the supply of them, both of which can vary among countries, is a powerful explanation for greater income inequalities or, to put it more broadly, the absence of social justice perceived by voters in many countries. This lag is one reason why the foundations of future prosperity can cause political tension.

However, there is more than new technology and the demand for a skilled workforce to some of the disparities in income and wealth we can observe today. Partly, of course, we all see the extremes so much more. We have become more conscious of the inequalities. Our screens and magazines bring us images of stock market frenzy, of great luxury, and also of famine and death. We walk down the streets of our greatest cities where some people enjoy a standard of comfort

> In the late nineteenth century . . . technology created a demand for certain workplace skills that were in short supply, depressing the incomes of those left behind relative to the lucky few who could forge ahead. But thanks in large part to schooling the supply caught up, creating subsequent generations that could reap the technological harvest as more productive, better-paid workers and also as consumers.

and affluence never seen before in human history and yet we see beggars and addicts sitting on their piles of damp cardboard outside a brightly lit designer clothes shop. There is a poverty problem on the one hand and a wealth problem on the other.

There are certainly a lot more billionaires than there used to be. The idea that there is an excrudescence of gilded-age wealth has been popularized in the phrase "winner takes all," based on an explanation by Sherwin Rosen in 1981 of why superstars could command such fantastic incomes. The basic point is that superstars can increase their output at zero marginal cost—a movie star only makes the movie once and it costs her no additional effort if another person wants to watch it. At the same time, consumers develop a preference for the best-known performers because they know what they're getting. A newcomer might be even more beautiful and talented than today's top stars, but you can't be sure. So when it comes to choosing what to go and see this Friday, the audience will still opt for the movie with the big names. This is why the publicity machine has to put so much effort into creating new stars.

Which brings us back to the question of technology. In the weightless economy these special supply and demand effects are becoming far more widespread.[11] They work for Bill Gates. Software is produced with high fixed costs—the development, testing, and marketing—but very low marginal costs. Programs can be copied at essentially no cost. And because of the "network effect" whereby a piece of software is more useful the more people use it, once Windows became established newcomers found it hard to dislodge from the number-one slot. Markets characterized by network effects, as most technological markets are, very often have a dominant leader. In fact, superstar economics operates more and more widely through the economy as new technologies cut production and distribution costs on the supply side and extend network effects on the demand side.

In other words, there could well be some inherent tendency toward inequality in the superstar effects of new technologies. But this is very much mitigated by the new opportunities technology is offering to outsiders. There are lots more winners and lots more chances to join their ranks. While the dot.com share price bubble has burst, it did make it clear that young people with no more than the basic benefits of a good education and solid middle-class background could reasonably aspire to much greater wealth. And the newcomers were not confined to the computer industry. In music and the media, retailing, travel, and a host of other service industries where there is no need to invest a huge amount of money in big factories and no need to jump high regulatory hurdles, the same technologies that have generated huge potential rewards have also lowered the barriers to attaining them.

This goes a long way to explaining why the pronounced increase in inequalities of income and wealth in the United States and UK in particular during the 1980s and early 1990s were uncontroversial. While many progressive commentators wrung their hands about inequality, it did nothing at all to dent the social calm. Rather than thinking about marching on the streets in protest, people were much more likely to turn their mind to devising their own money-making schemes.

> There could well be some inherent tendency toward inequality in the superstar effects of new technologies. But this is very much mitigated by the new opportunities technology is offering to outsiders. There are lots more winners and lots more chances to join their ranks.

The actual inequality of income was accompanied by far greater equality of aspiration.

It matters far more that our prosperous societies cannot eliminate poverty than that a small number of individuals are able to make unimaginable fortunes. Policies that aim to construct a fairer income distribution from the bottom rather than destroy an unfair one from the top address more directly the problem of poverty. This should be the higher priority for both moral and economic reasons. It is a much more serious and difficult problem.

There is no question the poor need to become less poor. It is not tolerable for those 1.3 billion citizens of the world to live on less than a dollar a day. It is certainly desirable for multinationals to apply the same standards in the developing world as in their home country. But the success of global capitalism since 1945 and especially since 1989 makes it apparent that it is the solution, and not, as those protesters in Prague claimed, the problem. It is hard to argue coherently, and in the face of a mass of evidence, against a very successful system. There is no other game in town.

The old tram lines of ideology have buckled and rusted, yet it is clear many people want to stick to them in preference to striking off into unmapped territory. Partly this is because the fundamental economic changes taking place now might well in the short term be creating losers as well as winners. At the very least, they mean the winners are pulling ahead of the rest to an unprecedented extent. Change in itself also often makes people uneasy; there is a natural tendency to abhor uncertainty. This attitude does not depend on objective suffering, on dry facts; as Manuel Castells has observed, being irrelevant is worse than being oppressed.

Being marginalized from the thriving New Capitalism, or the fear of becoming so, is one of the most unpopular and disturbing aspects of globalization. Alarmingly, uncertainty is marching hand in hand with prosperity. It might be your turn for marginalization next.

An Uncertain World

If unfairness appeared to be one undesirable consequence of the New Capitalism, new risks were another, risks in the job market because of industrial restructuring but also more widely in food scares or environmental change.

Uncertainty goes hand in hand with technological change, and on the face of it looks like another reason for having some serious reservations about techno-enthusiasm.

In 1996, after three years of solid growth and therefore when the economy was well into what turned out to be a record-breaking expansion, the *New York Times* published a special report called "The Downsizing of America." It captured the mood of the moment. Not only in the United States but also Europe and Japan, there was a widespread sense of insecurity, revealed in opinion polls and confidence surveys. Even in mid-2000, when U.S. unemployment had dropped below 4 percent or the workforce and consumer confidence was high, people reported to the pollsters a continuing sense of insecurity as workers.

This was partly a hangover from the recession of the early 1990s. During that downturn white-collar workers had suffered an increased risk of redundancy compared to the past, although needless to say it remained much lower than the comparable risk for blue-collar or unskilled workers. It is rare for the middle classes to get such a rude economic shock, and the reverberations are long-lasting. However, the public mood also reflected a deeper sense of uncertainty.

The same phenomenon occurred in the late nineteenth century when industrialization was turning society upside down. A clear sense of the forward march of prosperity coexisted with what Eric Hobsbawm has called the "profound unpredictability" of working lives. "If any single factor dominated the lives of nineteenth-century workers, it was insecurity," he writes.[12] Nor was this just the insecurity due to the possibility of illness or unemployment in an age before there existed a welfare state. "For the world of the established bourgeois was also considered to be essentially insecure." As J. K. Galbraith observed so brilliantly in *The Affluent Society*, the search for certainty and economic and financial security can explain a lot about the way our societies have developed. In stable times this quest is easier than in times of change. What we have now is not just change but revolution.

There are some obvious ways in which, as a number of sociologists have noted, risks of all kinds seem more widespread and threatening in our increasingly technologically complex societies. Examples are global warming and other potential environmental disasters; the outbreak of seemingly new diseases or their arrival from elsewhere, like BSE in Britain, Nile Fever in New York, AIDS, Ebola, and so on; or the unknown dangers posed by genetic modification of crops. Very few people feel well-equipped to assess the threats posed by such developments. If an awful disease emerges an ocean away, how much should we worry about it? One author anwers: "For many global citizens anyway, the perception of total interdependence brings with it a dark and paralyzing fear, at the root of which lies the awareness that there is no escape."[13] Worse, scientists and technologists, whom we might expect to tell the rest of us how much to worry, disagree with each other. The sight of one boffin confidently asserting one thing being followed by another saying exactly the opposite is a staple of the news bulletins.

Indeed, technological uncertainty has matured into an apocalyptic phase. In an influential article in *Wired* in April 2000 Bill Joy, the cofounder and chief scientist of Sun Microsystems, and cocreator of the Java programming language, announced his spectacular conversion from a techno-optimist to an extreme pessimist. He put the risk that new technologies would result in human self-extinction at 30–50 percent. The trigger for his conversion was the prediction by Ray Kurzweil, another titan of the computer industry, that a $1,000 computer would match human intelligence by 2020 and that machine intelligence would become self-replicating, taking the next big evolutionary step for intelligent beings.[14] (It is a prediction worth taking seriously: Kurzweil was a very early advocate of the idea that a machine could become clever enough to beat a human at chess, and got the date right to within a year.)

Like nuclear technology, Joy argued, computer and nanotechnology have the potential for use as weapons of mass destruction—and it will be a potential in the hands of every antisocial adolescent hacker ("high-performing sociopath" in Joy's phrase) burrowed in his darkened bedroom. In his *Wired* article, he writes: "The 21st century GNR [genetics, nanotechnology, and robotics] technologies have clear commercial uses and are being developed almost exclusively by corporate enterprises. In this age of triumphant commercialism, technology—with science as its handmaiden—is delivering a series of almost magical inventions that are the most phenomenally lucrative ever seen. We are aggressively pursuing the promises of these new technologies within the now-unchallenged system of global capitalism and its manifold financial incentives and competitive pressures."

When privately manufactured small arms kill millions of people each year, in a highly profitably $7 billion–10 billion a year industry, it seems odd to argue there is something dangerously new in the commercialism as such. Still, it is true the market for nuclear weapons is still a restricted one compared with the likely market for robotics. Ray Kurzweil also admits there is a problem: "My optimism probably accounts for my overall faith in humanity's ability to control the forces we are unleashing," he concludes. Little enough comfort there for pessimists.

The fear is the absence of control.

Who's in charge?

There is certainly a clear line of descent from the radicals of the 1960s who marched in protest against nuclear weapons to today's environmental and anti-globalization movement. It is easy to forget the dread of nuclear holocaust that was so widespread during the Cold War. Although I am too young to have marched with the Campaign for Nuclear Disarmament, I would have if I could: like many people of my age, I can still remember nightmares I had as a child about the end of the world in a perpetual, empty winter. The technological dangers must not be dismissed.

At a talk he gave in Paris, to an audience of business folk hoping to exploit the new technologies commercially, Bill Joy's underlying concern became clear, however. "We have an economic system that assumes change is always good, innovation is progress. But we might create a new life form that is out of control." The fear is the absence of control. Who's in charge?

The same fear appeared to lie behind the dramatic conversion of George Soros, the world's most famous financier, into a critic of the markets after the global financial crisis of 1997–98. He described global capitalism as a "wrecking ball," having posed the same question about who now could control the markets, and found that if he couldn't any longer, then nobody could. That the answer to the question "who's in charge" is always "nobody" is at the root of the pervasive sense of uncertainty. And that the economy is doing well is little comfort. After all, the economy is doing so well precisely because of the change, and because of that technologically based uncertainty.

It's the Economy, Stupid

Luckily, there is a huge upside to all this uncertainty, which arises from the changes that will create the basis for future economic growth and gains in human welfare. The uncertainty necessarily spills over into the everyday economic sphere. Changes in production methods, distribution channels, markets, and so on unleashed by the technological tide of "creative destruction" (in Schumpeter's apt phrase) are changing the business organization. In an influential book published in the mid-1980s, Oliver Williamson argued that the hierarchical corporation had developed as the best structure for coping with the kinds of uncertainty that prevailed in business for most of the postwar decades. It minimized the transactions costs and frictions due to unpredictability by internalizing them in a large, centrally run institution.

That is no longer a viable strategy. Technology is breaking down the old corporate hierarchies. It is no longer possible for the executives at the center to have all the information they need at their fingertips. So great is the extent of the unknowability of the future now, even quite near term, that the most efficient organizational structure is one that is prepared for anything. Many recent changes in company organization have been experimental, but a key goal has been increasing flexibility. Essential for rapid response to changing circumstances, and favorable to innovation, the network seems to be becoming the archetypal new form of business structure.[15] After a decade or so of alliance building, many of these are now becoming wired up through online supply chains and exchanges, for an even faster and more fluid response to changing market conditions and new opportunities.

As in the past, the car industry has been at the forefront of organizational innovation. The number of auto manufacturers has risen, contrary to popular impressions, mainly because of the entry of a number of new Asian producers. Behind the facade of huge mergers creating giant global auto manufacturers is a complicated web of cross-border alliances with suppliers and partners, marketing channels, and technological joint ventures.

The middle ranks of the corporate bureaucracies have been the sacrificial lambs of organizational change, with large-scale restructuring during the 1990s. No doubt many were *New York Times* readers. Thousands of fifty-year-old middle managers became just as technologically redundant as many a fifty-year-old miner or steelworker the previous decade. And facing the rest of the workforce, those still in jobs, was the demand for more flexibility.

This they delivered, at least in America, the crucible of this great transformation. (As Leonard Cohen puts it, "It's coming to America first/The cradle of the best and of the worst./It's there they've got the range and the machinery for change,/It's there they've got the spiritual thirst."[16]) Alan Greenspan pinpointed worker flexibility as an essential ingredient in the success of the New Economy in the United States. In one speech,[17] he said: "An intriguing aspect of the recent wave of productivity acceleration is that U.S. businesses and workers appear to have benefited more from recent advances in information technology than their counterparts in . . . . The relatively inflexible and, hence, more costly labor markets of these economies appear to be a significant part of the explanation."

Lower labor costs have resulted in a higher rate of return for the U.S. companies adopting the new technologies. Through the 1990s American corporations enjoyed rapid growth in profits, which led them to invest even more in technology, in a staggering vote of confidence in the future. Without embracing the upheavals in work and management patterns required to milk the new technologies effectively, those companies would not have gained the higher returns and would not have been able to invest even more in their future. The Fed chairman went on: "Here, labor displacement is more readily countenanced, both by law and by culture." And paradoxically, the fact that it is easier to fire American workers has led to a dramatic decline in the unemployment rate.

It is a lesson that seems unwelcome in many countries that value employment security, although companies outside the United States will also have to invest more in technology and even more crucially in new ways of work if prosperity is to increase. This argument is entirely consistent with the way unemployment in Europe ratcheted up to a persistently high level around the mid-1980s. Although those economies did not become any less flexible than they had been in the past, if technical change meant businesses actually needed more flexibility, then there would have been a new hesitation to do anything that might restrict future options, like hiring workers who could not then be fired more easily than before. Countries like the Netherlands and the UK, which introduced greater flexibility—quietly and pragmatically in the former case, triumphantly and con-

frontationally in the latter—subsequently saw a much faster decline
in unemployment. Flexibility is an important part of the story when
it comes to explaining unemployment patterns.

The Changing State

This is all very well for companies with the imperative of the profit
motive and corporate survival. But what about the rest of us? An outline answer of sorts is emerging. For example, education will be part
of it. However, there are profound political chasms ahead.

For the nature of the state as we know it has to change. Governments have to respond and become more nimble and flexible, just
as people and businesses do. If they do not, the clash between old
structures and new demands is likely to break them. While governments must still offer basics such as national defense, the rule of law,
and the protection of basic human and political rights, citizens'
wider demands of their political leaders are much tougher to satisfy
in this more complex and uncertain world. As Anthony Giddens has
put it: "States without enemies depend for their legitimacy more
than before upon their capacity for risk management."

On the face of it, this desire to address and limit new uncertainties has turned government into a more managerial or technocratic
matter. The old left-right political split makes little sense since the
end of the Cold War. Political parties of all lineages in all countries
have herded onto what we used to think of as the middle ground,
leaving their activists pining for the old ideological conflicts. The
choice for voters looks very much like a vote on competence.
Which of these identikit politicians will run the economy best?
Which can best reform public services or reduce crime? Politicians
all voice the same aims: stable employment, low inflation, a clamp-
down on drugs, better schools, a more efficient health service, and so
on. They argue about means, not ends.

Yet responses to the deep uncertainties that now face us are in
the end not technocratic or managerial but political issues. The de-

cisions cannot be left to the experts. The protests of the global anarchists are as much a protest against rule by a managerial elite, and in
favor of citizen involvement, as they are a protest against globalization. In this they are absolutely right, just as much as they are absolutely wrong in their analysis of the facts.

The welfare debate is a good example of the way political differences now lie along a new axis. Since the Second World War, governments in the developed world have promised their citizens economic security. Initially this took the form of a pledge of full
employment for male breadwinners and a pension on retirement.
Later with the advent of intractable mass unemployment, and other
social changes such as the entry of many more women into the
workforce and earlier retirement, it took the form of an income
safety net. Either way, the intermediation of the government allowed
citizens to pool the risk of income loss.

However, extraordinarily rapid growth in the social security
budget in many states gradually made it apparent that the strain on
this classic welfare state was increasing intolerably. High unemployment benefit was not the most important source of the increased
cost. Long-term sickness, additional housing or health benefits, pay-
ments to lone parents, and the rising bill for unfunded pensions contributed more to the fiscal burden. And the size of this burden led to
a vigorous debate about the corresponding tax burden. When voters
signaled their preference for tax cuts, rather than tax increases to pay
for more costly welfare or social security, government budget bal-
ances were the losers in most countries.

Of course, the 1990s have brought the public finances into better order in most countries, as politicians recognized the economic
damage being caused by excessive deficit finance. With social security the biggest single element of government spending, this has necessarily involved a degree of welfare reform. But the debate about
how to conduct this reform is by no means settled.

The UK offers a clear example of the dilemma. Gordon Brown's
"welfare-to-work" program has three main elements. First, using

both carrot and stick methods, reduce long-term unemployment through active labor-market policies. Secondly, improve work incentives through a minimum wage and in-work benefits. Thirdly, means-test benefits rigorously to ensure public money is directed to those who most need it. It is an approach that has chalked up early successes in reducing the number of people living only on benefit, and in reducing costs.

However, what it does not do is address the role of the social security system in sharing risk. Critics point out that extensive means-testing might indeed cut the bill for taxpayers but actually reduces the insurance element of the welfare system because what is received bears no necessary relation to the individual's past or potential contributions. This is more obvious in the case of state pensions, which are decreasingly related to the amount each individual pensioner has "saved" through the tax system.

This highlights a genuine political choice. We can have a welfare system that alleviates poverty effectively and therefore poses less of a tax burden but from which it is easy for the affluent majority to disengage itself. Those who pay and those who receive are on the whole nonoverlapping categories. This guarantees that welfare support will not be more than grudging, given the apparently robust voter resistance to increased taxes for this purpose. Or we can have a system that returns to the original postwar idea of "social insurance" for all citizens (whoever they are in an increasingly globalized world with greater numbers of people crossing national borders), updated for new risks and new social patterns. This would engage the vast majority in mutual support for the welfare system, but it could prove very expensive. It would take a brave politician to propose extending the scale of government right now, when the expansion in the size of government that began around 1960 has clearly come to a halt, not just in post-Reagan America and post-Thatcher Britain but also across the rest of the OECD.

Of course, this is not such a stark either-or choice in real life. The systems operating in most countries embed a mishmash of values, logical consistency never being the prime requirement. It does, however, reflect a real difference of political philosophy, one that straddles old partisan divisions. Welfare reform is not merely a managerial matter of reducing costs, rooting out fraud, and improving efficiency. It addresses fundamental questions about what kind of government we want—and also what governments are now able to do.

Taxes, of course, remain at the center of the debate about the power of government. Amongst those whose politics inclines to the romantic, there is still a hankering for governments to soak the ultrarich through higher taxes. It appears a clean, direct solution, but penal rates of taxation backfire. The ultrarich can easily evade them—in the end they just move to Monaco if that's what it takes. Higher tax rates do not even raise a lot of revenues because there are not all that many of the ultrarich; you have to raise taxes on the affluent middle classes to raise many billions.

The degree of government intervention in applying a strongly redistributive tax system also imposes a heavy burden in economic inefficiency. Growth is slower under such systems. It is more effective to use public spending for the purposes of redistribution. Any tax distorts the effort of those forced to pay, perhaps discouraging the second earner in a family from taking a job, perhaps driving the wealthy to convert their earned income to capital gains or set up offshore trusts, perhaps keeping new immigrants in low-paying jobs outside the formal economy altogether. It means governments need to think carefully about raising taxes—not that they should not do it but that it can be counterproductive to do too much or design taxes badly. Taxation designed to prevent rich people earning too much will certainly provoke them into avoidance measures. By the late 1970s the UK had a top income tax rate of 98 percent, but nobody paid it. On the other hand, especially when directed toward improved health and education, public spending helps the poorest most and creates a more productive workforce from which society as a whole benefits. It is a powerful tool for benefiting the poor more than the rich, helps the economy to the extent that it is invested in either human or physical capital, and commands a much greater measure of public support. Such expenditure creates the conditions for both greater fairness and faster growth, whereas redistributive taxes pose a trade-off between fairness and growth.

The Diffusion of Power

Many traditional government powers have started to seep away because of globalization. There is a deep political basis for this in the progressive withdrawal of citizens' acquiescence in government intervention in their lives since the end of the Second World War and again since the end of the Cold War. Even the most old-fashioned left-wingers would no longer want to have to get government permission to buy foreign currency for a trip abroad, for example, or need numerous permits to start a business. National governments are no longer in sole charge of their macroeconomic policies in global capital markets, in the sense that bad policies will ultimately reap a severe financial market punishment. Their powers to tax and spend have to operate within limits set by this threat and by the increasing mobility of goods, capital, and high-skilled labor. Their trade policies are set by a web of mutual obligations with other nations. Unions can still demand that politicians keep out certain exports or weaken the exchange rate, for example, but it is not at all clear either that the politicians could deliver or that it would make any difference if they could. Public bureaucracies parallel corporate hierarchies as command-and-control structures suited to a mass-production economy. In the emerging network economy they are increasingly dysfunctional.

But neither are multinationals as all-powerful as they once seemed to be—or still appear to be to some of their critics. They face much more competition from other corporations. Many of their markets are more rather than less regulated. Consumers are more demanding, so that even once all-powerful U.S. giants like Coca-

Cola and McDonald's have to respond to an increasing diversity of taste and sensitivity to price. Although managing a global network of customers and suppliers has become easier in some obvious ways because of information and communication technologies, the network itself has grown considerably more complicated and diffuse.

Governments are not shrinking, and corporate profits are almost as high as they have ever been. Yet one problematic aspect of the anticapitalist, antibusiness thrust of current protests is that it is getting harder to pinpoint the power structures against which it might be possible to rebel. Even as protesters accuse international agencies or multinational corporations of unprecedented abuses of their global power, the top officials and executives feel more powerless. They are certainly no more in control of events than the rest of us. Power, whether government or corporate, is growing ever more diffuse. To the extent that it is possible to identify power clearly, it lies in the United States and not the rest of the world, and hence the strong anti-American cast of the protests. (The French activist-farmer José Bové is not alone in identifying multinational power with American might, ignoring the increasingly international base of cross-border businesses.)

The diffusion of power makes the business of running a company, or a country, substantially more difficult. Formal rule-making from the center is increasingly having to give way to informal rules or norms of behavior that somehow have to emerge from a huge number of individual decisions dispersed through the network of workers, or voters. As Francis Fukuyama has pointed out, this kind of self-organization relies on a much greater stock of "social capital," or in other words accumulated social order, skill, and mutual trust.[18]

The technology at the root of this complexity does offer the promise of a future solution to the crisis of governance. As clouds of tear gas rolled over one anti-IMF demonstration, officials peering nervously out of the window of their bus were most amused by a placard that read "World Campaign against Globalization." The campaigners have used the Internet extremely effectively in organizing their rolling round-the-world protests. This suggests the Internet will indeed turn out to have great potential for political empowerment, a potential for now captured only by the most energetic and committed.

There is tremendous interest in egovernment. Some U.S. states have experimented with voting online. Different branches of the American gov-

One problematic aspect of the anticapitalist, antibusiness thrust of current protests is that it is getting harder to pinpoint the power structures against which it might be possible to rebel.

ernment have gone further than other countries in putting information and providing access on Web sites meant to be citizens' place of contact with their elected representatives. And certainly, this potential for openness and access is genuine. Many, many more people are able to find more and more information that was formerly closed to them. Those of us from other countries lagging behind can only be impressed by the openness, however limited, of the U.S. authorities. There are obvious concerns about privacy: we want to know what the authorities are doing without letting them know much more about us. George Orwell's terrible vision of Big Brother watching us from an ever present screen is extraordinarily potent in the Internet age. Still, it must be a step forward for democracy to be able to find out easily a politician's voting record, or official figures on unemployment in your area, or the breakdown for government spending on road building. And then perhaps compare the findings to what another government is doing. Online accountability will prove an increasingly powerful tool in the hands of citizens.

The point of this chapter has been to demonstrate, however, that technical progress does not guarantee social progress, but rather creates the conditions that make it possible. With today's information technologies there is a specific possibility that employees and citizens will become more empowered to have freedom and responsibility for their own lives. With earlier technological advances, the impact was indirect. Antibiotics and domestic plumbing improved health, electric light made reading for pleasure and self-improvement after work a possibility for the masses. But information technology, like printing, leads to a more immediate transfer of access to knowledge, making it more widely available outside the established elites. Needless to say, high hopes that technology will boost democracy or world peace are nothing new. Lewis Mumford wrote: "By turns, the steamboat, the railroad, the postal system, the electric telegraph, the airplane, have been described as instruments that would transcend local weaknesses, redress inequalities of natural and cultural resources and lead to a worldwide political unity. . . . In the course of two centuries these hopes have become discredited." It is sensible to retain a degree of cynicism about the potential of technology outside its material plane. Such potential can never be realized without a struggle.

End of An Era

The events of 1989 with which this chapter opened torpedoed Communism. Television viewers around the world had ringside seats as the people of Eastern Europe ousted their governments. What was not so obvious still is that capitalism in its present form was also holed below the waterline. The anti-globalization demonstrations taking place every few months now are not causing its collapse in any direct way, but they are evidence that centralized, command-and-control capitalism is as defunct as centrally planned Communism. Both have been made extinct by the switch to a new technology-based economic system. The slow death of the system of capitalism as we have known it in favor of a new and potentially better version explains many of the strains and conflicts of modern life. As the earlier chapters showed, long-term economic growth is driven forward by new technologies, which in the end represent the efforts of human beings to forge a better life. And it works. In terms of real income levels, access to goods and services, health and longevity, and quality of life, not only the rich and the average but also the poorest people in Western capitalist societies are unimaginably better off than their grandparents and great-grandparents. Those living in the formerly Communist societies are trying to catch up as rapidly as possible. The very poor developing countries where technological progress has had no impact at all on everday life, where living standards have scarcely advanced for a hundred years, are those that have not had in place the economic and political framework to translate technical changes into personal changes. Technology is part of a social system, not an abstraction.

So the technological advances that will deliver the next step of change in world prosperity are also at the root of extraordinary social and political tensions, in every group of countries. This is one fundamental paradox of prosperity. We want it and at the same time don't welcome it. Human beings do not on the whole like change or find it easy. But, as Paul Romer put it, "Wealth is just another word for change."

What's more, I believe the technological revolution offers the opportunity to shape society for the better. It can undermine the rule of elites, which is always fundamentally rotten even when those elites are managerially competent. State bureaucracy is past its sell-by date. Governments are everywhere unpopular or, at best, irrelevant. Corporate hierarchies are faring little better. Twentieth-century capitalism is ripe for replacement by a fairer and more democratic version in the twenty-first century, a transition information and communications technologies will make possible. The anti-globalization campaign already demonstrates how effectively the new technologies can be harnessed for political organization, even if its activists have not yet found the ideal focus for their firepower.

Our societies are likely to have to cope with an unprecedented degree of technological change in the next twenty to fifty years. Even the optimistic Ray Kurzweil predicts: "The challenge to the human race posed by machines is fundamental enough that a violent reaction during this coming century is a strong possibility."

Whether or not that proves too pessimistic, it is safe to predict ex-

The technological advances that will deliver the next step of change in world prosperity are also at the root of extraordinary social and political tensions, in every group of countries. This is one fundamental paradox of prosperity.

treme tensions. The next section of this book looks in more detail at paradoxical aspects of the present wave of growth in the advanced economies, at the costs to be paid for the enormous potential benefit to our living standards from new technologies. Examples of the costs include the incredible speed of modern life and the great time drought; the redundancy of places in the Old Economy as the New Economy relocates; and the problem of needing to trust when everything becomes less trustworthy. Exploring this detail lays the foundations for proposals, in the final section, about the responses needed from all of us as individuals, from corporations, and from our governments.

4

Vanishing Borders

Barbed wire was invented to control the movement of cattle in the American West in the 1870s, as land was parceled out under the Homestead Act and cattle-raising made the transition from ranging to ranching. In 1873 Henry Rose, a farmer from Waterman Station in Illinois, attached sharp strands of wire to planks of wood along a fence to prevent his livestock from roaming. A year later six patents for barbed wire had been registered, and by 1880 50,000 miles were in place. Later uses of this new technology were not so benign. Barbed-wire fencing went on to be used to surround concentration camps in the Boer War and later defend trenches in the First World War. It was cheap, light, and virtually impassable. Cutting through a tangle of wire left frontline soldiers appallingly exposed to fire.

So, according to Reviel Netz, barbed wire is a "key element in the modern texture of power." But as the historian notes in the same article, many of the most important and powerfully defined areas of space have no physical form but are symbolic. "Mark out, on the two-dimensional surface of the earth, lines across which no movement is allowed and you have one of the key themes of history. . . .

Draw an open line preventing movement in either direction and you define a border."[1]

Borders are also one of the key properties of economies, although in this case it is a theme long submerged in the uniformity of conventional theoretical economics, with its study of identical rational agents, disembodied from any specific context. It is only recently that economic geography has enjoyed a revival.[2] This professional interest reflects the growing importance of place as a criterion for economic success.

The invisible barriers that divide one country from another, or put one neighborhood on the wrong side of the tracks, have always divided real-world economies into the fundamental units of analysis. When we speak of "an economy" it is usually shorthand for the economic activity taking place within the boundaries of the nation state, or perhaps the administrative regions of a nation like the U.S. states or German Lander. Very few economists have ever thought about other units. Karl Marx was one exception, basing his analysis on class, and Jane Jacobs has analyzed the economies of cities. But the profession as a whole today does not consider either to be an economist.

However, in an increasingly globalized world, with distance supposedly irrelevant, the specifics of place are paradoxically more important than ever, not less. Pundits who predict that place will no longer matter thanks to information and communication technologies that allow the rapid reorganization of production around the globe, or that can make working from home in rural havens the norm, could not be more wrong. We are no more seeing the end of geography than the end of history, and the reason lies precisely in those technologies.

This seems, to many people, counterintuitive. After all, the point of the technology is supposed to be that you don't have to be there, wherever "there" is. Modern communications technology and globalization have supposedly turned the world into a single marketplace, a playground for multinational companies, and on the face of it this ought to make the details of ge-ography increasingly irrelevant. As the eminent management theorist Peter Drucker expresses the business logic of globalization: "National boundaries are impediments and cost centers."[3]

Yet the paradox is real. If you can lo-cate anywhere thanks to the Internet and cheap communications, or to

In an increasingly globalized world, with distance supposedly irrelevant, the specifics of place are paradoxically more important than ever, not less.

deregulation and globalization, you might as well locate in the best possible place. And the best place is likely to be one that is already very successful. The clearest example is the way Silicon Valley and its hinterland have turned into one of the most powerful economic magnets ever. It is possible to set up a dot.com company anywhere. But the most ambitious entrepreneurs only want to base theirs in that small area in California.

Everybody knows Silicon Valley is where it is because Dave Packard and Bill Hewlett, Stanford University graduate students, founded an electronics company in the garage of Hewlett's house in Palo Alto in 1939. Within fifteen years there was a decisive cluster of precursor computer companies. By 1999 there was nowhere else on earth ambitious software and hardware entrepreneurs wanted to be. The world's supply of workers with relevant skills gathers there.

Nor can the base of specialized suppliers be replicated anywhere else. As writer Po Bronson puts it, you can't just throw together some programmers, venture capitalists, and electronics stores and season with money, because the Silicon Valley stew has been cooking on high heat for fifty years. It has generated all kinds of extremely spe-cialized functions, like headhunters who bring engineers from Sin-gapore, VCs who fund only video chips, writers specializing in tech-nical manuals, agents (the human kind) for software programmers, and so on. A telling example is the fact that you can find people who specialize in refurbishing the partitions used to create individual of-fice cubicles in software companies, as featured in Dilbert cartoons.

In fact, there are many partition refurbishers. It's a highly competitive industry. So we might talk loosely about Silicon Fen and Silicon Glen and Silicon Alley but frankly there is only one outstanding geographical success story in the computer business. Bronson writes: "By car, by plane, they come. They just show up. They've given up their lives elsewhere to come here."

Geography, explaining the here, is one of the key frontiers in economics. As a profession we have a much better sense of how economies change over time—or at least how to avoid mistakes in macroeconomic policy over the course of a business cycle. But there is scant understanding, and less evidence, about how economies work over space. The fact that it is an intellectual frontier also means there is little systematic, fine-grained evidence. This intellectual and empirical deficiency is not just an untidy gap. It matters more now than in the past. The contrast between the places that get something right—like Silicon Valley, or the cosmopolitan capitals like London or Shanghai, the new technology clusters like Munich in Germany or Cambridge in England—and those that do not, whether third-world cities or the desolate inner-city areas in all Western countries, is becoming extreme. It is another dimension of increasing inequality that campaigners see as a badge of the undesirability of globalization, as a reason for resistance. Without being at all explicit about the mechanisms, they portray geographic success as parasitical, as if a thriving center of economic activity were an ugly sister needing to exploit the Cinderella regions in order to get to the ball.

The here is more important now. There are multiple forces pointing to greater geographic concentration. The transition to a weightless or "new" economy is reducing the share of output accounted for by traditional manufacturing. Not only are the developed economies continuing the long-standing shift toward service-sector occupations, but also toward higher-value processing within manufacturing. Both aspects make it more important for people to be where other people already are. In many service industries there is a compelling basic need to locate where the customers are, creating a virtuous circle whereby the businesses set up where there is a ready market, and more customers are attracted because there are lots of suppliers offering a wide choice. Think of any restaurant district, where rival businesses choose to locate close to one another because potential customers will already be looking for a place to eat, and where customers know they will get a choice of restaurants and a pleasant buzz of activity.

One of the most fashionable restaurants in London as I write is the Ivy, notoriously hard to get into. One June day, I called to try to book a table for my husband's birthday treat the following January. Sorry, they said, we aren't yet taking reservations for next year. Out of curiosity, I asked for a table any evening in the next six months. They had none. If I had pretended to be Madonna I might have had more luck. Still, my experience backs the evidence that in a number of services congestion actually generates additional demand: as it is in the nature of the transaction that you don't know what you're getting until you have already consumed it, customers look for other evidence of quality, like popularity with other people or sheer trendiness. Faced with a choice of two neighboring fruit and vegetable stands in a market, one with a line of customers and one without, most people will join the line. If there's a line outside a restaurant, it must be good. Besides, it's more exciting to be eating somewhere all the fashionable folk prefer; it makes you feel fashionable, too, and who knows who will be at the next table? (I obviously need to work on my celebrity status before I try the Ivy again.)

> The transition to a weightless or "new" economy is reducing the share of output accounted for by traditional manufacturing. Not only are the developed economies continuing the long-standing shift toward service-sector occupations, but also toward higher-value processing within manufacturing. Both aspects make it more important for people to be where other people already are.

In any personal-service industry, moreover, it is essential to be in the same place as the customers. Consultancy, banking, and design can be delivered over a distance, but nurses, security guards, and waiters have to be right there. And it is not just low-paid services to which this applies. So do interior decorators, IT support staff, personnel managers, lawyers, and a host of other professionals. It is simply in the nature of the service.

The forces for agglomeration are not restricted to person-to-person services, however. In many industries new technologies have reduced transaction and transportation costs. While cotton mills needed to be near ports and soft water, few modern industries have such a pressing material reason to be in a particular spot. That means they might as well locate near their customers and near a pool of available labor. These are Alfred Marshall's original explanations (in his classic 1870 text) for the existence of cities as hubs of economic activity. As industries are increasingly less restrained by other locational pulls, these reasons suggest there will be even more agglomeration in either old, big cities or newer urban clusters.

Another explanation for clustering offered by Marshall—the exchange of ideas so that "the mysteries of the trade become no mystery but are, as it were, in the air"—also operates far more strongly. The exchange of ideas is a bigger part of economic activity in the weightless world; it is at the level of ideas that value is added. Moreover, in New Capitalism industries the ideas being exchanged are increasingly complex or subtle. Just as academics have always congregated in universities, software programmers or options traders want to work in a community of peers. This reinforces the advantage of particular locations even if, like Silicon Valley or the City of London, there was a good pinch of historical accident involved initially. Certainly, financial services firms for which the cost of transporting the product is negligible are willing to pay an extremely high price (around £100,000 an employee in London's financial heart) for their key "knowledge workers" to be present at the heart of the flow of information.

People Power

It is worth emphasizing the importance of face-to-face contact in the ideas industries. For many years I worked in a big, noisy, open-plan newsroom. Visitors often comment that it must be hard to concentrate, and it is. But concentration is unimportant compared to the ease with which ideas flow around in an open space; it is relatively easy to concentrate but very hard indeed to have a good new idea. Very few of my colleagues on the newspaper have a separate office. One who does is the editor. But he rarely has it to himself for quiet reflection. When there is not a large meeting taking place in his space, he is rarely there and can more often be found sitting at the news desk in the middle of the action or out and about seeing contacts. Similarly, when people ask why I can't work more often from home, now that it is so easy to get raw news and information over the Internet, I have to explain that it is not the basic facts alone that matter. Rather, it is the discussion with colleagues about what's important and why, and the coordination about who will do what and where in the newspaper something should go, and what kind of graphic or image is needed—all the value of interpretation and understanding that can be added to the raw materials.

So, being not just in the office but in a big office without physical barriers is essential. And that's before you even get into the office politics—spotting who is having lunch with whom, who has been summoned in to see the editor, which people are having rows, which having affairs, and so on. This kind of interchange used to take place among different newspapers in London, when journalists were able to exchange gossip over a drink in famous bars and pubs like El Vino's and the Printer's Devil around Fleet Street. Alas, the rich investment banks and law firms scattered the UK's only sporadically profitable newspapers to a number of cheaper bases around the city. The press is the poorer for the breakup of its original Marshallian cluster. But it is unimaginable that the flow of ideas and gossip could be eliminated within a newspaper.

The success of the Canary Wharf development in London's Docklands is a great testament to the importance of the flow of ideas face-to-face in an appropriate physical space, at the frontier of the weightless economy. The deregulation of the financial markets in 1986, a move by the Thatcher government widely described as "Big Bang," transformed a static closed-shop industry into a dynamic and growing one in which innovation became crucial for profit and even survival. It was also the start of the Docklands regeneration project, designed to breathe life into a moribund and poor area of the capital after the decline of the traditional port industries. Although there were financial incentives for companies to move to Canary Wharf, the decisive factor for the first big banks to do so was a difference in planning regulations compared with the Square Mile of the City of London. The regulators of the self-governing City were forced to allow new buildings in the late 1980s but only in Canary Wharf; it wasn't until some years later that these allowed to be big enough for the huge open-plan trading floors now considered essential in investment banking. The tardiness on the part of its planners in recognizing the importance of space torpedoed the City's traditional dominance in financial services, although luckily only dispersing that business to other nearby parts of London.

Small differences in the physical environment, such as the route to a particular colleague's desk, can make a huge difference in the quantity and quality of the information shared.

Indeed, the management will often shift groups of traders, salesmen, and analysts around the floor, the configuration depending on the flow of business of different types, in order to make sure the people who need to speak often are within easy calling distance of each other. Even though moving a workstation, with its multiple screens, might cost £3,000 ($4,500) each time, it is often worth moving people a few meters or tens of meters every few months. "The business shifts so much you need to move people to capture the varying synergies," according to one senior manager. "It's well worth the cost of moving the workstations." The bankers can literally do much more profitable business in new buildings with totally flexible floor space. Small differences in the physical environment, such as the route to a particular colleague's desk, can make a huge difference in the quantity and quality of the information shared, because although physical transport costs are almost irrelevant in financial services, like many weightless industries, the information transport costs are high indeed.

Using information technology in place of personal contact is no substitute. The quality of the exchange is not as high, at least as the technology now stands. In fact, communications technologies probably complement, rather than substitute, personal meetings. In other words, the greater ease of contact via email and the Internet actually increases the demand for face-to-face meeting because people want to complete and enhance conversations they have begun electronically. Making communicating with other people easier and cheaper in one way—online—boosts the demand for communicating in other ways, like face-to-face meetings. It should not be a surprise that business travel is soaring, that even cyber-gurus spend all their time in airports traveling to speak at conferences, or even that some couples are getting married after a first meeting in an Internet chat room.

The Urban Future

With more and more work either in service industries or in ideas industries, the demand for personal contacts means the economy of the future is even more urban than it is today. Urbanization is almost a synonym for economic development. It is one of the variables most strongly linked to measures of a country's prosperity. More than ever, cities will be the hubs of economic success. This conclusion will no doubt be challenged by many of those who are uneasy about technology and growth. There is a strong movement of antiurban environmentalism ranging from overworked young professionals to anxious parents who believe the quality of life is higher outside the city. Much of the comment about cities concerns the negatives: pollution, congestion, crime, physical dilapidation, poor schooling, and so on. There are also more ominous tensions, such as the very marked concentration of immigrants and nonimmigrant ethnic minorities in urban areas. The problems are real, but this litany misses the very basic point that a greater and greater proportion of the modern economy's output is generated in big cities because that is the source of ideas and creativity. These inputs need concentrations of people, and diverse types of people. It is essentially a self-fueling process, although one that policy makers and businesses need to open their eyes to.

> A greater and greater proportion of the modern economy's output is generated in big cities because that is the source of ideas and creativity. These inputs need concentrations of people, and diverse types of people.

The nature of urban economic dynamism is changing, however. In 1883, the novelist Émile Zola described the department store, just introduced in Paris, as the "cathedral of modern business." In department stores, for the first time prices were fixed rather than negotiable, set by management rather than salespeople. Employees in the stores lost the personal discretion to close a sale. These physically magnificent and imposing new emporia, like the Galeries Lafayette close to the Louvre, symbolized the decisive bureaucratization and centralization in the New Economy emerging in the late nineteenth century, and were one of the most ostentatious and impressive manifestations of the bureaucratic revolution. The people flocked to gawk at them.

The modern equivalent is the art gallery or museum. Many cities have refueled by building a prestigious new gallery designed by a famous architect. Often in the past these were pure manifestations of personal or national pride, the egos of rich and powerful people clad in concrete, glass, and metal; but increasingly they are seen by local authorities as an important component of urban regeneration. An early example of this phenomenon was the Richard Rogers–designed Pompidou Center in Paris (soon popularly renamed the Beaubourg, after its immediate district rather than a stuffy politician). Frank Gehry's Guggenheim has given Bilbao a much-needed shot in the arm and started the process of reversing its industrial decline. A potent example in contemporary London is Bankside, a massive former power station that fueled the Old Economy transformed (by Swiss architects Herzog and de Meuron) into Tate Modern, an art gallery pumping electricity into the New Economy of cultural and intellectual exchange. Bankside—which still contains an electricity substation whose humming is clearly audible in the massive entrance gallery created out of the old turbine hall—has been linked by a new footbridge direct to the City of London, one of the global economy's key locations. The captains and colonels and generals of the global economy can now power-lunch overlooking the city and overlooked by the fantastically valuable icons of modern art.

The energy for economic dynamism has shifted from electricity to ideas and creativity. The critic Stephen Bayley writes: "In many art museums, the building is much more impressive than the paintings or sculpture. . . . Now the museum is the distinctive building of our age, the one in which all the symbolic values of our civilization are invested." Just as Victorian city leaders expressed their economic confidence in magnificent, architect-designed power stations, factories and stores, and of course town halls (hubs of bureaucratic power), so now they seek the vastly ambitious and physically commanding museum for their cities.

In the introduction to a British Council exhibition on landscape, filmmaker Patrick Keiller observed: "Capitalism destroys and creates places, but the places it creates seem always, at least to begin with, less substantial, less rich, than the places it destroys—as in the cases, say, of the mechanization of agriculture or the replacement of mining and other industries by landscapes of distribution and retailing." The dark satanic mills, the pit head, even the flood of workers pouring out of a factory gate as the whistle blows, these are romantic images. Yet even the iconic Silicon Valley itself is hardly romantic or impressive, merely bland. If you watch TV reports on the economy, the difficulty in finding visual symbols of modern economic activity becomes very plain. After all, an office worker at a computer screen makes a dull image, while a cleaner or sales assistant does not conjure up dynamism and growth. The reporter usually opts instead for a production line, which is certainly no longer characteristic.

Keiller continued: "On the other hand, modern capitalism also gives place high value, partly by making its sought-after qualities scarce, partly by concentrating power in the global system in particular places—New York, Tokyo, Frankfurt, London etc. In the interstices of all this—in more or less dilapidated spaces as 'consumers'— we live our lives." The trophy gallery is the physical symbol of this concentration of global economic power. Its symbolic force lies in the fact that growth in weightless economies depends almost entirely on cultural and intellectual activity, on the exchange of ideas, and the creative human spirit. While much of the urban landscape is drab and featureless, or worse in the poorer areas, the politicians and businessmen who have most power in the big cities are giving physical expression to economic success in the shape of dramatic new galleries and museums, much as the city fathers in Victorian times built splendid town halls and libraries. Ed Glaeser, an urban economist at Harvard University, argues that in addition to their classical Marshallian advantages like the division of labor in a big job market, cities speed the increasingly important accumulation of human capital: "Because cities bring together people from different walks of life, they foster transmission of ideas." Although many inner cities have seen a population exodus, only partly reversed by recent gentrification, property values have been soaring and many city centers also witnessed a massive building boom during the 1990s. This indicates at the least no reduction in the demand for an urban presence, especially in what are clearly key global centers such as London and New York, or Berlin and Shanghai.

Endogenous growth theory suggests that the benefits of innovation extend socially, beyond the private return to the innovator. An economy can proceed along a virtuous circle of self-fueling invention and technical advance. Originally, this process was modeled as the presence of increasing returns to scale within an industry, so that the more it grew, the more it could grow in the future.[4] However, the (limited) empirical evidence suggests that the kinds of spillovers of knowledge beyond the innovator that can boost growth, in line with endogenous growth theory, are actually those that take place among different industries in those urban centers with a wide range of industries.

Glaeser links this finding both to Jane Jacobs' emphasis on the importance of urban diversity and to recent work by Martin Weitzman, also at Harvard, on "recombinant growth." The notion is that new ideas are combinations of old ideas. Or as Weitzman puts it: "Knowledge can build upon itself in a combinatoric feedback process which may have significant implications for economic growth. . . . The ultimate limits to growth lie not so much in our ability to generate new ideas as in our ability to process an abundance of potentially new ideas into usable form." There are hugely increasing returns to knowledge: the outer envelope of this process grows according to the formula two to the power N (rather than the more sedate N squared). However, the human ability to manipulate ideas appears to increase at an altogether slower pace than either. As Weitzman puts it: "The evolution of technology basically exhibits a declining degree of determinateness. . . . We end up on just one path taken from an almost incomprehensibly vast universe of ever branching possibilities."

The signs are that the quality of the path taken, or in other words people's prosperity and well-being, depends on combining ideas that are in some sense

Diversity is likely to prove more productive than similarity. There is little innovation from people who think alike and offer one another little fresh stimulation.

far apart. This is intuitively obvious. The more surprising a new idea, the more unlikely and the more valuable it will be. But another way of putting this is that diversity is likely to prove more productive than similarity. There is little innovation from people who think alike and offer one another little fresh stimulation. History offers some classic examples of the economic cost of impermeability to distant ideas. One is China's loss of technical leadership and long stagnation when its leaders closed the country to the rest of the world in the fourteenth century. Another is the contrast in Japan's fortunes before and after the 1868 Meiji Restoration, when a new ruling dynasty opened the country to the outside world in order to industrialize, a process so successful that within a hundred years it had become the world's dominant industrial economy.

This argument helps explain why cities, or more generally face-to-face contact, are so crucial. It is because the flow of ideas, especially those that might not in normal circumstances brush up against each other, is central to economic growth. I think this is similar to Edmund Wilson's notion of "consilience," or a holistic approach to knowledge. He writes: "Access to factual knowledge of all kinds is rising exponentially while dropping in unit cost. . . . Soon it will be available everywhere, on television and computer screens. What then? The answer is clear: synthesis. We are drawing in information while starving for wisdom. The world henceforth will be run by synthesizers, people able to put together the right information at the right time, think critically about it, and make important choices wisely."[5]

Exchanging ideas is inherently a nonmarket transaction. There is no possibility of sampling the product before deciding to buy it, or returning it to the seller if faulty. An idea is a "nonexcludable" product whose "ownership" by one person does not prevent another "owning" it, too. It has never been expressed better than by Thomas Jefferson: "No-one possesses the less because every other possesses the whole of it. He who receives an idea from me, receives instruction himself without lessening mine; as he who lights his taper at mine receives light without darkening me."[6] But as the metaphor suggests, just as tapers are best lit by someone standing close by, ideas are best ignited by somebody in the same room. Mediation by the telephone line or TV network excludes the kind or quality of personal interaction made possible by direct contact. As Glaeser puts it: "These interactions tend to be determined by spatial proximity. Social influence decays rapidly with distance. . . . The effortless transmission of ideas and values depends on sight or hearing in many cases."

Empirical research suggests clustering is most pronounced in precisely those industries where knowledge spillovers matter most. So in the U.S. computer industry, for example, the Silicon Valley cluster accounted for 42 percent of the innovations recorded in one year in the early 1980s, and the Route 128 cluster in Massachusetts for another 10 percent. In other words, two centers generated more than half the innovations in the industry.[7]

What's new in New Capitalism is therefore the unparalleled importance of face-to-face human networks. While they always were important in creating successful market economies, they are fundamental now. This explains the new interest of economists in social capital, the metaphor borrowed from sociologists and political theorists and treated as roughly analogous with human capital. (The human and social are linked, of course; building human capital depends on the quality of the social capital available, and vice versa.) The interactions that occur in social networks are rife with externalities, explaining the endogenous nature of modern growth, or in other words the importance of apparently insignificant spillovers from one event to another that can have large and entirely unforeseen consequences.

> What's new in New Capitalism is the unparalleled importance of face-to-face human networks.

For example, an increase in transport costs or other barriers will reduce the number of interactions or exchanges of ideas, whose social returns might be vastly more valuable than the cost increase. This is why financial firms are prepared to pay small fortunes for their employees to be kept close to the flow of information at the hub of the great cities. And thus it is that small differences in architecture or the work environment can make a huge difference in the quality of the social connection between coworkers. Or conversely a chance encounter or unexpectedly different idea can have a huge payoff. Network effects are highly sensitive to small changes in the cost of networking.

The Benefits of Diversity

It is one of the paradoxes of the globalized New Capitalism that local details are crucially important. As the old slogan puts it, think globally, act locally. But what does local detail really mean? Certainly the physical environment, the cultural amenities, the transport and telecommunications infrastructure, and so on. More than such abstractions, however, it means the relationships among people and all the institutions that mediate human interactions. People are the most important resource in the weightless economy. The people who have potentially the most to gain are those who have least now. And if diversity is in itself an economic benefit, those who contribute the main elements of diversity, whatever is outside the current mainstream, will be the biggest beneficiaries. It isn't possible to suck the essence of new ways of thinking and cultural attributes out of their human hosts; the new economic resources are inextricably embedded in people.

This adds up to a powerful argument for ensuring our cities are full of vitality, beauty, and cosmopolitanism. This sounds bland enough, but its implications are controversial. For example, it highlights a clear economic benefit in increased immigration, one of the most sensitive of political issues.

In the shadow of Nicholas Hawksmoor's austerely beautiful church of Christ Church, Spitalfields, in east London lie a few narrow streets of seventeenth-century houses. They were first occupied by Huguenots seeking asylum in England from religious persecution in their native France. These were the first of many waves of refugees who found a haven of sorts in this part of London, so close to the docks. By the late nineteenth century the patch was almost entirely peopled by Jews from Eastern Europe. By the late twentieth century most of the locals were Bangladeshi; nearby Brick Lane still offers some of the capital's best Indian restaurants and the street signs are written in Bengali as well as English. Each wave of the poor and persecuted has eventually prospered and moved out to richer areas, leaving Spitalfields to needier successors. But as the twenty-first century dawns this pattern has changed. The new influx consists of the gentrifiers, with wealthy bankers and fashionable media moguls bidding up property prices and restoring the 300-year-old housing stock.

It isn't possible to suck the essence of new ways of thinking and cultural attributes out of their human hosts; the new economic resources are inextricably embedded in people.

In this little warren, at number 19 Princelet Street, stands a still near-derelict house that tells in its fabric this tale of centuries of immigration into London. Mid-terrace, its top floor has the telltale windows letting in maximum light that say it used to be a weavers' shed, and a bobbin hangs outside signaling the same trade. Compared to its neighbors, however, the brown front door has been noticeably widened. Step into the entrance hall and it becomes clear that the house at the front, extended at the top into a workplace, was turned into a synagogue at the back. It is a replica of a synagogue that had had to be abandoned far away in Poland, built over a former garden. On this little plot of land history is transmuted into stone, wood, and glass, into dust and shadow. Even empty and silent this building is crowded. You find yourself mentally muttering "excuse me" to the ghosts of century-old women as you push through the dusty atmosphere to the front of their gallery for a better view.

Before long, subject to fundraising, 19 Princelet Street will become a museum of immigration, London's first permanent celebration of the repeated infusion of cultures that has made it perhaps the world's greatest city. It has become a controversial project. Far-right extremists, unsurprisingly, find nothing to celebrate in cultural and ethnic diversity. Brick Lane even suffered a bomb attack in the spring of 1999. But mainstream politicians too have latched onto fear and hatred of immigrants, tagged as "bogus asylum seekers," as a safe, populist electioneering issue.

No other single issue could better symbolize the profound lack of understanding amongst many political leaders and members of our technocratic elite—and not just in Britain—of the changes taking place in the world economy. Anti-immigrant sloganeering ignores the forces of globalization, pretending that while money must be free to move, people cannot—or at least not without satisfying stringent minimum wealth requirements. It ignores all the evidence about what makes global cities great. This includes the fact that the more people of more varieties are there already, the more other people and new businesses will want to be there, too. If all a city has to offer is nice parks and designer boutiques, it is a sterile place, not a great, throbbing economic engine. Cultural complexity is the fuel powering the advanced economies. In developing countries the dynamism of megacities as opposed to the stagnation of rural life provides an even greater contrast. The pace of urbanization is moving even faster outside the West. Although conditions in the slums are utterly atrocious, the informal economy generated by incomers pouring into the city from elsewhere is the main source of growth in a number of poor and middle-income countries.

More subtly, the xenophobic populism signals closed minds, a defensive and inward-looking instinct that is exactly the opposite of the openness needed to thrive in the New Capitalism. Ideas and creativity are no respecters of boundaries, whether these are geographical, social, or institutional. The most interesting intellectual developments are those on the borders between different disciplines, whether economics and psychology, or biology and chemistry. No organization can thrive any longer on internally generated knowledge. Even corporations with huge teams of their own researchers, like the pharmaceutical or auto giants, need to draw on other disciplines, the chemists turning to geneticists, the engineers to information technologists. Even if an organization does contain the seeds of an innovation within itself, it might well take an outsider to recognize it. John Seely Brown and Paul Duguid recount the failures of engineers at the Xerox PARC to recognize the importance of the graphical user interface that they had invented.[8] It was taken up by Apple instead, Steve Jobs seeing with his outsider's eye the importance of the innovation. Ideas languish until somebody brings a fresh way of understanding to them. Institutions—and countries— that only look inward, hauling up the drawbridges to the outside world, will atrophy and die.

As we saw in earlier chapters, all long-run economic growth, everywhere, throughout history, has been driven by technical progress, or new ideas about how to grow or make things or provide a service. What's new about the New Capitalism is that ideas are vastly more important. Human ingenuity and creativity is the key resource, rather than land or machines or muscles. New ideas germinate from old ones. As Isaac Newton put it: "If I have seen further, it is by standing on the shoulders of giants." Or in the less poetic terminology used earlier in this chapter, growth is recombinant.

Institutions—and countries—that only look inward, hauling up the drawbridges to the outside world, will atrophy and die.

As we saw, there is no economic payoff from obvious ideas. Innovation demands surprising juxtapositions and connections. Sameness is bad for innovation, diversity good. Ideas, whether purely scientific or creative, are embodied in people.

It is my firm belief that this is a crucial time for encouraging an openness to a greater diversity of people. After all, it's estimated that a third of Silicon Valley start-ups in 2000 were founded by immigrants from South or Southeast Asia.[9] Even America, the most scientifically advanced nation on earth, can't innovate without fresh blood.

The contribution past immigration has made to the cultural life and attitude of mind both of countries like America that have celebrated the melting pot and of those like Britain that have been more ambivalent about it—contributing some of that openness and creativity so necessary to the economy—should never be underestimated. The arrival of migrants brings fresh ideas, new ways of doing business, and delivers a jolt to tired and inflexible ways of thought. Moreover, the experience of exile seems to spur the migrants to astonishing heights of creativity. The example of émigrés from Nazi Germany to the United States during the 1930s offers a vivid demonstration of this, making inestimable contributions to the sciences and arts, to business and education.

London's success in the global economy is in large part explained by its cosmopolitanism and dynamism. Businessmen certainly think so. In a London Chamber of Commerce survey there was an unexpected finding: cultural diversity headed the list of the capital's attractions as a place for international companies to locate. Fully 73 percent said it outclassed the rest of Europe on this. The hugely successful cities have always been those with a vigorous and varied mix of people from all over. And conversely, decisions to seal off an economy from "pernicious" foreign influences, as in China in the fifteenth and sixteenth centuries or Japan before the 1868 Meiji Restoration or more recently in autarkic states like Albania and North Korea, have always been economically damaging.

Thanks to the New Economy boom in the United States and skill shortages in the computer industry in other Western countries, politicians have demonstrated a glimmer of understanding of this, but just a glimmer. "Skill shortage" is a finite problem they can get their minds round, and so a number of countries have relaxed immigration restrictions for people who can show they have relevant qualifications. The Web site of the UK's Department for Education and Employment thus has a list of specific skill needs in the IT industry, drawn up by officials who have never worked in the IT industry and presumably do not know how to program. It is an absurdity Soviet planners could have been proud of, applied to one of the least predictable industries in the modern economy.

In fact, the focus on skill is another way of controlling the border. It transfers a small group of would-be migrants from their no-go homes to the privileged locations of the advanced economies, in a token recognition of the powerful forces of economic change.

However, the economic benefits of admitting outsiders bear no relation to the pieces of paper they might carry signaling qualifications or asset holdings. Some of the biggest potential contributions might come from those with nothing. As Susie Symes, director of the Spitalfields Trust, which hopes to turn 19 Princelet Street into a celebration of immigration into the UK, puts it: "You just can't tell which skinny little child entering the country with nothing is going to turn into a captain of industry or patron of the arts." The individual's human qualities are what count, not their luck in birth. Simply wanting to move, to choose exile over home, to leave behind everything that's familiar, signals more courage and enterprise than most of us ever need to demonstrate.

Glass Walls

The invisible boundaries in the modern economy do not just keep out immigrants from other countries, however. All Western cities have their homegrown excluded. Some places seem doomed to poverty and depression by apparently insuperable barriers to the kind of social and creative networks that mark economic success. We have a kind of internal exile more rigorous than anything devised by Stalin, and it involves no physical confinement at all. In any big city poverty goes cheek by jowl with wealth. It is a matter of crossing an invisible line on a street, no less real for the absence of barbed wire.

Step over the imagined boundary and everything changes. There will be boarded windows, dank concrete, and litter blowing along the streets. The residents of that foreign land will be much poorer and sicker, with lower life expectancies. They are more likely to be members of ethnic minorities, disabled, single parents, illiterate. They will lack bus routes and banks, their schools will have much worse exam results, and they are more likely to be the victims of theft and violent crime. If the symbol of one city is the prestige art gallery, the symbol of its negative must be graffiti on the canvas of a concrete wall.

The apparent existence of glass barriers around particular deprived areas, typically inner city, is one of the puzzles in economics. Why is there such high unemployment in Hackney when the neighboring City of London is crying out for workers, unskilled as well as skilled, and soaking up massive amounts of illegal and legal immigrant labor? A Treasury paper published in 2000, as the national unemployment rate fell to its lowest in twenty years, showed that in the UK there is a "tail" of fifteen to twenty local authority districts with high unemployment, low employment, and a concentration of all the other indicators of economic disadvantage and detachment from the job market.

The paper said: "While these pockets suffer multiple and complex problems, they do not face a simple lack of jobs. Almost without exception, areas of high unemployment lie within easy travelling distance of areas where vacancies are plentiful." Even within these fifteen to twenty places, the ratio of number of claimants to number of vacancies is only slightly higher than the national average.

What is it, then, that bars the people from the nearby jobs? Why is an unemployed young person in Tower Hamlets unable to work in a nearby City of London coffee bar when an unemployed young person from New Zealand or student from Taiwan can do so? Or work as an office cleaner when Somali refugees do so?

Manuel Castells explains it as a feature of the underlying trend away from the production of goods in industrial locations toward the generation of flows of services globally. He writes: "It is this distinctive feature of being globally connected and locally disconnected, both physically and socially, that makes megacities a new urban form," and goes on: "Elites are cosmopolitan; people are local. The space of power and wealth is projected throughout the world, while people's life and experience is rooted in places, in their culture, in their history."[10] His vision is a New Capitalism of global flows superimposed on existing local economies and barely connected to them.

While it has become widely accepted that there is a footloose global elite moving freely around the key centers of the global economy, I think the significance of the globocrats is exaggerated. There are explanations closer to home for the glass walls carving up our cities, and for the disconnection of the modern urban underclass from the conventional world of work and worldly success. For example, racism might well play a part, and so might a lack of family resources so important to launching young people successfully into the world with their first suit, their first season ticket, and their first month's rent. Some jobs are genuinely unattractive to all but the most desperate, being either illegally or legally exploitative.

However, an important part of the explanation lies in the nature of the social networks in these geographical pockets of deprivation. Their inadequacies are more important as the economy becomes increasingly weightless. The types of failure prevalent in the ghetto matter more now than twenty years ago, and are more likely to exclude residents from the mainstream job market. Nonmarket interactions like the flow of ideas or transfer of values, enthusiasm, and "soft" workplace skills such as verbal fluency and sociability are playing an increasingly important role in the economy. They are essential in more and more occupations. And they are all determined by spatial proximity. They are learned through role models, peer pressure, and social norms. The transmission of ideas and values depends very much on face-to-face contact, on the presence of respected peers and mentors who are connected to the mainstream. This makes it easy to see why living in a place where other values predominate can easily become a trap. Of course, this pretty obvious statement is in some ways thoroughly unhelpful. As the old joke goes: How many psychiatrists does it take to change a lightbulb? Only one, but the lightbulb's got to want to change.

Support for this argument can be found in the evidence that only a part of the difference between individuals' earnings can be explained by measures of innate ability or formal schooling. Much of it is related to skills that are acquired outside school. The real cost of living in a ghetto is the inability to acquire human capital there, because of adverse peer effects and the transmission of values outside the mainstream, such as the acceptability of violence and illegality, or the downgrading of success at school.

Nonmarket interactions like the flow of ideas or transfer of values, enthusiasm, and "soft" workplace skills such as verbal fluency and sociability are playing an increasingly important role in the economy. They are essential in more and more occupations. And they are all determined by spatial proximity.

This is well demonstrated by places that suffer an economic catastrophe throwing many people out of work simultaneously. Many urban areas of multiple deprivation are former manufacturing areas that suffered exactly this kind of catastrophe with the closure of a big factory or decline of a traditional industry. When few prime-age workers in a community have jobs, the deprivation will have hardened into place by the time the next generation has grown. With many of the industrial jobs lost being well paid compared to the alternatives, unemployment rapidly became a social norm. Vast amounts of public money have been poured into old industrial regions in the UK without solving this problem. There is no doubt money can help in mitigating economic problems, but unfortunately you can't buy values. The public-policy problem is far harder than spending more on benefits or business subsidies.

The Role of the Illegal Economy

In a few communities any solution to economic problems cannot ignore crime and violence. Crime rates vary enormously in different places and different times, with little of the variation accounted for by obvious factors such as unemployment or poverty rates. The principal explanation seems to be precisely the prevailing social norm, or peer pressures, especially in the case of crimes against property.[11]

In many pockets of deprivation there is already an alternative New Capitalism, an "informal economy," with its own distinct set of values and skills. A report by the UK's National Criminal Intelligence Service put the size of the illegal drugs business at nearly £10 billion a year, prostitution at £500 million a year, and the entire "organized'" criminal economy at £50 billion a year. Add in less sinister illegalities such as tax evasion and benefit fraud, and it is obvious that this parallel but separate economy, concentrated in the areas we are thinking about, is easily big enough to support those communities. The entire "shadow" economy is estimated to be equivalent to at least 10 percent of UK GDP. To set the NCIS figures in context, annual UK consumer spending is about £560 billion, and the government's total annual benefit bill is £100 billion.

> In many pockets of deprivation there is already an alternative New Capitalism, an "informal economy," with its own distinct set of values and skills.

Violence and crime offer clear evidence of the dissolution of economically healthy social networks. This turns policing and security into aspects of economic policy, although as with any vicious circle the problem looks like a chicken and egg one—do you start by tackling the crime to boost the local economy, or start with the economy to reduce the crime?

Yet not all illegality is so sinister. On the contrary, some of it constitutes an informal economy providing the only source of wealth and dynamism in the locality. The entrepreneurs in this economy have exactly the same characteristics so much praised, in an approved context, by policy makers. As Hernando da Soto has pointed out, the informal economy in some developing countries dwarfs the formal economy. He gives the example of an apparent economic slump in the Brazilian construction industry, which reported just 0.1 percent growth in 1995, contradicted by the reality of soaring sales of cement, up 20 percent in just six months. According to a Deutsche Morgan Grenfell report he cites, around two-thirds of the country's construction never makes it to the formal records.[12] Bureaucracy and corruption prevent the members of the informal sector making the transition to legality. While the globalized economy of organized crime is clearly undesirable because of its violence and tendency to undermine the normal fabric of society, this informal economy is clearly beneficial. Governments should be looking at reducing the regulatory burden and official corruption instead of stamping on the most dynamic part of their economy.

While the scale is different in the advanced economies, the informal economy is undoubtedly growing, and much of its growth is concentrated in the poorest areas. Evidence collected by researchers for the International Monetary Fund shows a strong upward trend in the size of the shadow economy relative to the formal economy in OECD countries,[13] to the extent that in countries like Belgium, Italy, and Spain it amounts to more than 20 percent of official GDP, the same scale as in some developing countries. Even in law-abiding, conformist Germany one in five people work at least partly in the shadow economy, perhaps through an undeclared second job, and in Italy it is nearly one in two.

> Not all illegality is sinister. On the contrary, some of it constitutes an informal economy providing the only source of wealth and dynamism in the locality.

The size of the tax burden is one clear culprit for the trend and helps explain why the shadow economy is smaller in the low-tax United States than elsewhere. However, even in America it has more than trebled in size since the 1960s. The legacy of inappropriate government regulation of the changing economy is the main cause.

For it is when the law is an ass that large numbers of people are perfectly prepared to ignore it. Certainly many conventional entrepreneurs started out with a bit of rule-breaking and corner-cutting. As Keith Hart, who originally developed the notion of the informal economy from his anthropological work in Ghana, puts it: "The only way the poor can acquire surpluses, short of working impossibly hard, is to fiddle a slice of the social cake to which they would not ordinarily be entitled."[14] When they achieve success, these former cowboys find they are celebrated as rough diamonds. This necessary social hypocrisy is coming under strain now that so many ordinary workers and consumers, not just the most ambitious and energetic, feel compelled to break the rules.

In developing countries, the legal obstacles most often take the form of having to acquire trading licenses or land titles. In most of the advanced economies the problem is now inflexible tax and benefit systems that do not recognize the fluidity of many people's working lives, or social protection legislation, drawn up with the best of intentions to prevent exploitation but actually preventing the creation of borderline jobs in micro-businesses. The hassle of claiming a benefit for a while, working in a full-time job, switching to a part-time job to study, and then making a fresh legitimate claim persuades many people to keep up one continuous claim even when for a time it is fraudulent. Registering and de-registering for value-added tax for a small business of borderline size is so onerous that it is better not to register at all. And somebody working as a cleaner would have to be mad to declare herself a self-employed businesswoman just because of the red tape, never mind the tax bill.

The time has come to face up to the hypocrisy involved in celebrating dynamism amongst the successful but ruling it out of order for the poor. The people those on the center-left or liberal end of politics most want government to help are precisely those opting out of the formal, government-approved economy in droves. Governments are no longer able or willing to provide the cradle-to-grave assurance against financial insecurity that characterized the twentieth century. Mass welfare was a feature of mass production. It worked because of the employment of breadwinners by big companies that acted as bureaucratic extensions of government for the purposes of collecting tax and administration. For the most part citizens led stable working lives, staying in jobs for long periods, with an occupational pension if they were the family breadwinner. This pattern is no longer the norm—except perhaps in government bureaucracies, and there not for much longer. Somebody starting her working life today will experience a far more fluid career. There has been some recognition of this, for example by the U.S. government when it legislated for savings plans such as Individual Retirement Accounts and 401K investment plans. For those who are able to perform in the job market and earn good pay, it is possible to cope with the legacy of an inflexible tax and pensions structure.

Not so for those only tenuously connected to the job market who might need to turn to the state for help in bad periods or assistance in jumping over hurdles to bettering their lives. For them, the informal economy offers a flexibility lacking in the formal economy and benefit system. However, it confines them to parts of the city that are disconnected from the mainstream of prosperity. The price—exclusion in the literal as well as metaphorical sense, confinement to specific geographical areas—is high.

> If the traditional support and welfare available from governments is serving its supposed beneficiaries so badly that they are opting out, it's worse than useless.

If the traditional support and welfare available from governments is serving its supposed beneficiaries so badly that they are opting out, it's worse than useless. Taxpayers are financing a mass system of state benefits that is not achieving its aims and whose main beneficiaries are the officials administering it. Without reform, more and more people are likely to opt out, and especially in the biggest cities, where inflows of immigrants, often illegal, operate outside the benefit system, anyway. The forces of globalization and growth are likely to wash over the old welfare structures, eroding them like waves crashing over a sandcastle as the tide advances over the beach. What's more, without reforms, the people who most need help probably won't get it.

With the problems different from country to country and city to city, there will not be a one-size-fits-all policy prescription. Experiments and pilot projects to reconnect people to the formal economy are called for. These will include programs that equip hard-to-employ people for the formal job market, and, equally, measures to make the transition easier by removing red tape and regulations that act as barriers. It will also be important to think more clearly about which people should be counted as part of the community and who is responsible for their welfare. The answer is unlikely to be only the native-born on the one hand and only the national or local government on the other. Businesses and nonprofit groups will share responsibility, and for a community that could well be self-selected rather than those who are citizens by accident of birth. This will be a radically different polity, and one that will make those who are now thriving in the globalized economy deeply uneasy.

New Solutions

There are some interesting alternative proposals. One is social en-
trepreneurship. The think-tank Demos has identified people who
provide innovative services for social ends in neighborhoods failed
by conventional public-sector programs. It describes them in this
way: "Social entrepreneurs are driven, ambitious leaders, with great
skills in communicating a mission and inspiring staff, users, and
partners." It notes they achieve impressive results with scant financial resources. The main resource, it seems, is the values they embody personally, the example they set, and the inspiration they
provide. Many work in places where nobody else at all challenges
the prevailing nonmainstream value set. The social entrepreneur
provides an alternative, a bit of competition to the local criminal
baronies.

The work done in Boston by the Initiative for a Competitive
Inner City, founded by Harvard Business School professor Michael
Porter, also addresses the social network. It aims to weave the city's
deprived areas into the same economic networks that are thriving
thanks to Boston's university and high-tech base. Work in the United
States is also looking at the "soft" infrastructure needed to prevent or
eliminate negative clustering, in an intellectual tradition going back
to at least Jane Jacobs. These might include bus routes, the presence
of shops and banks, day-care centers, parks and benches, and so on.
The deprived areas that really make the heart sink are those with
ranks of low-grade social housing, a corner shop covered in grilles,
and nothing else.

In Britain the urban taskforce led by architect Richard Rogers
rightly put much emphasis on the look and feel of depressed areas.
"The physical and the social must go together," according to Lord
Rogers. His report pointed out that of the £200 billion a year in public money spent in English cities and towns, mostly spent on health,
education, and welfare, only 4 percent goes to buildings and transport. Some of the most successful urban renewal projects have in-

volved physical transformation, like Hulme in inner-city Manchester, which was essentially razed to the ground and rebuilt.

The Costs of Borders

The new solutions have a long way to go before they make a dent in old prejudices. It is depressing, although perhaps not surprising, that increasing geographical disparities create in some quarters a desire for higher, rather than lower, barriers. Security guards in city apartment blocks, "indoor" public spaces like patrolled shopping malls, gated communities, the famous—or notorious—Disney township of Celebration, are familiar features of the landscape by now. For many commuters driving from an affluent suburb to a high-paying job in the center, their closest contact with much of their city takes the form of speeding past it on the motorway. This phenomenon of raising the drawbridge against disadvantaged fellow citizens has become a familiar one.

The disconnection between winners and losers in the New Capitalism is also taking place on a global scale. The same concerns about inadequate social capital and economic networks that help explain the failing pockets of urban deprivation in first-world cities also apply to entire third-world countries.

The detailed links from social capital to economic success remain hazy but there is no longer any doubt they exist. And their increased salience reflects the growing economic significance of social capital in the weightless world. There is ample evidence of the fact that economies with failing or corrupt institutions, high levels of crime, low trust, excessive degrees of inequality, and so on perform consistently worse than economies that are more equal and have fair and efficient institutions.[15]

The same concerns about inadequate social capital and economic networks that help explain the failing pockets of urban deprivation in first-world cities also apply to entire third-world countries.

As Professor Nick Crafts puts it in his survey of twentieth-century economic history: "Broadly speaking, it seems clear that strong commitment to the enforcement of property rights, the development of a legal system that reduces moral hazard and opportunism, and policies of openness toward international trade are all good for growth." Economists such as Douglass North and Mancur Olsen have left no doubt about the potential impact of institutions and social context on the operation of markets and the evolution of economies. And recent work by, for example, the World Bank and United Nations Development Program have documented the extensive economic costs imposed by a bad institutional and social framework.

One of the biggest dangers globalization poses to very poor countries is their possible exclusion from it; some of the poorest countries are only tenuously linked to the huge flows of trade and investment across borders. But it is unimaginable that globalization in goods and money, so warmly welcomed by the technocratic elite, can occur without globalization in the movement of people. If national boundaries are becoming irrelevant for some purposes, they will come to seem irrelevant for others. The logical consequence is increased migration—it is how the global and local geographies map into each other. Its absence so far is one of the key differences between this episode of globalization and the one that occurred a century ago. Between 1881 and 1915, emigration from Europe to the New World countries averaged 900,000 people a year, while in the century before 1915 the United States, the main recipient country, saw nearly 32 million people immigrate. Flows on this scale dwarf even the increased cross-border migration the world has seen since the early 1990s.[16]

However, although recent increases in the numbers of people on the move have been firmly resisted by fearful governments, the national border is nevertheless losing its meaning. As Jeremy Harding points out in his excellent book, European immigration officers have now been dispatched to countries from which there are high immigration flows into the EU—not consular officials, but home-office officials. "This may seem trifling, but it alerts us to the disappearing distinction between inside and outside, and the speed at which nations are ceasing to be what they were."[17]

The reaction amongst most Western governments to the growing desire amongst poor people to enter the lands of the rich has been to fortify their boundaries. Along land borders, like that of Ceuta, a Spanish and therefore EU enclave in North Africa, or the Mexican-American border, this might well mean more barbed wire. It also means more officials at airports and ports, fines for airlines or trucks that carry in illegal immigrants, more coastguards, and so on.

Although recent increases in the numbers of people on the move have been firmly resisted by fearful governments, the national border is nevertheless losing its meaning.

Shoring up the borders is a grave mistake, however. It will damage the potential for greater prosperity in the emerging economy of the twenty-first century. That the "haves" of the new global economy recognize the "have-nots" as a resource is illustrated by the repeated plundering of ideas from ghetto culture by the music, movie, and fashion industries. Similarly, Western companies lift "content" from African music or Indian herbal remedies. This is, of course, the imperialism of the twenty-first century. In the weight-less economy creativity and culture matter more than land and minerals. But this potential for economic advantage is not being shared with the owners of the key resources. And one of those resources is pure difference. Attempts to raise the drawbridges, internal or external, to keep out the marginalized will hold back future gains in prosperity by throttling the free flow of ideas and the fruits of diversity.

It will also undermine the political basis of support for the emerging economic order, with all its potential for improving the quality of life and human well-being. In an assortment of protest movements, whether affluent young Americans demonstrating against the World

Trade Organization in Seattle, or European green activists occupying trees to prevent new road-building schemes, we see what the French sociologist Alain Touraine has called a *grand refus*. There are inescapable parallels with the anticapitalist protest movements of the late 1960s, another time of promise and prosperity. The activists reject conventional political solutions such as the "third way" or *neue mitte*, in complete agreement with the Texan wisdom that there ain't nothing in the middle of the road but white lines and dead armadillos. Their resistance hits home at both the global and local scale.

Start with the former. If it becomes harder for people to enter countries legally, they will do it illegally, and indeed some die in the attempt. If governments were to succeed in stopping the movement of people, it would also mark the diversion of the benefits of globalization to serve only the interests of the rich countries. There is already enough uneasiness about whether globalization is as good as it's cracked up to be. The economic benefits can only emerge if it is politically acceptable, and that means it must work for poor countries, too. Migration is what human beings do; they always have. And now it is cheaper and easier than ever before in history to move. People also know more about other parts of the world; thanks to the mass media, abroad is no longer a frightening unknown in the way it was in the past. And for those in the poorest parts of the third world, the gap between reality and promise grows wider daily. Nothing changes in their daily struggle for existence or even survival, while the images dangled in front of them by satellite TV show lives in the affluent West that to such viewers are almost literally fantastic. Or as Harding puts it: "Market capitalism is always taunting the poor, and now it has far more scope to do so."

The best solution for the poor and desperate would be for them not to be driven to leave home, by war or persecution or gross economic mismanagement by their own governments. How much better if their own economies could develop in ways that gave people longer life, health, and happiness. But those who want to move to better their lives and create new hope for their children should have some chance of doing so. Very many Westerners want to haul up the rope ladder behind them so that none of the frightening poor can scramble up behind them. My uneasiness about some Western politicians' grudging admission that a certain increase in the immigration of people with high skills is not just that it makes no particular sense economically (because an incomer's value to the economy is not well captured by her having one particular type of diploma rather than another—the market will be a better judge of who is needed than any number of immigration officials). It also boils down to saying: if you're rich and, preferably, white, the globalized world is your oyster. If you're poor and brown-skinned, not a hope.

To imagine it's sustainable that money and goods can be free to move across national borders but people will rest content with impenetrable boundaries is unrealistic. It's also immoral and not a verdict I'm prepared to accept. The freedom of people to move where they choose is the missing link in globalization.

> Those who want to move to better their lives and create new hope for their children should have some chance of doing so.

Likewise, the borders between the worlds of affluence and poverty at the local scale are both politically unacceptable and economically costly. Inequality can undermine the chances of growth and prosperity. For although there is no systematic relationship between inequality and lower growth, if improvements in equality take the form of equipping the poor with more assets, whether land or education that builds their human capital and earning power, then overall economic growth will be higher. So while old-fashioned income redistribution via the tax system as practiced in some developed economies during the 1960s harmed long-run growth prospects, a redistribution of opportunities would have the opposite effect.

We need to ask ourselves what effect the determined exclusion of the poor from the places of the rich has on our social capital, which as we have seen has an increasingly important economic significance. Whether it is the confinement of fellow citizens within the invisible walls around inner-city ghettos or of would-be migrants in detention centers for refugees and illegal immigrants, the stark geographic inequalities cannot possibly benefit the wider economy because they damage the host societies.

Places lose some of their economic sparkle if, alongside the glittering art galleries and thriving business clusters, lie the scars of entrenched poverty and exclusion. In his account of barbed wire, Reviel Netz describes the way it had to be supplemented by walls in the concentration camps of the 1930s. The wire topped high walls so the boundary prevented passers-by seeing in as well as keeping in the prisoners. Visiting a center for refugees in rural Oxfordshire just after reading his article, it was impossible to keep the comparison out of my mind.[18] The detainees here too were penned behind walls and barbed wire, essentially for nothing more than getting on a plane—or perhaps simply being the wrong kind of person. Most faced deportation. If they were to die then of hunger or preventable disease or as victims of violence it would at least be on some other national territory.

> Prosperity depends on two complementary strategies. The first is maximizing the beneficial possibilities for contacts among people; the more possibilities, and the greater the diversity and openness of such contacts, the better. The second is tearing down rather than building up the barriers between places.

However, while keeping the poor out of sight through the geographical translation of inequality might make for a more comfortable life for the majority in the short term, it will dent the longer-term promise of prosperity.

Social capital is specific to time and place. It is built by the people who live and work in particular places. Despite the distance-gobbling aspects of technology, the details of place, of who does what, where, and when, matter more than ever, whether the positive aspects of personal contact in a cosmopolitan and dynamic economic cluster or the negative ones of geographic exclusion. Prosperity depends on two complementary strategies. The first is maximizing the beneficial possibilities for contacts among people; the more possibilities, and the greater the diversity and openness of such contacts, the better. The second is tearing down rather than building up the barriers between places. Carving inequality into the physical landscape will not only end up damaging the social framework of the economy at all levels from the very local to the global, but it will also increase the danger of a political backlash against economic progress. What's more, this danger is pressing. We are already on red alert.

The places of the rich and places of the poor meet at two different scales, the local and the global. In both cases, the affluent society is energetically reinforcing the boundary, piling up more sandbags to hold back the flood. It is the wrong response. The barriers between the two types of space must fall if we are to avoid conflicts that will ultimately impoverish everybody. This is not an idle fear. After all, a bitter battle between losers and winners saw the first era of globalization end in hyperinflation, depression, and total war.

5

Time as Capital

"Were there but world enough and time,
This coyness, lady, were no crime."

So begins the famous seductive poem by Andrew Marvell, "To His
Coy Mistress."

The theme that life is too short to cram everything in is nothing
new. *Carpe diem*. You're only young once.

Yet the sense of being constantly busy and under pressure is
surely more intense now than in the past. It is another paradox of the
modern economy that increased riches and technological advances
do not seem to make us any happier. On the contrary, they make
some people deeply uneasy. One of the engines of the protest movement against global capitalism is a genuine, even spiritual, search for
a better quality of life and a sense of meaning in a world in which
work seems to eat more and more into time for family, friends, and
self. A small number of people actively "downshift," trading off more
time for less income, although larger numbers still work manically.
Those hanging on in the rat race always place a high priority on the
problem of work-life balance, however. Surveys suggest a majority of

workers would prefer more flexibility in their working time. One UK poll found that more than half agreed with the statement: "I often dream about doing something completely different with my life." Each of us is pondering the question: What's it all for?

In this chapter I argue that the pressure on our time is a result of the increased demand for intrinsically human qualities such as new ideas, creativity, and kindness in the creation of economic value. Employers are short of people and want to sweat their human assets once they've got them. But it is a short-term, transitional pressure. A potential resolution will lie in making work more satisfying and transferring control over work from employers to all of us. We each do, after all, for the first time in history own one of the key means of production as we move into an era in which growth depends on what goes on in people's heads and hearts. In the past it would have been impossible to produce without land or without finance and machines. Now we have plentiful physical and financial capital, and future production will be impossible without new services and ideas and creative insights. If the New Capitalism is one in which value lies in our thoughts and dreams and imagination, it will thrive only if we are able to generate these serendipitous and fragile intangibles and are appropriately rewarded for them.

> It is another paradox of the modern economy that increased riches and technological advances do not seem to make us any happier.

It is inescapably true that time appears to have become more precious than ever in the modern world. One of several recent books about how short of time we are sums it up: "Our culture has been transformed from one with time to fill and time to spare to one that views time as a thing to guard, hoard, and protect."[1] We're all so busy. So busy we now have a twenty-four-hour society, so that we can shop or go for a meal (no time to cook at home) or do the laundry in whatever spare slivers of time are left over by the pressures of job and family. The work ethic is taken to extremes in Silicon Valley, where programmers notoriously sleep

under their desks and live on takeout pizza. But what harassed working mother, what dual-earner professional couple, what young person starting out on the career ladder does not feel the pressure of
time weighing heavily on their shoulders?

It is hard to open a newspaper or magazine without finding a feature about this weariness. "We're stressed-out, debt-ridden, exhausted. We have less time for our families than we feel we should
have. We take fewer pleasures from our consumption and entertainment than we expected. We feel less connected to our communities than we ever did. In our workplaces we subject ourselves to
routines and duties which at best seem pointless and at worst un-
ethical or immoral. Yet we also feel like hollow citizens, too weary to
respond to any political treaty with anything other than a shrug,"
went one multipage, full-color version of the complaint in a British
Sunday newspaper.[2] Phew!

This is not just media hype. Researchers have found that while
poverty and unemployment definitely make people unhappy, increased incomes do not necessarily make them happy. Andrew Oswald, an economist at Warwick University, reports that there is little
sign of an upward trend through time in happiness, as recorded in
U.S. survey data, although a declining number of respondents say
they are "not too happy." Happiness was increasing, if anything, over
the period 1972–90, but it was a very slight improvement. Evidence
for a number of European countries shows wide variations and no
sign of a uniform upward trend in happiness. Again, there appears to
have been a slight increase in the European average level of happiness since the early 1970s. For the United States and UK, which
have more detailed survey data, the evidence also shows that unemployment is definitely bad for happiness, but on the other hand,
there has been no increase in job satisfaction over time.

Some sociologists go much further, arguing there has been a distinct decline in work satisfaction because of the rush of paid work
and its invasion of "free" time. Richard Sennett argues that work in
the modern economy has led to the "corrosion of character" in its

embrace of hasty values: "The codes of conduct which rule the modern work world would shatter families if taken home from the office: Don't get involved, don't commit, think short-term."[3] Pervasive short-termism, and the sheer disposability of people as workers, has undermined trust, loyalty, and mutual obligation, he argues. The quality of life is being eroded irretrievably.

His is a particularly passionate and eloquent statement, but there seems little doubt that the pressure of work is definitely weighing heavily on modern shoulders. There is something a little bizarre about the apparent shortage of time, however. The statistics show that everywhere outside the United States hours worked have been on a decisive long-term downward trend. According to figures from the International Labor Organization (ILO), annual average hours worked had declined from 1,810 in 1980 to 1,656 by 1997 in France, 1,742 to 1,560 in Germany, and 1,775 to 1,731 in the UK. Japanese workers were still clocking 1,889 hours a year in 1995, but this was more than 10 percent below the 1980 level of 2,121. This is exactly what you might expect as a result of increasing levels of productivity. Workers should divide the productivity gain between higher real incomes and shorter hours worked, and for the most part that's what they do. While the reduction in the workweek was most pronounced in the nineteenth century, partly as a result of campaigns to set legal limits on what exploitative employers could demand of their workers, it continued throughout the twentieth century. France recently reduced the legal ceiling on hours worked to thirty-five a week.

America is the main exception, driven by a more powerful work ethic and having correspondingly higher real incomes per head than most other countries. The United States was the only country for which the ILO figures are available to have logged an increase in working time, from 1,883 in 1980 to 1,966 in 1997. Even in the United States, however, the rise is three and a half days a year over nearly two decades. Economist Juliet Schor calculated a bigger increase, nearly seven days in twenty years, including unpaid "productive" work like housework and child care.[4] The joke in the 1996 election campaign went: "Bill Clinton has created 10 million jobs and two of them are mine"; still, the potent idea of the "overworked American" rests on real but not startling evidence.

More detailed evidence on the amount of free time available in Britain comes from a time-use survey for 1995 and 1999 published by the UK's National Statistics office. This clearly showed a reduction in the average time spent in paid work, from 214 minutes a day for men and 121 for women down to 189 minutes for men and 106 for women in that four-year period.[5] Other changes were minor: people were doing a bit less cleaning, a bit more laundry. Most of the minutes saved on paid work seemed to go to travel and gardening. Women, of course, spent far longer than men on unpaid work in the home, putting in fifty-one minutes a day on housework and sixty-five on cooking and washing up, compared to the idle male tally of a mere thirteen minutes of cleaning and twenty-eight minutes on cooking.[6]

Yet even with that female "second shift," most people in the industrial world have, if anything, a little more free time, not a lot less. The changes in time use have not been dramatic. The length of the typical working life has also shrunk in all industrial countries, with early retirement having become increasingly common. One study found 71 percent of men in the UK between the ages of eighteen and twenty-four were working in 1999, down from 85 percent in 1975. And of those aged between sixty and sixty-four, only 39 percent were working, down sharply from 82 percent in 1975.[7] Longer educations and earlier retirements make for far more nonworking years in a lifetime. (This might change as aging populations present too big a pensions burden in the next decade or two, forcing retirement ages up again for the first time since the 1970s.)

Of course, there are questions about how free time is distributed. No longer do most households consist of a breadwinner and a housewife, whose unpaid work left the income-earner able to relax when he got home. In many Western economies there are more two-income households (and no-income households) than in the past, and it is easy to see why the combination of work and domestic duties would weigh heavily on the free time of these couples. And, as Schor points out, technology means work has invaded leisure time. Pagers, mobile phones, laptop computers have erased the boundaries that used to confine work time to the workplace. But these changes, invasive as they have been, do not seem entirely enough to explain the paradox of feeling busier yet working less.

It would certainly be possible to find explanations such as the increased complexity of modern life; chores that used to be swift, like paying the bills or getting clothes clean or commuting, have become more burdensome rather than less. Some feminists have long argued that labor-saving devices in the home actually create more work because they simply set new standards for the diligent housewife.

Yet I believe the underlying key lies in the shift in the resource base of the weightless economy. Land and physical capital are now relatively abundant, compared to the demand for them; human capital is relatively scarce. Ultimately, this will be good news for humans, especially those who have lacked resources in the past. Human capital is the economist's term for the skill and knowledge a human being brings to her work, usually measured by educational attainment. Education is just a summary measure, however, for experience—for the number of hours spent reading books rather than buying them and adding them to a towering pile, perhaps. We have not so much an information or even a knowledge economy as an intelligence economy, and the ultimate scarce resource in that case is time. And if something is in short supply, its price will go up. Ultimately, this will be good news.

> The ultimate scarce resource in that case is time. And if something is in short supply, its price will go up. Ultimately, this will be good news.

The Quick and the Dead

Just as it is becoming clear that the economic value of our time is growing because of its scarcity, the need for speed is also becoming greater. We have to do more, and we have to do it faster. There is nothing new in this sensation of being always in a rush. The telegraph gave the Victorians the same anxieties; Henry Adams said it had "annihilated both space and time." And a century ago the Futurist manifesto glorified the acceleration of life in the machine age: "We declare that the splendour of the world has been enriched by a new beauty: the beauty of speed. . . . We are on the extreme promontory of the centuries! Time and Space died yesterday. We are already living in the absolute, since we have already created eternal, omnipresent speed."[8]

Now, as then, technology is forcing the pace. Today's new technologies are vastly speeding up the process of production. It started innocuously enough with the invention and export to other countries of the "just in time" production system in manufacturing by Japanese corporations, Toyota its pioneer. Supplies are delivered to the factory, or components between parts of the factory, just when they are needed. Predating the widespread use of computers, the just-in-time system initially allowed a reduction in levels of stocks of materials and work in progress, saving money, and also an improvement in quality because it devolved a good deal of decision making to teams on the shop floor. Information technology allowing extremely detailed monitoring of the flow of supplies and goods has extended just-in-time enormously. So, for example, supermarkets are now supplied from depots on this basis, and indeed the entire complex logistical framework of the economy is pretty much just-in-time.

One consequence has been a tremendous reduction in the time it takes to produce anything and get it to the final customer. Dell famously does not manufacture a computer until it has been ordered. It does not hold much in the way of inventories (although its suppliers still do); on the contrary, it has a sales backlog instead. Not only do the buyers get exactly the machine they want, they also get it fast. But it is not just in computers that the life cycle of a product has shrunk thanks to information technology. The time it takes to get from drawing board to consumer has fallen sharply across manufacturing, from high-street clothing to aircraft. Computers have speeded the process of research, design, production, and distribution, and have made the links between each stage almost seamless thanks to computerized inventory systems, satellite coordinated trucking, and the ubiquitous bar code.

This is a tremendous benefit, eliminating huge economic inefficiencies. As Alan Greenspan has pointed out, it has helped reduce the fog of uncertainty, the information void, in which business has had to operate in the past, boosting the productivity of labor and capital. "Before this recent quantum jump in information availability, businesses had limited and less timely knowledge of customers' needs and of the location of inventories and materials flowing through complex production systems." Businesses had to carry large inventories and spare labor and capital to guard against the unexpected. He continued: "The remarkable surge in the availability of real-time information has enabled businesses to reduce unnecessary inventory and dispense with labor and capital redundancies. Intermediate production and distribution processes, so essential when information and quality control were poor, are being bypassed or eliminated."[9]

The speeding up of the economy goes beyond the factory floor. For instance, computer modeling has slashed design times in architecture, so buildings can go up much faster. It takes just one to two years to put up a tall modern office block from scratch. Medical diagnoses can be made more swiftly, and treatment hastened. Capital markets reallocate funds from one industry to another, or one country to another, at almost literally the speed of light.

At the same time, what companies measure now as an indicator of success is not their static market share but rather "customer lifetime value," implying a continuing relationship. Specific customer needs must be met quickly in order to retain customer loyalty. The downside, however, has been the generation of fresh uncertainties during the period of transition, a vigorous wave of what Joseph Schumpeter labeled "creative destruction." In particular, staying at the crest of that wave, rather than being washed away by it, demands constant innovation and improvements in efficiency. Companies have to stay ahead of their competitors to thrive and perhaps even to survive. There is no scope to take decisions in leisurely fashion. One of Kevin Kelly's rules for the New Economy is: "No harmony, all flux. As turbulence and instability become the norm in business, the most effective survival stance is a constant but highly selective disruption that we call innovation."

Certainly, speed is everything on the Internet, where one year notoriously equates to four in the normal business world. As John Norton puts it: "Without the need to assemble a huge manufacturing and distribution operation, just about anyone could get into your market and gain a sizable share of it in the blink of an eye. All of which meant that from now on there are only going to be two kinds of successful operations on the Net—the quick and the dead."[10] The rate at which new Internet businesses are born, mature, and die is phenomenal. Commentators have long understood that concepts of time change with technology. In a famous essay E. P. Thompson noted that the Industrial Revolution and factory system changed people's understanding of the passage of time, from a natural to a mechanical process, regimented by the clock rather than the sun. The mechanical clock standardized time, and, Thompson writes: "Time has become a currency which we spend rather than pass." Now, however, the economy moves to a faster beat than minutes and seconds, as computers operate at speeds faster than human perception. In the twenty-four-hour, global information economy, the mechanical clock has been overtaken too.

> There are only two kinds of successful operations on the Net—the quick and the dead.

The Performance Economy

Some enthusiasts for the New Economy believe it is characterized by abundance, as indeed it is in some ways. The basis for this is a special characteristic of ideas, infinite expansibility. Ideas are shared, not traded. If I pass one on to you, you have the idea and I do, too. Any number of people can share it, in fact, without reducing my possession of it at all. Thomas Jefferson put it eloquently: "If nature has made one thing less susceptible than all others of exclusive property, it is the action of the thinking power called an idea. . . . Its peculiar character, too, is that no-one possesses the less, because every other possesses the whole of it. He who receives an idea from me, receives an instruction himself without lessening mine; as he who lights his taper at mine, receives light without darkening me."[11]

Yet despite the infinite expansibility of an economy based on ideas, scarcity, the basic concept in economics, has not been abolished. The Nobel Laureate Herbert Simon put his finger on what it was that is now scarce: "What information consumes is rather obvious; it consumes attention. Hence a wealth of information creates a poverty of attention and a need to allocate that attention efficiently among the overabundance of information sources." Or as writer John Seabrook translated it: "Ideas may be infinitely expansible through space, as Jefferson said they were, but time is not. That's why they call it real time."[12] Attention uses up time.

For Hamlet, it dragged wearily: "Tomorrow, and tomorrow, and tomorrow, Creeps on this petty pace from day to day, To the last syllables of recorded time." If only he had had the Internet and other modern media to while away his dreary days. The dimensions of the modern scarcity of time are demonstrated by a survey on the annual production of information carried out by the School of Information and Management Systems at Berkeley. The research team, led by Peter Lyman and Hal Varian, noted: "Soon it will be technologically possible for an average person to access virtually all recorded information." So they set out to estimate how much information there is, published and stored, in all formats, on paper, film, and optical and magnetic media. The staggering answer is that the amount of information produced in just one year, 1999, was 1–2 exabytes (an exabyte is ten to the power eighteen bytes, and five exabytes would take care of all the words spoken by human beings so far in history). That is around 250 megabytes for every man, woman, and child on earth, or the equivalent of 250 short novels each, 125 photographs, or 12.5 full floppy disks.[13] Annually. This does not count, either, the information produced digitally but not stored systematically, notably email. The report estimates annual email production at 610 billion messages, requiring roughly 11,285 terabytes if it were stored, or the equivalent of more than 1,000 times the printed collection of the Library of Congress.

No wonder the researchers conclude: "It is clear we are all drowning in a sea of information." They add that consumption, as opposed to production, of information, is hardly rising at all. Indeed, it could not be otherwise. Because the consumption of information is a process that takes place in time and competes with all the other activities with which we pass the days. With this mushrooming in the amount of information supplied, the relative value of time spent processing it has increased dramatically.

It is not surprising, therefore, that time is more salient in an economy that depends increasingly on information. In fact, it could be characterized as a performance or experience economy as much as a knowledge economy or weightless economy. Economic value is increasingly generated by processes that take place in real time. John Perry Barlow, the Grateful Dead's lyricist, noticed this as long ago as 1994, when he argued that it would prove impossible to apply the old model of property rights to ideas rather than things. As you might perhaps expect from a musician, he suggested that because information is a process that is experienced rather than a thing to be possessed, information workers will be performers rather than producers: "Information is an action which occupies time rather than a state of being which occupies physical space. . . . Information is experienced, not possessed."

He continued: "Information economics, in the absence of objects, will be based more on relationship than possession." Value would lie in real-time relationships. "Your future protection of your intellectual property will depend on your ability to control your relationship to the market. . . . The value of that relationship will reside in the quality of your performance, the uniqueness of your point of view, the validity of your expertise, its relevance to the market and, underlying everything, the ability of that market to access your creative services swiftly, conveniently and interactively."

The performance aspect of production is clear in the case of many services, which only exist at the time they are performed. However, it is just as valid in the case of many stages of manufacturing, and certainly in those that add the most value, like the design or engineering. As workers we perform and as consumers we experience. Both are actions that take place in time. In *Neuromancer* and other novels William Gibson imagines a technology that can shortcut time, in the shape of microchip implants that people can slot behind their ear, a technical fix for the absence of time spent acquiring certain bits of knowledge. It would be a way to speak a foreign language without ever having slogged for hours memorizing vocabulary and grammar, a direct implant into the brain's memory circuits. As yet, however, there is no technology that can substitute for personal experience, or to put it another way, time logged in processing information.

The spending of time is another way of saying the economy is demanding more and more human capital. However, it would be wrong to imagine an out-of-control capitalist machine that has found new ways to chew up workers and spit them out when their usefulness has been exhausted. Being the owners of the scarce type of capital will enable people to gain more control over what they do. One trend will be that more people will insist their work is meaningful or even fun. . . . After all, there is even a good living in being an anticapitalist, working as a lecturer or author or think-tank pundit, in an economy that values ideas and debate.

Nor will the well-heeled professional classes be the only ones to benefit. Not only does that presumption make the mistake of assuming there is no scope for meaning or satisfaction in "ordinary" jobs, it also ignores the interplay between human and social capital. Individuals add up to society, and the unfolding history of a society is also increasingly important in today's and tomorrow's economy, as the next section shows.

Frozen Time

Somewhere in the Southwestern desert in the United States there will be a clock, made mainly of steel, intended to last for a thousand years, in a complex carved right into the rock of the mountains. It will be a huge, lasting monument, like the pyramids at Giza or a vast Gothic cathedral, perhaps. Once every century it will chime. It is meant to make visitors slow down and reflect on a time scale vastly beyond anything they have experienced in their rushed quotidian lives. In his account of the origins of the Clock of the Long Now, Stewart Brand, futurist, writer, and inventor, notes that the U.S. Weather Service has a nice little business selling old weather reports. The market? Lawyers, preparing court cases, who want to know whether it was raining on September 17, 1985. Brand concludes that we have no idea what will be valuable in the future. But one safe conclusion is: "Bad things happen fast; good things happen slow."[14]

Being the owners of the scarce type of capital will enable people to gain more control over what they do. One trend will be that more people will insist their work is meaningful or even fun.

It is a wise observation. Companies can destroy a reputation built over decades in a few days or weeks, by reacting stupidly to problems such as health scares that threaten a brand. Business cycles are not symmetric; rather, a slow, steady economic expansion gives way to a short, sharp recession triggered by a wrong-headed policy or a bad harvest.

The building of prosperity is a particularly slow process, even in a high-speed information economy. Slower than ever, in fact. The reason is that in an economy where economic value lies in processes that must take place through time, the understanding of ideas and decoding of information, the stock of wealth is no longer land or mineral ores or machines. It is history. The resource of human capital can only be used in real time, as it unfolds from day to day.

There is a code word for this accumulation of experience currently much in vogue in economics and political science: social capital. Its definition and measurement are a little hazy. As Francis Fukuyama notes, many definitions in use really apply to manifestations of social capital. He defines it as: "An instantiated informal norm that promotes cooperation amongst two or more individuals."[15] This can cover everything from cooperation among family members and friends to organized religion, and the institutions and habits that embody such relations. Close synonyms are civil society, trust, networks, and so on. Vague as this might be, economists and others are clear about its importance. In a classic 1993 book, Robert Putnam linked the divergent economic performance of northern and southern Italian regions to the presence or absence of social capital.

Fukuyama has since documented many examples of the role it has played in a number of economies.[16] In particular, he notes that in modern economic networks where decisions are delegated and management hierarchies flattened, there is a tremendous gain in efficiency that rests entirely on the trust between managers and workers. There can be better use of local knowledge and faster decision making; but if the trust breaks down, instant paralysis. "This is in effect what happened to General Motors during the strikes of 1996 and 1998 when a single dissident local (angry, in the first instance, over the outsourcing of brake parts) was able to shut down the company's entire North American operations."

There is plentiful evidence that high-quality social capital delivers economic results. "Trust" is associated with lower inflation and higher per capita GDP growth, and the effects are "statistically significant and quantitatively large," according to one survey.[17] Building on the work of institutional economists in the 1970s and 1980s (they were then a brave minority), the World Bank and United Nations Development Program have documented the importance of the political and social institutions of liberal democracy for the economic development of poor countries. In short, the presence of an abundant

In modern economic networks where decisions are delegated and management hierarchies flattened, there is a tremendous gain in efficiency that rests entirely on the trust between managers and workers.

stock of social capital is seen as essential to the health of the dense forest of relationships and institutions that underpin a successful modern market economy.

There is such an intellectual fad for social capital that Sam Bowles, an economist at the University of Massachusetts, is right to be somewhat suspicious. "Once everyone realized that market failures are the rule rather than the exception and that governments are neither smart enough nor good enough to make things entirely right, the social capital rage was bound to happen."[17] History's hard knocks have revealed the bankruptcy of the markets versus planning debate, he observes. He therefore prefers a different term, "community," but the point is the same. "Communities . . . may make an important contribution to governance where market contracts and government fiats fail because the necessary information to design and enforce beneficial exchanges and directives cannot effectively be used by judges, government officials and other outsiders. This is particularly the case where ongoing relationships among community members support trust, mutual concern, or sometimes simply effective multilateral enforcement of group norms. This idea—old hat in sociology—long predates recent interest in social capital even among economists."

Thus in the *Wealth of Nations* Adam Smith emphasized the merits of self-interest: "It is not from the benevolence of the butcher, the brewer, or the baker, that we expect our dinner, but from their regard to their own interest." However, he was also the author of the *Theory of Moral Sentiments*, which made it plain that self-interest was only one of the elements of natural order, others including sympathy, the desire for freedom, and a sense of propriety. Kenneth Arrow, the father of modern welfare economics, likewise stressed that the merits of competitive, free-market economic equilibrium depended on institutions of trust and cooperation.

While social capital—the investment a society makes in itself through the passage of time, or its history—has always been important for economic outcomes, it does now matter more than ever. That is because economic value is increasingly created through processes involving the transfer of information or ideas, something whose very essence is that it takes time. It can't be speeded up, and it can't happen outside any specific context. An economy's prosperity depends on its unfolding history more than ever because the nature of people's accumulated experience over time is precisely what creates value. The future is not someplace you go to, it's something you build, as the slogan goes. Building future prosperity depends on the individual economic players, on their relationships with others, and on the personal qualities they bring to their efforts and the quality of attention they pay.

This could be good or bad news, depending on a given society's inherited history. An engineer might call it path-dependence. Karl Marx observed: "Men make their own history, but they do not make it just as they please; they do not make it under circumstances chosen by themselves, but under circumstances directly encountered, given and transmitted from the past."[19] While a factory owner might scrap old machines to install a gleaming new vintage (although examples of starting with a clean slate are actually very rare), it is impossible to throw out a moth-eaten stock of social capital and replace it with new. Rather, it has to be woven and darned into what's already there. This is slow, painstaking, and difficult.

How difficult can be seen from the failures of the richest

economies to learn from one another. Each has specific traditions and institutions that make it hard to import a framework of production from elsewhere. Japan has never been able to make its own advanced fighter planes, despite its abundance of skilled engineers and high-tech manufacturing expertise, for example; the skill of weaving together the components and systems in such an aircraft, the systems integration, has proven impossible to replicate. While American and European corporations did adopt Japanese just-in-time production, this took more than a decade and would not have happened without direct investment in factories elsewhere by Japanese manufacturers during the 1980s. In fact, one of the reasons for the importance of direct investment is that it is the only known way to transfer the management know-how and work culture, the tacit knowledge and social capital needed.

It is hard to glorify the new and exciting without denigrating the past. Much that is written on the New Economy devalues the past in order to emphasize the promise of the future. But while we increasingly feel time is passing at breakneck speed in a headlong rush into the future, the accumulation of past moments is becoming more important. Perhaps it is best to leave the final word to a poet; T. S. Eliot wrote, in *Four Quartets*:

> *Time present and time past*
> *Are both perhaps present in time future*
> *And time future contained in time past.*

The importance of social capital therefore rules out quick fixes in economic policy. However, the vital role played by the interdependent connections among people and by business and social networks in the economy is profoundly democratizing. While not all the bits of the network matter equally, they do all matter. While it perhaps used to be possible for an economy to grow even if there were great inequalities or bitter social conflicts, delivering the gains in prosperity to a lucky few, this is decreasingly viable because trust and the flow of ideas amongst different people have grown so much more valuable than in the past. Inner-city poverty and the high rate of incarceration of ethnic minority men are two examples of social problems in the United States that exact an economic cost. They did nothing to halt the 1990s boom, and many anticapitalist critics would argue that they were even side products of the booming economy, in an expansion that created great wealth for "globocratic" professionals and left the poor behind. But I believe long-term growth in the economy will depend on repairing such damage to the social fabric. It will be hard to sustain networks of trust and tacit knowledge in an economy where some groups of people are left so far behind the majority.

> While it perhaps used to be possible for an economy to grow even if there were great inequalities or bitter social conflicts, delivering the gains in prosperity to a lucky few, this is decreasingly viable. . . . It will be hard to sustain networks of trust and tacit knowledge in an economy where some groups of people are left so far behind the majority.

What's more, this applies on a global scale. A world in which 20 percent of the people control 80 percent (and rising) of the income will be one where political tensions would damage hopes for improving prosperity and also one squandering the crucial resource, human capital, on an enormous scale. Human capital is certainly not evenly distributed, depending on the natural endowment of talent and on access to education and rewarding experiences, but it is at least shared more equally than any of the previously essential factors of production. This point is well understood by many, though certainly not all, leading multinational executives and also political leaders. The tremendous capacity of capitalism for enlightened self-interest will work in favor of building both global and local social capital.

The Value of Time

Britain's Chancellor of the Exchequer made an announcement in May 1999 that caused a storm of outrage. He had decided that the Bank of England would sell a portion of its reserves of gold and invest the proceeds in interest-bearing securities issued by other G7 governments. It was a move symbolic of the inherently democratic potential of the weightless economy. It seemed to make good sense, anyway. The return to the treasury would be higher, and after all, gold is not of much use anymore. The Bank of England's gold vaults have always been a place of great mystique. Few people have seen them, even amongst Bank of England employees. Journalists are hardly ever allowed in. One BBC team that thought it was being granted rare access to the secret vaults was in fact shown an antechamber where some of the glistening ingots were temporarily stored. I was told by one of the lucky few who have visited the vaults that they are a huge place of great beauty, their gleaming contents set off to best advantage by bright Mediterranean blue paintwork.

Gordon Brown's decision outraged traditionalists. However, other central banks had already started quietly shedding their gold reserves. The long-run decline in the price had made it a depreciating asset. And as one analyst commented after the announcement, the sale marked the democratization of money. No longer would value rest in any way on an unequally distributed natural resource. Money had all but gone fully electronic. Its evolution is continuing, as money becomes increasingly an indicator of people's time and effort. Although governments are likely to remain dominant providers of money, or at any rate the formal kind, people will be able to generate for themselves other forms of money. It will depend on mutual agreements about what's valuable.

Information technology has already

Money has all but gone fully electronic. Its evolution is continuing, as money becomes increasingly an indicator of people's time and effort.

revolutionized money, which is no more than zeros and ones, appropriately labeled electronic impulses stored on a large number of magnetic tapes and servers. It should not be surprising that if the nature of value is shifting toward a metric based on time, then a parallel shift is taking place in the way value is recorded. The financial markets are in the vanguard of the rest of the economy in the fact that transactions will soon for the most part take place in "real time," or in other words will be instantaneous and recorded as happening when they do happen.

Scott McNealy of Sun Microsystems once speculated that it would be possible to have global spot markets for all goods, in a return of haggling via auction sites on the Internet. This is not feasible, of course; time is the main constraint on making markets in everything all the time, and we are all too busy to want to haggle over the price we'll pay for flour and milk, or T-shirts and CDs for that matter. However, computers do make markets for money—all sorts of money—not only possible but likely.

It is easy to underestimate the radical change taking place in the nature of money, partly because the subject is pretty mysterious. Few people, few economists even, understand the process by which commercial banks create money in the modern fractional reserve system. Bankers like to mystify money, too, because they would prefer customers not to notice its intrinsic worthlessness. Money is a collective illusion, subjectively valuable only as long as we all value it. Societies choose to value the same money because of the three indispensable functions it serves: it is a medium of exchange, taking economies beyond barter; it is a unit of account, measuring worth; and it is a store of value, permitting saving for the future.

Although governments are likely to remain dominant providers of money, or at any rate the formal kind, people will be able to generate for themselves other forms of money. It will depend on mutual agreements about what's valuable.

In his intriguing book, *Money in an Unequal World*, Keith Hart suggests that the era of state monopolies over money is drawing to a close. As the weightless economy has less to do with making and distributing physical things and more to do with what human beings can do for each other, he suggests an older tradition of personal credit will be revived. "Money is an expression of trust between individuals in society, an act of remembering that allows us to bring calculation to some of our interactions and relationships," he writes.[20] It acts as a record of personal obligations and exchanges, in other words. "In the context of more democratic access to money, it will become clearer that its main function is to help us keep track of those exchanges with others that we choose to calculate. We will make money in many different ways as a means of remembering."[21]

This is a little abstract, so it is worth reflecting on the fact that there are already some competing private monies in existence. One of the best-known examples is Air Miles. Some localities have started issuing their own currencies for community economic activities. One of the most successful is Edgar Kahn's "time dollars," a record of hours worked that can be exchanged for other services. So far these monies have been limited in their application, mainly intended to operate in a very local economy. But one British entrepreneur, Peter Dawe, has a far more ambitious plan to allow the launch of many private currencies in a parallel Internet banking system.

The American artist J. S. Boggs does only one kind of painting: images of U.S. banknotes. For the most part they are as big as a desktop and could not be mistaken for forgeries, although the artist has been able to "spend" his paintings on restaurant meals, when a picture is accepted in lieu of payment. However, Boggs is not a popular man with the federal authorities; he has been pursued through the courts for the offense of passing off forged dollars. It makes the authorities look rather silly, of course.

But the idea that the state has a monopoly on money is an important fiction in our economies. According to the textbook definition, money is something that serves three purposes: it is a medium of exchange, a unit of account, and a store of value. In principle many things could fill these functions. In practice, too, there are many "moneys." As one old textbook puts it, before proceeding to ignore the complexity: "There are many financial assets which perform these functions to a greater or lesser degree." Most of what we think of as money is not cash, in which national central banks retain a pretty secure monopoly, but assets issued by commercial banks, under more or less strict supervision by the central bank, and financial assets issued by companies.

Nevertheless, the issuance of money in modern economies has been pretty centralized since the late eighteenth century. And as with any near-monopoly, it is in the interests of the money issuers to keep it that way. National governments, in particular, receive significant "seigniorage" benefits from the power to print cash. Yet, given that most money is no longer metal or paper but rather information stored as an electronic impulse in computers, it is natural to ask whether the Internet revolution is going to make central banks redundant. Pundits who have gleefully predicted the privatization of money by digital means have been mocked, not least because some early experiments in electronic cash, such as DigiCash and Cyber-Cash, failed. These electronic monies did not do anything people could not already do with credit cards, so few wanted to use them.

However, the new technology from one of the pioneers of the Internet in Britain makes it not just possible but easy to issue and use electronic currencies. The software is about to be launched by Oakington, a new company founded by Peter Dawe, who launched the first UK ISP, Unipalm Pipex. It will allow any company, not just banks, to issue electronic tokens that are, in effect, money. The software can fulfill in a decentralized way the functions currently carried out by the relatively centralized banking system. Oakington's role is essentially that of authenticator of the issuance of tokens and of transactions. Suppose, for example, Microsoft wanted to issue MS-dollars. It would go to Oakington, whose servers would record the number of MS-dollars issued and their transfer to users of the new currency. MS-dollars could then be used as a medium of exchange, with transactions once again authenticated by Oakington. The software seeks to establish a financial transaction protocol. The company would keep a tally of users' electronic piggy banks, making the tokens a unit of account. The question mark hangs over their use as a store of value; the founder admits trust in his monetary system will be slow to build. For one thing, the new monies will not have a government guarantee that they will keep their value; cash does have that guarantee, as do some types of bank account, albeit an assurance profoundly undermined by inflation.

It sounds a slightly megalomaniac scheme. Can a cyber start-up really make the Federal Reserve Board and Bank of England extinct? But if you reflect on the inherently bizarre nature of money in the first place, the Oakington scheme sounds better and better. After all, Microsoft already issues shares, which people willingly trade for conventional dollars. Different types of financial assets are already fungible, though with varying rates of exchange, such as the share price. The only thing to distinguish the value of a shareholding from the value of a dollar bank account—both expressed as series of zeros and ones in banks' computers—is the way it is described by the software. If Oakington really has addressed the problems of feasibility, scale, and security with its software, I cannot think of any reason why the current monetary system should not start to feel the brisk winds of competition. The company has even gone out of its way to make its alternative monetary system acceptable to governments. It has, for example, written into the software the ability to deduct the appropriate taxes on transactions at the source and pay them—in the relevant tokens—into government coffers. It has also made it possible to identify the parties in suspicious transactions if provided with an appropriate court order. As Peter Dawe puts it: "We're just selling the arms, not fighting the war." Still, these features are a sort of courtesy to the authorities, given their sensitivity on the money question. Central banks could be in for their first real competitive battle in more than 200 years.

Could a cyber start-up really make the Federal Reserve Board and Bank of England extinct?

Schemes like Oakington's use technology to substitute for the accumulation of trust we place in existing national monies. The technology keeps track of the exchanges among people and the value placed on these exchanges. Keith Hart observes: "Property must endure in order to be property, and that depends on memory."[22] The sorts of property we are creating in the weightless economy are increasingly abstract—intellectual property. In his essay on intellectual property, John Perry Barlow notes: "Since it is now possible to convey ideas from one mind to another without ever making them physical, we are now claiming to own ideas themselves and not merely their expression. . . . We have taken to patenting abstractions, sequences of virtual events and mathematical formulae— the most unreal estate imaginable. . . . As we increasingly buy information with money, we begin to see that buying information with other information is simple economic exchange without the necessity of converting the product into and out of currency." He goes on to argue that it will be gravely misleading to think of the economy in monetary terms, but perhaps instead it is the nature of money that will change.

There are signs of this in the frequent comparison of the Internet economy, and especially the open-source movement, to a gift economy.[23] The Internet's frontiersmen seek to trade information as much as exchanging effort for money. Here is where the indistinguishability of money from other sorts of electronic impulse becomes apparent. Computer technology means different kinds of value can be compared more immediately, as all are obviously forms of information. For the privileged knowledge workers (or performers) on the frontier of the New Economy, it is easy to see that payment could take on a variety of disembodied, digital forms, only one of them money. (For workers with less of it, the money of course matters a lot more.) The esteem of peers is particularly important in this community. The programmers are committed to giving away their software for free. The code is posted on the Internet and improved by other users. The only condition of use is that any changes you make are also freely available to other users. It has turned out to be a fantastically powerful approach to software development. The Linux operating system is perhaps the best-known example, one whose technical excellence is the direct result of its development by a global cooperative. There is no better method of quality control than peer review. This is why peer review is so crucial in the academic world, where ideas are the final product as well as the key input.

Linux experts make their monetary living by selling support services and consultancy, and some have made plenty of money by launching and floating dot.coms. Linus Torvalds, the originator of Linux, has moved on to cofound the chip company Transmeta. There is so much money around in this business that it seems paying the rent is a minor concern. Skilled programmers just don't seem to fret about being able to get enough money-paying work. The more highly valued reward, because it is so much harder to come by, is the esteem in which they are held by their peer group if they contribute a particularly successful improvement to the software. The parallel with a gift economy, in which status and wealth are reflected by how much you can give away, is compelling. Those blessed with much information, or the skill to generate it easily, give away much information. (Of course, esteem easily turns into fame, and fame makes superstars of people. High esteem can therefore deliver exceedingly high financial rewards, too.)

The open-source community has a strong ideological commitment to keeping software, specifically, free. But the young Internet generation has been labeled "dot communist" because of its broader opposition to the property rights and work ethic of the old industrial economy. Its is a more radical analysis of the changing nature of work and money than that espoused by "downshifters," for example, who trade off time for money in the old framework.

Conclusions

The importance of time as a resource is one of the most profound reasons for optimism about the weightless economy. For it is allocated equally amongst people. While landowners were few in number, and the capitalist class still relatively small, the variety of human talents is distributed far more equally, and every one of us has just twenty-four hours in every day. In principle, every human being has become, for the first time ever in history, the owner of the key means of production.

Some authors find instead grounds for pessimism. Jeremy Rifkin argues that capitalism is now commodifying human time, rather than things or places, plundering cultures and relationships in order to find something else to sell. "When time itself is bought and sold, and one's life becomes little more than an ongoing series of commercial transactions . . . what happens to the kinds of traditional reciprocal relationships that are born of affection, love and devotion?" he asks.[24]

This is similar to the charge leveled against the information-based economy by Richard Sennett and other critics of "short-termism" or "flexibility" or any of the other code words for the increased value of time. Sennett writes: "The short time frame of modern institutions limits the ripening of informal trust." However, even if it is true that it is harder to build such trust, or social capital, in the workplaces of the New Economy, that does not mean that trust is crumbling. On the contrary, as we've seen, it is more crucial than ever, so the incentives to build it are all the stronger. The modern economy is underpinned by a fine and complex web of qualitative transactions, hard to measure and monitor. It is easy to be sure how many machines of given quality are delivered by a manufacturer but much harder to know how much and what quality is being delivered by a software expert, derivatives trader, scientific researcher, or for that matter teacher or security guard. Most jobs now imply more trust, not less. They depend more on reputation and mutual esteem, and not, as in the Old Economy, on supervision and monitoring. The quality of personal relationships in the workplace becomes considerably more important when the bosses cannot measure the workers' effort directly.

This could turn out to be a tremendously powerful force for social change, and change for the better. Although it is certainly true that today some corporate fat cats are paid obscenely more than their typical employee, this disparity might well prove unsustainable in the longer term. For such skewed corporate hierarchies will almost certainly not be high-trust organizations. Sam Bowles argues that this will generalize to whole economies: "The conclusion seems inescapable that highly unequal societies will be competitively disadvantaged in the future because their skewed structures of privilege and material reward limit the capacity of community governance to facilitate the qualitative interactions which underpin the modern economy." Or to put it another way, what sort of effort could an employer expect from a worker not given an appropriate degree of respect and reward when that effort cannot be measured directly but has to be taken on trust? Despite the winner-take-all forces operating in the labor market, superstar rates of pay that

> Most jobs now imply more trust, not less. They depend more on reputation and mutual esteem, and not, as in the Old Economy, on supervision and monitoring. The quality of personal relationships in the workplace becomes considerably more important when the bosses cannot measure the workers' effort directly.

are widely felt to be undeserved could prove temporary. Indeed, that is the message of the bad publicity generated by corporate fat cats.

Others go even further in their criticism of economic trends, condemning the transition to full-blown "cultural" capitalism, seen as appropriating culture, "art," and indeed all of lived experience to package up and sell to consumers. The feminist author Naomi Klein has a similar objection to the "hijacking" of street culture by global brands such as Nike and other corporations that use consultancies to predict what young consumers will find fashionable. She complains that capitalism has invaded every moment of every life. It certainly makes it harder to rebel when big business can turn a tidy profit on whatever types of outfit teenage rebels can devise. While some multinationals play down their ubiquity and emphasize the need to fit in to local culture, others revel in conformity, like Gap, which used its "Everyone in khaki" (or whatever it was that season) advertising campaign all over the world. In my youth, in the heady days of punk rock, no company had thought about tearing jeans deliberately and inserting safety pins before selling them. I think a crest of pink-and-green spiked hair would still work as a shock tactic, however, although we middle-aged former rebels would probably react in a disappointingly blasé way, unlike our own parents. The next chapter looks more closely at the cultural paradoxes of the weightless world.

Here I want to conclude by arguing that the fact that time has become a dimension of economic value is enormously encouraging. We all have it in equal measure. What's more, if how we spend our time is the key determinant of future prosperity, it opens up the prospect of work becoming much more meaningful. To put it bluntly, more quality time will spell more prosperity for more people.

Time is the ultimate scarce resource. It is in fixed supply. How will all of us, all owners of time and experience, react to the growing value of this resource? The answer is likely to be work less and spend more of it on ourselves. Downshifters, high-profile women managers seeking a better work-life balance, have set the trend. Musician Pat Kane has started a "play ethic" movement in the UK, intended to be far more radical by persuading people to take seriously the idea that the pursuit of happiness should be their ambition, and that work is not an end in itself. It is obviously a movement born of the prospect of prosperity, of not having to worry about earning enough to meet basic needs. Kane sees the play ethic as a replacement for the work ethic of the industrial era, and as an overall theory for the anti-globalization movement, which is better at knowing what it's against than what it's for.

But the numbers of people altering their lives in such ways have, so far, been small, and it is also a risk taken only by privileged professionals like programmers and artists. However, there is likely to be an explosion in demand amongst many categories of workers for a variety of patterns of working time. It has long been established that once hours worked go beyond a certain point productivity decreases. In the future, employees will be able to add to this familiar argument another: that any experiences, whether at work or not, can contribute to their value as economic performers. Who can say whether a visit to a museum or time spent helping at the kids' school might not trigger a creative insight or recharge the mental batteries? Most employers will hate their loss of control over their key input, the human brain, but it is gratifyingly inevitable.

6

Chaos, Control, and Culture
in the Information Age

A November evening in central London's Soho Square. It's pitch-dark, raining heavily; the leaves of the trees are shuddering in the wind. There are eerie noises in place of the daytime rumble of traffic, and overlaying the bass track of the rain: odd abstract music, a strange voice intoning words just beyond the edge of hearing, a rhythmic knock, knock, knock. The knocking sound, it seems, is being made by a giant hand projected onto an office building across the square. The face of an old man drifts toward the watchers in a cloud of smoke. A woman's features appear in the tallest of the sycamore trees, shifting with the leaves and branches. Computer code is projected in a constant scroll down the trunk of another.

The phantasmagoria was, it became apparent after a startled minute or so, an installation, *The Influence Machine*, by the New York video artist Tony Oursler, sponsored by London's Artangel. It tapped into an idea that has always haunted new communications technologies, that of the ghost in the machine. The event, which took place every evening for two weeks, was an unforgettable manifestation of the spirit world of the information age. As Arthur Clarke observed, any sufficiently advanced technology is indistinguishable from magic. It can be truly spooky. The technological capacity to capture and transmit unlimited quantities of information takes humanity into new territory, but it is more challenging than the tangible expansion of the globe that the sailing ship or the telegraph brought within reach in past centuries. This age of discovery is instead an inner voyage. Doron Swade, who was the senior curator for computers and information technology at London's Science Museum—responsible for building Charles Babbage's Second Difference Engine for the first time in 1991, to celebrate the two hundredth anniversary of Babbage's birth—argues that even though automation was by the 1830s not at all new, the machine was nevertheless a landmark. "In the case of textile machines or trains, the human activity they replaced was physical. The 1832 engine represents the ingression of machinery into psychology," he writes.[1]

The power of television and new media to insinuate themselves into our lives is Oursler's main preoccupation. He explores "introjection," our unconscious absorption of the language and values of the movies, TV, and the Internet, not in any obvious ways but by the same process by which people come to look like their dogs or married couples begin to behave and think alike. He commented: "My main focus is the position of the individual in relation to the mass of information we are fed and the manipulation we undergo by the powers that be, such as large conglomerates." The mass media hold us, he said, in a "hypnotic thrall." His concern is part of the zeitgeist, featured in popular movies like *The Matrix* and *The Truman Show*, and, in an even more paranoid version where the manipulation is direct, *eXistenZ*. What makes us humans special in a world where machines have broken our monopoly on intelligence?

The ever more intelligent machine frightens as many people as it excites. It raises concerns about the degree of control or its opposite, the degree of chaos, made possible by information technologies.

The great technological leap forward we are experiencing also poses profound ethical questions in the case of genetic advances, and then there's Bill Joy's worry about the lack of safety of nanotechnology and robotics if they fall into the wrong hands. Oursler's installation updated the Victorian gothic fears that haunted an earlier era of great technological advance. He summoned up both the shades of London's fog-wreathed past, the spirit world whose tapped messages and ectoplasmic discharges were brought into being by the telegraph and Morse code and electricity, and at the same time the strange and obscure otherworld of Neal Stephenson's or William Gibson's cyberspace, where disembodied avatars and intelligent entities echo and manipulate real life in the digital dimension. Gibson and coauthor Bruce Sterling had also tapped into the parallels suggested by the Victorian era in their novel *The Difference Engine*, a counterfactual history based on the success of Charles Babbage in building his prototype computer. "A rejigged Victorian London seems to serve," observes the critic Francis Spufford, "as a favorite kind of artificial unconscious, where anxieties can be condensed, and discharged, on the understanding that this lurid place is definitively other."[2]

Twin Fears

The concerns aroused by new technologies, by globalization, by the renewed and sometimes destructive vigor of capitalism, need to be properly addressed. As in that earlier epoch of tumultuous technical change, anxieties abound. While the sunny side of today's technological progress is the promise of greater prosperity, better health, longer life, all spread more fairly around the globe, the dark side is more apparent to many. According to Erik Davis: "For many global citizens, the perception of total interdependence brings with it a dark and paralyzing fear, at the root of which lies the awareness that there is no escape." He continues: "Boundaries of time and space that once kept the demands of the market at bay are dissolving into an enveloping sea of silicon."[3] The fears include that of drowning in a Babel of pointless information in a disordered world, calling to mind Kafka: "So now there are a great many couriers; they post through the world and, as there are no kings left, shout to each other their meaningless and obsolete messages." And in addition to such fears of disintegration and meaninglessness, there is a logically contradictory but nevertheless equally genuine alarm about the risk of centralization, conformity, control, cultural imperialism. The twin fears are cultural fragmentation and Disney imperialism.

Like all such deep-seated fears, they are exaggerated. Diversity does not amount to disintegration, nor does a changing order inevitably spell disorder, while the case for a global monoculture is often made to hang on the pretty slender thread of the existence of some well-known global brands. However, the human heart does not speak the language of logic, and the practicalities of the New Capitalism depend on policies that speak to the heart as well as the head.

> In addition to such fears of disintegration and meaninglessness, there is a logically contradictory but nevertheless equally genuine alarm about the risk of centralization, conformity, control, cultural imperialism. The twin fears are cultural fragmentation and Disney imperialism.

Part of the difficulty in addressing the public concerns about new technologies is that, while inviting generalization about its effects in an attempt to understand them, the technology actually makes generalization next to impossible, with diversity the order of the day. The information is easily at hand to contradict any too-sweeping statement, and oversimplification about the complexities of the globalized economy can be readily unmasked. We can see the world in all its glory and its squalor. Nevertheless, a paradox is that technology that will permit empowerment and has the potential to boost democratic control is in fact generally felt to be disempowering and facilitating central control. Access to information is a weapon in itself, with official and corporate secrecy becoming ever harder to sustain. Governments are under pressure to make more of their information hoards available, because they can: the principle of transparency has firmly embedded itself into the democratic ideal, even if not yet put into practice. What's more, the Internet has started to democratize the broadcasting of information. For all the corporate stranglehold on both wires and content, and despite governments' legal powers over service providers, the traditional power centers cannot close down alternative voices. Just as the birth of alternative publishing played an important role in the political and social changes of the late 1960s, the possibility of Internet publishing will prove a powerful radical force now. There are already celebrated examples of its use, in Mexico's Chiapas rebellion, for instance, in which a battered laptop in the hands of rebels ultimately led to the overthrow of decades of one-party rule in Mexico, or in the organization of the anti-globalization protests. Linking people around the world as never before, information technology also highlights its deep divisions.

A paradox is that technology that will permit empowerment and has the potential to boost democratic control is in fact generally felt to be disempowering and facilitating central control.

In his book about Michael Jordan and the Nike Air Jordan marketing campaign, Walter LaFeber puts his finger on one of the many paradoxes evident in the New Capitalism: "The power of the new post-1970s technology lay here: while creating unimagined wealth more rapidly than ever before, it could also raise fundamental questions about the society that generated that wealth. It could raise such questions more rapidly and intensely, and to billions of viewers, moreover, than ever before."[4]

The questions are certainly being asked. The growing opposition movement includes the international raggle-taggle of idealists and agitators stalking the meetings of the WTO, IMF, and World Economic Forum, the angry activists working in inner-city ghettos or third-world shantytowns, young rebels fed up with the complacency of their baby-boomer parents. The new technologies fuel the burning anger of this movement. They do this both by creating an awareness of injustices around the globe, thanks to the instant access to plentiful information, and also by creating new injustices in terms of the "digital divide" or access to medicines and so on. At the same time, the technologies make it possible to organize opposition and protest, and will also, although many critics would not accept this, create the prosperity that could help us build a fairer and happier society. The technophobic paradox is perhaps at its intensest on environmental issues. The deepest green campaigners dislike much of humankind's technological development and would indeed turn the clock back on some aspects of it, yet political support for environmentalism is strongest in the richest and most technologically advanced countries, while the index of environmental conditions devised by Yale University's Center for Law and Environmental Policy is also highest in the same countries.

New technologies create an awareness of injustices around the globe, thanks to the instant access to plentiful information, and also by creating new injustices in terms of the "digital divide" or access to medicines and so on. At the same time, the technologies make it possible to organize opposition and protest, and will also, although many critics would not accept this, create the prosperity that could help us build a fairer and happier society.

Wealth combined with awareness is proving a potent political mix. My former colleague, the writer Andrew Marshall, covering the 2000 U.S. election campaign, which left America unable to decide between two dull middle-of-the-road candidates, predicted that the movement's anger and idealism were gathering a big enough head of steam to derail the mainstream express. "I have met many people in the past few years who care deeply about their country and their fellow citizens, some in Seattle and some in Philadelphia, though precious few in Washington," he observed.[5] One of the inadequacies of mainstream politics is in fact its failure to address citizens' deepest fears.

This is not so much due to a lack of understanding as a failure of political leadership.

Writers, academics, and policy makers have provided plentiful warnings. One rather dry OECD economics paper, one of many forward-looking documents published by the organization, writes of "an enormous strain on people's ability to tolerate the foreign and the unknown." It concludes that the social and economic institutions built for national industrial societies are inadequate for the global, weightless society.[6] Francis Fukuyama makes the same point: "Social norms that work for one historical period are disrupted by the advance of technology and the economy, and society has to play catch up."[7] However, conventional politics has so far proven unable to depart from its tradition of debate about which policy levers to pull and how far, on tax, welfare, or military action. The mental model remains one in which elected politicians or appointed officials are in charge and decide what to do—even amongst those who have signaled, whether through a search for a "third way" in politics or anti-Washington rhetoric, that they know it does not mesh with the new global reality. But then the search for a new model of governing has always fizzled out. The rituals of power clearly exert a strong pull. Change is likely to emerge from the opposition, and the powers-that-were will react to those forces.

The Parallels with Revolution Past

This is true of every period of rapid technical change. The Industrial Revolution spawned extraordinary social changes after all, changes likely to prove similar in magnitude in the information revolution. Social change in turn led to an extraordinary period of political reform, such as the spread of universal suffrage and formation of unions. The railways made massive urbanization viable by allowing the transport of fresh food into cities. The Great Western lines from Berkshire and Wiltshire into London were known as the Milky Way because the founder of Express Dairies, whose electric floats still chug around the early-morning streets of the capital, making deliveries to people's doorsteps, used them to ship fresh milk in from the countryside. The railroad from Lake Erie into New York brought fish to metropolitan dining tables in a dietary revolution. Paris, in whose history bread riots had many times proven politically decisive, saw a similar surge in workers' protein intake as meat was brought in by train.[8] Mass politics is urban and communications-hungry. The social and political change spurred by rail and other technologies, such as the telegraph or the chemicals industry, is reflected in the novels of George Eliot and Charles Dickens, Mrs. Gaskell and George Gissing, or across-the-Channel writers like Gustave Flaubert, Victor Hugo, and Émile Zola. All air the social conscience stirred by observing those people damaged by the great technological leap forward and the resulting political tumult. Upheaval in human affairs is hardly desirable but it does make for great literature.

Can the changes under way now really be compared to the scale of the transformation that took place in earlier industrial revolutions? I believe so, for several reasons.

One of the most obvious changes is feminism, which, although it predates the most recent economic trends, is embedded by the diminishing importance of physical strength and increasing importance of social skills in the workplace. As male steelworkers and miners have become redundant, "female" jobs in retailing, the caring professions, and other service industries have grown. The potential economic independence of women has transformed family life, resulting in households where both parents are out at work, single-parent households, and high divorce rates. The exact nature of the social spillover is hotly debated, but its existence cannot be in dispute.

More immediately, the diffusion of information via computer and phone lines, like earlier communications revolutions, has the potential to overturn established elites, just as newspapers (the first mass medium, dependent on the telegraph for information and rail for delivery) played an essential part in the formation of an informed electorate and the end of aristocratic or oligarchic rule. That the laboring classes were getting above themselves, and forgetting their place, was one of the great fears of Victorian conservatives. All elites depend on special knowledge, the secrets of the trade, handed down by one generation to the successors they select themselves. All the professions have established their power and wealth thanks to the tight control of a body of knowledge. Now their area of expertise is shrinking fast. Lawyers, doctors, management consultants, government officials; all are finding that they are dealing with some very well-informed clients. Not all will bother to gather the knowledge, nor can discovering something on the Internet substitute for professional experience and judgment. However, the danger that they will have to justify their judgments to a customer or patient who knows exactly what they are talking about will fundamentally undermine the traditional authority that depends on knowing better than those on whose behalf the decision is taken.

> The diffusion of information via computer and phone lines, like earlier communications revolutions, has the potential to overturn established elites, just as newspapers . . . played an essential part in the formation of an informed electorate and the end of aristocratic or oligarchic rule.

Thirdly, the changing nature of the economy is clearly creating winners and losers, with coalitions of support building up for the latter, not only the obvious groups ranging from blue-collar workers in traditional industries in the West to the desperately poor rural laborers in developing countries, but also powerful corporations whose monopolies and customer bases are under threat from the new technologies. Perhaps it is inevitable that there should be some new frontline in the class struggle whenever the economic cake increases appreciably in size, just as capitalists and workers fought in the nineteenth century over the distribution of the profits of the factory system, with the campaigns for better conditions and higher wages and the violent conflicts over unionization the battleground. Of course, the battle lines have changed. At the beginning of the twenty-first century the struggle for the fruits of growth is being waged on a global front. The scale of the fortunes being made in the New Capitalism and the new visibility, thanks to pervasive media, of poverty and squalor on the one hand and gilded-age wealth on the other present an unsustainable contrast. It makes the haves uneasy and the have-nots resentful. Globalization gives this contrast its novel flavor. And the crusade waged by the disaffected in the rich countries is being waged mainly in the name of the most deprived inhabitants of the poor countries.

The Challenge of Rebellion

One of the most blatant paradoxes, of course, is that many of these disaffected, the anti-globalization campaigners, are just about its biggest beneficiaries. The movement is dominated by well-off young Americans and Europeans who are passionate and articulate about their opposition to the New Capitalism. No matter that they are just about the most wired people on earth, that they work in the most weightless businesses, that they (or their parents) are in the top percent or so of the global income distribution. It is a middle-class campaign born of a prosperous era when enough people do not need to worry much about getting a job or other bread-and-butter matters. The Western campaigners have forged links with their counterparts in developing countries, but the latter could not have achieved nearly as much international political momentum by themselves.

The radical middle class has often been in the vanguard of political change, as Lenin recognized. I return in a later chapter to the directly political consequences of the technology. However, it is in the cultural field that the extent of social change is perhaps most apparent, in a number of intense contradictions and paradoxes. The New Capitalism has indeed been labeled "cultural capitalism." This should come as no surprise: if ideas are increasingly the raw material of the economy, culture, the terrain of ideas, becomes the new frontier, rich in resources for the plundering. This analogy is made by the writer Jeremy Rifkin, a perpetual pessimist about the direction of economic change, in his book *The Age of Access*. The central argument is that in the weightless economy of New Capitalism the exchange of physical property is replaced by the leasing for a period of time of access to services or some form of intellectual property. But he goes on to say that as Western societies approach saturation point in terms of the amount of stuff consumers want, capitalism turns to buying and selling lived experience, including manifestations of cultural life. Life is a performance, and that's the ultimate commodity we have to trade. The thought is taken to its logical conclusion in the enormously successful TV shows *Big Brother* and *Survivor*, whose stars, if that is the right word, have become B-league celebrities simply by virtue of leading their everyday lives on camera for a few weeks.

The analysis would not be unfamiliar to radical French thinkers like Guy Debord, or Gilles Deleuze, who writes: "The operation of markets is now the instrument of social control." Nor to Umberto Eco, whose analysis of the "hyper-real" United States dwells on the commodification of key cultural icons, like the Last Supper or Babe Ruth. Yet the process has expanded beyond their wildest dreams—or worst nightmares. Anything, even poverty, it seems, can now be marketed. The fashion and music industries habitually plunder inner-city street fashions in order to design the next hundred-dollar pair of sports shoes or the next best-selling rap CD praising drugs and violence.

The apparent invasion of everything by the market explains why

The radical middle class has often been in the vanguard of political change, as Lenin recognized. . . . However, it is in the cultural field that the extent of social change is perhaps most apparent, in a number of intense contradictions and paradoxes.

Naomi Klein's *No Logo* struck such a chord amongst those attracted to the emerging opposition movement. She notes that almost every rebellion against capitalism can be sanitized, packaged, and sold — even No Shopping Day, whose organizers could not resist marketing T-shirts displaying their message. Indeed, the stylishly minimal cover of Klein's book has its own rather nifty, and trademarked, red and white logo. An ironic move, perhaps, but one that is sure to prove financially shrewd. Her analysis pins the blame on global brands whose owners want more than buyers; they want in effect adherents who sign up to live the Nike lifestyle or the Disney lifestyle when they acquire the product. I think this view is in the slightly patronizing tradition of critiques of consumerism, dating back at least to Aldous Huxley's *Brave New World*, which usually imply that the masses have rather doubtful taste and don't really know what's good for them. It sneers at the lack of originality and exaggerates the passivity of consumers, who in reality choose a brand for its signal of quality and consistency as well as the lifestyle image it encourages them to aspire to. Whatever you think about McDonald's, eating at the sign of the golden arches will give you a reliable and cheap meal above a certain minimum standard. Some people even like the food. I can still remember, when they first reached the UK, what a treat it was to go out for a real burger after the dreary experience of eating at a Wimpy, the only native fast-food chain at the time.

Still, would-be dissenters from the mainstream deserve some sympathy. Their task has been growing harder. In the days of James Dean youthful rebellion was a novelty, one of the luxuries permitted by growing prosperity. Teenagers of that generation were the first to have spending money and free time. Several generations of teenagers on, when those who reached twenty in the 1950s have started becoming grandparents, it is very difficult to rebel properly. Even punks, probably the last cohort to inflict genuine shocks on mainstream society, had to resort to extreme tactics; body piercing now seems fairly tame but vomiting on others is still considered right out of order by most of us. As Francis Fukuyama notes: "Each generation finds the task of norm violation harder because there are fewer norms left to be undermined and fewer people who can be shocked out of their complacent conformism."[9] When rioters break the windows of a Starbucks in Seattle on the West Coast of the United States or destroy a part-built McDonald's in Millau in southern France, they attract ritual condemnation from politicians or judges who must safeguard law and order, but one thing they do not do is manage to shock many people. However, one thing that might work still as a means of rebellion is condemning the whole system, and globalization is after all pretty mainstream.

In short, it's harder and harder to find effective cultural signifiers of dissent and rebellion. Pity the teenage girl buying a pair of stupidly high platform shoes, only to find her mother, with a tatoo on her shoulder and torn jeans, reminiscing about having worn just such footwear in the 1970s and suggesting a trip to the costume gallery at the Victoria and Albert Museum in London to see what real platforms look like. However, even if braided hair and body piercing or even a bold disregard for personal hygiene (all too obvious at some of the camps set up for international protests like that in Prague) no longer have any power to shock, political activism works as cultural dissent, too, and works best for those people who seemingly benefit most from the system as it stands.

A related part of the opposition to brands derives from the conformity they impose. Cities throughout the West are often said to be looking more and more like one another, with the same chain stores on every high street and in every mall as retailers go global. This trend has given rise to the notion of two worlds inhabiting the same planet, the world of the well-heeled cosmocrats who travel around the globe from air-conditioned mall to mall, never needing to connect to the second world, that of the poor rather than the rich, the local rather than the global, and also the distinctive rather than the bland.

Independent traders in cities like Manchester, Leeds, Nottingham, and Glasgow are linking to resist the "blanding" of city centers caused by omnipresence of high street chain stores. Nick Johnson, cofounder of one such group, the Independents, said: "It erodes and undermines the cultural difference of a city and undermines the economic base. They are employing people but the profits are going to shareholders who are often outside the city." Manchester's Northern Quarter is seen as the last bastion of diversity. Once the main commercial center, in the age of textiles, it is a slightly bohemian and shabby home to many small restaurants, bars, design and multimedia agencies, galleries, and shops. The businesses see it as one of the few areas that make Manchester different and special. Now there is a £50 million redevelopment of the former wholesale market into a mix of market stalls and independent shops. However, success in a large-scale redevelopment could push rents higher and threaten the viability of independent stores.[10]

This has happened in other gentrifications, past and present. Gentrification is both desired and despised. Take the change in San Francisco's Mission District with the recent influx of dot.com dollars. The pickup in the area's fortunes has been much resented by some of the natives. Inhabitants have formed the Mission Anti-Displacement Coalition, taking over from the direct action of the anarchist Yuppie Eradication Program, which preceded it. Its leaders point out that even the dot.com industry needs a service industry whose workers have to be able to afford to commute to work there. But some of those workers make a more philosophical point. According to Lee Burick, a doorman at the Beauty Bar in the district: "Yuppies are homogeneous. Their demeanor is always the same. They don't buy art, they don't support local bands, they don't go to galleries. All they do is take, take, take. Yuppies are moths eating the cultural fabric of the city."[11] It would be equally unacceptable for them to buy the art and support the local bands, however—literally patronizing the local culture.

The tensions demonstrate that the edge of bohemian raffishness and difference that attracts the first gentrifiers is eventually submerged under a tsunami of later arrivals who bring the sameness of everywhere else along with them. While cultural difference can breed economic success for an area, it also carries the seeds of its own destruction, death by absorption into the mainstream. Like an idea skirting around the edge of the mind that evaporates when you try to get hold of it directly, cultural innovation thrives in the margins and gets flattened in the middle of the road. The New Labour government in Britain tried to celebrate the national talent for creativity, grabbing hold of the idea of "Cool Britannia" when modern British culture had been featured thus on the cover of *Newsweek*. Before too long the most creative were turned off by the mundanity of public life and the politicians were left with the naff and second-rate. Cool Britannia turned out to be a huge embarrassment. Culture resists packaging.

The Myth of Cultural Imperialism

Outside the United States the blanding process is very often interpreted as American cultural imperialism. The French, for example, are in principle highly offended by the onward march of this global uniformity (while at the same time being some of the most ardent admirers and imitators of the tackiest American pop culture). McDonald's is the target of choice for French activists, whether Breton nationalists or the ecological and anti-globalization campaigner José Bové. Although McDonald's does as well in the French market as any other, to French intellectuals it is a natural representative of both the cultural and the economic expropriation of their patrimony. The upsurge in intellectual anti-Americanism in France currently carries strong echoes of the late 1960s when *Le Défi Americain* by Jean-Jacques Servan-Schreiber became an influential best-seller. It, too, warned of the danger of ever growing dominance of other countries by successful and ruthless American multinationals.

Such arguments overlook the fact that very many successful multinationals are European and Japanese. Non-American global corporations like Sony or Nokia or Bertelsmann do not suffer any-

In the case of cultural
traffic it is a mistake
to interpret the flow as
a one-way process from
West to East.

thing like the same degree of obloquy outside their own national boundaries. That's because this is not really a debate about business or economics, about national competitive success, but rather about culture, a far more sensitive area. It is fine for foreigners to make money, but not acceptable for them to do so by shaping our daily lives into their alien stereotype. The power of American TV and movies almost certainly accounts for the broader anti-American sentiments.

However, even in the case of cultural traffic it would be a mistake to interpret the flow as a one-way process. In the late 1980s and early 1990s, American cultural resentment against Japan grew as Japanese car makers opened U.S. plants and Japanese companies bought prime real estate in U.S. cities, even taking over a Hollywood studio. The reversal of economic fortunes later, as Japan slumped into a decade-long stagnation while America enjoyed a decade-long boom, removed such concerns, for success makes it harder to keep up victim status. However, that earlier tide of sentiment, fueled by a number of best-selling hysterical books about the demonic power of Japan, does demonstrate that cultural influences are more subtle than they might seem at first glance.

In a fascinating article Theodore Bestor, Professor of Anthropology at Cornell University, explores the links between the globalization of sushi—and the tuna-fishing trade—and Japanese cultural diffusion.[12] Tuna caught off the coast of Massachusetts is priced in the Tokyo fish market and either flown to Tokyo or sold into the domestic U.S. market to meet the growing American appetite for sushi. He noted that U.S. consular offices in Japan grant more than 1,000 visas a year to sushi chefs, tuna buyers, and other workers in the global sushi business.

"The tuna trade is a prime example of the globalization of a regional industry," he writes. "North Americans tend to think of cultural influence as flowing from West to East: James Dean, baseball,

Coca-Cola, McDonald's, and Disneyland have all gone over big in Tokyo. Yet Japanese cultural motifs and material—from Kurosawa's *The Seven Samurai* to Yoda's Zen and Darth Vader's armor, from Issey Miyake's fashions to Nintendo's PlayStation, and Pokemon— have increasingly saturated North American and indeed the entire world's consumption and popular culture. Against all odds, so too has sushi. . . . Sushi has even become the stuff of fashion, from 'sushi' lip gloss, colored the deep red of raw tuna, to 'wasabi' nail polish, a soft avocado green." It's easy to list many other Japanese influences on the Anglo-Saxon and European cultures: "minimalist" design, Dragonball Z, just-in-time manufacturing, cyberspace in science fiction, and so on.

"Japan" is a good brand, too, unlike the faintly declasse flavor that clings to some American brands overseas. The UK electronics retailer Dixon calls its own brand goods, made in Scotland and elsewhere, Asai because consumers trust the Japanese-sounding name. In the same vein, Bestor writes: "Just because sushi is available, in some form or another, in exclusive Fifth Avenue restaurants, in baseball stadiums in Los Angeles, at airport snack carts in Amsterdam, at an apartment in Madrid (delivered by motorcycle), or in Buenos Aires, Tel Aviv, or Moscow, doesn't mean that sushi has lost its status as Japanese cultural property. Globalization doesn't necessarily homogenize cultural differences nor erase the salience of cultural labels. Quite the contrary, it grows the franchise. In the global economy of consumption, the brand equity of sushi as Japanese cultural property adds to the cachet of both the country and the cuisine. A Texan Chinese-American restauranteur told me, for example, that he had converted his chain of restaurants from Chinese to Japanese cuisine because the prestige factor of the latter meant he could charge a premium."

> Globalization doesn't necessarily homogenize cultural differences nor erase the salience of cultural labels. Quite the contrary, it grows the franchise.

In the article, he concludes: "Fishing is rooted in local communities and local economies — even for fishers dipping their lines (or nets) in the same body of water, a couple hundred miles can be worlds away. Now, a Massachusetts fisher's livelihood can be transformed in a matter of hours by a spike in market prices halfway around the globe or by a disaster at a fish farm across the Atlantic."

The conclusion holds for many trades in many countries. Cultural influences, like economic interconnections now, flow every which way between countries. Big countries with concentrations of mass-media ownership have a head start in spreading their national culture. The United States will always have a special status because of its cultural dynamism. A huge and diverse country, it simply generates more cultural raw material than any other, which makes it hugely and profoundly resource-rich in the weightless economy. It is impossible not to sense an undercurrent of envy in the complaints of those who argue their own cultures need special defenses against American invasion.

But does the globalization of culture, the fact that consumers can find the same brands, the same coffee bars, the same music in the stores or online, the same fashions or cuisines, amount to "blanding," anyway? The novelist Mario Vargas Llosa insists that, on the contrary, globalization is helping defeat the coercive idea of a national cultural identity, a concept he believes is dangerously oppressive and conformist. "The concept of identity, when not employed on an exclusively individual scale, is inherently dehumanizing and reductionist." He continues: "Globalization must be welcomed because it notably expands the horizons of individual liberty." It will even, he argues, revive forgotten and marginalized local cultures stamped out by the nationalism of the industrial era.[13]

I would agree that a wider menu of ingredients will, in fact, allow a greater variety of individual recipes everywhere. Twenty or thirty years ago in most of small-town Europe or America it would have been extremely uncomfortable not to conform to the same lifestyle as everybody else. Being different generally meant escaping to the big city. Now, it is easier to differ, to find Chinese food even if most of your neighbors prefer McDonald's, to listen to world music instead of Anglo-Saxon pop. The cultural result of globalization is not like mixing too many colors of paint to end up with muddy brown everywhere; instead, it is kaleidoscopic, intricate, and everywhere different.

The Greed Complex

"Greed is good," decreed Gordon Gekko in the movie *Wall Street* that came to symbolize the excess of the late 1980s boom. The Reagan-Thatcher ideological revolution made it in a way easy to tell right from wrong. The application of the profit motive to all areas of life was, for many opponents, clearly inappropriate. Greed was obviously bad, and its elevation as a principle exacted a terrible social and cultural toll. Naturally, Gekko got his comeuppance in the film, and his sorcerer's apprentice learned in the nick of time the importance of old-fashioned values.

The triumph of globalization in the subsequent decade is also condemned by its critics for elevating money above all other values. Nevertheless, one of the effects of the Internet boom, especially in Anglo-Saxon cultures, has been to make making money as acceptable, even as fashionable, as it has ever been. Becoming an entrepreneur and making millions is seen as a reasonable ambition. After all, it is a quest for more than money, involving also creativity and a contribution to employment and the wider society. The question is more likely to be, why not? Richard Sennett recounts meeting a group of computer programmers sacked by IBM. Although they started out bitter about being made redundant, their reaction evolved into self-blame. Why hadn't they personally left the corporation earlier to found a start-up computer company? Because after all, so many other people in their business had done just that. That raw fact left them no excuses.

With a new millionaire created every ten minutes at the height of

Becoming an entrepreneur and making millions is seen as a reasonable ambition. After all, it is a quest for more than money, involving also creativity and a contribution to employment and the wider society.

the U.S. stock-market boom in 1999, the making of a large sum of money was demystified and democratized. Everybody was to get their fifteen minutes of fortune.[14] Rich men like Bill Gates or Ted Turner (creator of a more old-fashioned fortune through old media) or George Soros (who made his fortune in an even more old-fashioned way, by financial speculation) are rather revered. People now generally tend to admire their hard work and luck. Likewise the wealthy founders of computer start-ups are heroes, not villains. They are certainly not cast in the mold of the robber barons of capitalism a hundred years earlier, or the financial arbitrageurs and wide-boys of the late 1980s. It helps that many of the Internet pioneers actually rejected the easy-money options earlier in their careers, dropping out of college to pursue what seemed a bizarre dream, avoiding jobs in investment banking or management consultancy like the plague.

Yet at the same time the elevation of moneymaking is widely regretted as signaling a corresponding moral and cultural impoverishment. A decade on from the straightforward message of *Wall Street*, *Boiler Room* painted a darker, more complex picture of the epicenter of global capitalism. There was a harking back to gentler times. As one critic described its message: "Everything is electronic and split second except morality. That always takes time so who could have diary space for it?"[15] Similarly, the journalist Michael Lewis wrote: "If you place an absurdly high value on the future, you place an absurdly low value on the past." The New Capitalism is seen as a harsh place, with more winners perhaps but unfortunately incredibly tough on the losers. Most of us do not want our personal finances and security in old age to depend on victory in a gladiatorial economic contest, even if there are more winners and they win big-time. Making money is still an inadequate moral foundation for our societies, in the hip and democratized new millennium mold as much as in the 1980s.

The emerging critique of cultural capitalism is right to condemn the mainstream inclination to write off the losers, with a shrug of the shoulders, even if it is accompanied by a renewed sense of regret or guilt. The public conscience that seems to have developed since the "greed is good" era, reflected in the election of centrist governments and in the new protest movement against the dark side of global capitalism, makes the result no less harsh.

A New Cultural Context

Yet it would be absolutely wrong to indulge in unremitting pessimism. The global markets cannot devour culture unsustainably. Because it is culture, in the broadest sense of specific human interactions in a specific social context, that makes markets work. Capitalism does depend on culture—it always has—but the New Capitalism does so more than ever because the creation of economic value depends precisely on what happens in people's hearts and minds. However, this dependence on ideas and creativity and emotion is not necessarily the vampirism diagnosed by some of its critics. Communications technologies in fact demand of the mass market increasing sophistication and intelligence, increasing interconnection and shared references. The increasing technological complexity is a cohesive force, requiring increased social capital. Francis Fukuyama puts his finger on it: "It is hard to turn ideas into wealth in the absence of social connectedness, which in the age of the Internet still requires something more than bandwidth." The New Capitalism based on ideas can be a culturally richer, warmer, and more connected

> Capitalism does depend on culture—it always has—but the New Capitalism does so more than ever because the creation of economic value depends precisely on what happens in people's hearts and minds.

version, and if it does not become so, it will never achieve its potential.

In fact, we are utterly mistaken if we interpret technical change as being only something to do with machines. A new technology is a system incorporating machines and people in a specific institutional framework and cultural context. Technological progress makes demands on the whole system, not just the machinery. Simon Schaffer, a philosopher of science, says: "The intelligence attributed to machines hinges on the cultural invisibility of the human skills which accompany them. . . . If such machines look intelligent because we do not concentrate on where their work is done, then we need to think harder about the work which produces values and who performs it."[16]

There is an optimistic alternative to the easy criticisms of cultural capitalism, which make lazy reference to the gothic vision of technology gone out of control and devouring its creators, like Frankenstein's monster. The very awareness of the rest of the world, of other values and cultures, delivered unremittingly to our living rooms and desktops, to the posters we pass in the streets and the movies we see, could help build a new mainstream. It would be more diverse and tolerant of difference but less willing to tolerate poverty, squalor, and gross inequality. Whatever the resonance of the grim cyberpunk visions of the future, science fiction is doing its traditional job of taking current technological and social trends to extremes that we hope never to see. Perhaps, in fact, turbo-capitalism is right now giving birth to the very critique that will limit its excesses and build for itself a strong social and cultural base, just as earlier epochs of capitalism have turned out to develop, in the political reaction to change, their own self-regulating mechanisms.

This is the great upside to the new wave of anti-globalization protests. After all, young people are taking to the streets to protest against injustice in the biggest demonstrations in thirty years. They have a number of specific causes, whether third-world debt or the environment, animal rights or civil liberties. Their broad cause is opposition to corporate power. Many of the protestors will never have to work for an IBM or General Motors, or even Merrill Lynch or McKinsey. Thanks to the new technologies they can reasonably expect to work for a small company or start their own, and with low or at least falling unemployment in many OECD countries they can feel optimistic about their own prospects.

Turbo-capitalism is right now giving birth to the very critique that will limit its excesses and build for itself a strong social and cultural base, just as earlier epochs of capitalism have turned out to develop, in the political reaction to change, their own self-regulating mechanisms.

It is in just such prosperous and expansive times, when the market economy is thriving, that people feel most able to point to its flaws and unfairnesses. And the pressure of protest is working. Whatever hopes the cultural despoilers in multinational corporations once had of ruling the world, they must have tempered them now. At a minimum they all have to pay lip service to their social responsibilities. Some even mean it. And none can control or even manipulate easily demand in the huge, sophisticated, and interconnected consumer markets they have created since 1980.

Out of Control

We are those vast, out-of-control markets that have become such a heavily criticized aspect of the New Capitalism. This is a cause for celebration rather than fear. In their pursuit of profits and growth, big corporations have themselves undermined—perhaps irrevocably—the grip they once had on our lives.

In particular instances it is not obvious that this is so. In the titanic clash between the giant music corporations and Napster, for example, the Goliaths might well have inflicted a complete legal defeat on David. But even if they succeed in the court battles, they will lose the war. Simply taking action against Napster back in December 1999 alerted millions of teenagers to the possibility of swapping music, and increased Napster's number of users from not much more than zero earlier in 1999 to reach its early 2001 subscriber base of 50 million. The publicity spawned other file-swapping services, so Napster users will simply migrate to these. What's more, the industry has alienated some of its best customers, young and well-off music lovers, and will anyway have to end its stranglehold on distributing music in expensive album-sized bundles instead of cheap single songs now that consumers know it is feasible to buy music one song at a time online.

The Internet can clearly be a means of control as well as a means of escaping control. Yet it has breached the dike holding back a flood of consumer power. Big companies, like other existing hierarchies of power, are being forced to justify themselves over and over again. In the case of the music industry, the profitable oligopolistic stranglehold on the distribution system has been exposed and cannot survive in its present form. If the industry defeats Napster, other ways around its approved channels can and will be found. It is characteristic of new technologies that they benefit consumers, not companies, in the end.

Douglas Rushkoff argues that young people understand that the mass media have become "a natural system capable of responding to our societal needs." Older generations are more prone to seeing dark conspiracies because they still think there is an underlying order. "They wanted to change the numbers on the dots so that the lines would be drawn in a different order and the picture would come out different."[17] They want to regulate human behavior, on different models depending on their political views. However, the communications technologies have vaporized the possibility of imposing a consistent centralized order on society or culture. We will get whatever emerges from the millions of decisions of individual human beings about where to work, what to watch, what in the world to buy. Kevin Kelly, the *Wired* guru, has compared the New Economy to an emergent system of the sort familiar from the natural world.[18] This is a type of model a growing number of economists are also finding a useful guide to how modern economies behave, able to explain financial market movements, fluctuations in business confidence, fashions, and in fact many of the phenomena that make free markets look so alarming and unpredictable.[19] They are in fact unpredictable, and become more so the more the postwar system of corporatist control crumbles. Predictability was a feature of the controlled economy and the controlled society and culture that formed its framework.

Ian Clarke is the founder of Freenet, free software for distributing files of any sort over the Internet in an entirely dispersed way, one of the cousins of Napster. It does not depend on central servers that the law courts could easily shut down at the behest of big corporations. He has said: "I think people will look back in twenty to forty years and look at the idea that you can own information in the same way as gold or real estate in the same way we look at witch burning today." Smell smoke, anyone? The ghosts looming out of those digital mists are haunting the capitalists.

It is characteristic of new technologies that they benefit consumers, not companies, in the end.

7

The End of Bureaucracy

The 1990s were an unmistakably fin de siècle decade. There was a lot of "endism" around, and not just amongst strange millennial cults. The decisive end of Communism in 1989 clearly played a large part in creating the sense that a line had been drawn under an old era. Many influential books celebrated the end of one thing or the death of another. Authors like Francis Fukuyama and Kenichi Ohmae lowered the final curtain on history, geography, ideology, distance, economics, borders, the nation-state, and much else. While they might have been guilty of exaggeration, like the report that mistakenly proclaimed the death of Mark Twain, it is hard to avoid the conclusion that obsolescence has become a compelling theme of our times.

What is it, then, that is obsolete? Obviously not anything on the above list. History definitely continues and nationalism goes from strength to strength in a thoroughly alarming manner. The obsolescence lies not in the abstract but rather the specific; not geography as such but rather the spatial divisions of the world that are the most significant; not economics as a method of understanding human behavior but the specific processes by which we organize our work and consumption and the metaphors through which we understand it.

The fact that the technological basis of society is changing is profoundly altering the social and economic processes by which we interact, and hence the day-to-day developments in politics, the economy, and diplomacy. I think this explains the renewal of interest in Karl Marx, just at the time when you would expect him to have been thoroughly discredited. The interest was rekindled by a *New Yorker* article by John Cassidy in 1997, and has recently produced the first English-language biography of Marx in twenty years.[1] While the bearded prophet, whose tomb in Highgate cemetery in North London is still a shrine to old Communists, might have got many details wrong, he was the last really influential thinker to have tackled the links from the technical and material "substructure" via the organization of economic activity to the social and political "superstructure." Manuel Castells might yet emerge as the Marx of the Information Age, through his magisterial analysis of the network society, but the economic framework is still only lightly sketched in.

In his trilogy, *The Information Age*, however, Castells outlines the political transformation clearly. It is a new addition to the list of ends: the end of bureaucracy, of mass politics and assembly-line government. The dominant organizational form of the industrial era, the bureaucratic elite, is crumbling. As he puts it: "Because current political systems are still based in organizational forms and political strategies of the industrial era, they have become politically obsolete." And he portrays this as a profound crisis for liberal democracy, occurring paradoxically just at the time when the demise of Communism might have seemed to lay the foundations for its triumph. Castells continues: "The new institutional, cultural and technological conditions of democratic exercise have made obsolete the existing party system, and the current regime of competitive politics, as adequate mechanisms of political representation in the network society. People know it and feel it, but they also know, in their collective memory, how important it is to prevent tyrants from occupying the vanishing space of democratic politics. Citizens are still citizens, but they are uncertain of which city and whose city."[2]

Here I explore the end of bureaucracy, of mass government, by looking at three specific aspects: taxes, defense, and education. In the first two, taxes and defense, at least in the democratic West, we find they no longer have unquestioned power over their citizens, who increasingly are convinced they have a choice and often choose to say no. As poll after poll in country after country showing the decline in respect for traditional institutions demonstrates, the unquestioned authority of old hierarchies of power is no more. That specifically applies to the state's power to demand money, and even life itself, from its citizens. Both are examples of the way the authority of the state is limited by the New Capitalism.

The third issue, education, is widely sensed to be crucial in the way we equip our children to cope with this brave new world, and widely felt to be failing. This has direct economic spillovers as the quality and quantity of education builds human capital, perhaps the key building block for future prosperity. In most OECD economies the state provides the bulk of its population with their education at primary and secondary levels, and in many cases also their higher education. The majority of teachers are civil servants, bureaucrats who process children rather than paper. Education is the key example of one of the main challenges for governments, an issue where public policy is widely felt by citizens to play a crucial role but where just as many believe government is failing to deliver.

A Tax Revolt?

On Sunday, September 10, 2000, it was my son's tenth birthday party, and his father had nobly volunteered to take him to the bowling alley with some friends. There had been a news report that farmers and truck owners were blocking an oil depot in South Wales in protest of the high price of gas, or petrol, and excessive taxes. They were copying the tactics of a French haulers strike the previous week. That had been so successful in bringing the country grinding to a halt, and wringing speedy tax cuts out of the government, that the British truck drivers—some of whom had actually been trapped by the direct action in France—decided to follow suit. Our car had a quarter tank of fuel left, easily enough for a few days, especially for my husband, who sees the orange petrol gauge light on the dashboard as a first hint rather than a final warning. But as the daughter of a woman who had stashed kilos of coffee and sugar away in the cupboards at home during the 1970s commodity crises, I rushed out and filled up the tank. Wisely, as it turned out. If you are going to panic-buy, do it early. My instinct kept us mobile throughout the following ten days of crisis.

And what an extraordinary ten days it was. The prime minister made emergency statements to the nation on three successive evenings as panic-buying not only emptied the gas stations but also swept the supermarket shelves clean of milk and bread[3] (yes, my freezer was full), shut down bus services, closed schools whose teachers could not get to work, and halted postal deliveries. No more than a few hundred special-interest protestors shut down a modern postindustrial economy within days. Fights broke out on gas-station forecourts—surprisingly few, perhaps. The viewing figures for the BBC's main news bulletin—always the people's first port of call in a national crisis—more than doubled, reaching their highest levels since the previous general election. The Labour government's opinion poll ratings plunged catastrophically, putting the party behind the Conservatives for the first time since Britain's exchange rate crisis in September 1992, all the more extraordinary given the ineptitude of the opposition Conservative leadership. Even when the fuel was at last flowing out of the depots again, a chance remark by a presenter on Red Dragon Radio, a small independent station in Wales, set off a rumor that the blockades would restart. The false rumor spread across the country within a couple of hours, by phone, email, and pager, triggering more panic-buying and once again emptying some of the newly restocked gas stations.

Media pundits compared the febrile national mood to the extraordinary wave of emotion that followed the death of Princess Diana. The once phlegmatic British had become a nation of hysterics. As someone who regards Star Trek's Mr. Spock as a role model, I think there is something in this. Elaine Showalter noted that the turn of centuries have often brought epidemics of hysteria. "Hysteria not only survives in the 1990s, it is more contagious than in the past," she commented. "Infectious epidemics of hysteria spread by stories circulated in self-help books, articles in newspapers and magazines, TV talk shows, films, the Internet . . . The cultural narratives of hysteria multiply rapidly and uncontrollably in the era of mass media, telecommunications and e-mail."[4] However, the easy conclusion that the national character has changed ignores the fact that the fuel tax protests were in fact pan-European. From Bristol to Berlin truck owners, hysterical or not, blocked city centers and picketed gasoline stations, broadly supported by the voters even as they were sweeping the shelves clean of perishable foodstuffs. In fact, the crisis brought out the traditional British stiff upper lip, as motorists were forced to join long lines for buses and trains and the desire to chat and compare notes broke through the characteristic national reserve. One fellow-queuer put his finger on it when he said to me: "This is cool. People power!"

That was exactly how it was perceived. The people were saying: Enough! All the European governments impose much higher rates of tax and duty than the United States. While it is highest in the UK, even in Spain, which has the lowest tax rate in the EU, fuel costs the driver twice as much as his or her American counterpart. The price of gasoline had become a political issue even in the United States, with its low tax rate, because of the trebling of the price of oil in the year to fall 2000. Europeans, however, can only weep with envy at the thought of $1.74 a gallon for fuel, the level that ruffled voters in the Midwest. At that point it cost $4.30 a gallon in the UK. Although the increase in the market price of oil was clearly to blame for fomenting the discontent over the retail price of gasoline, helping make the tax burden more, well, burdensome, and although the protests reflected the actions of a small group of gasoline users, this was nevertheless a genuine, continent-wide movement. There was strong opinion-poll support for the self-employed farmers and haulers blocking fuel supplies. Ordinary motorists had had enough, too.

The Limits to Taxation

This was quite a shock to politicians. For some years British governments of all stripes had regarded huge increases in the taxes on fuel as an easy option when resistance to other taxes was building up. After all, on a low oil price it was barely noticeable, and it could be dressed up in environmentally friendly clothing for anybody who did notice. The explanation for the very high UK duty was that the Conservatives had introduced in the early 1990s an automatic "escalator," raising the tax by a fixed amount above inflation each year. It was actually ended in the spring of 2000 by Gordon Brown, the Labour chancellor who later in the year got the blame for the excessive tax rate, thanks to the time bomb his predecessor had primed.

This was not a special British case. Across the Atlantic, the promise that the big and sustained surpluses of the federal government would be returned to the people in the form of a $1.6 trillion ten-year tax cutting plan formed a centerpiece of George W. Bush's presidential election campaign. It won him crucial votes despite the Democratic administration's glowingly successful economic record. There can be little doubt that many voters agreed it was their money and should be given back. At the state level, tax-cutting propositions have been winning occasional success ever since the Reagan era. However, the United States is a low-tax economy by comparison with other Western nations, arguably limiting the scope for reductions. What about the high-tax countries? In some of those, too, there is evidence of a mounting taxpayer resistance. France and

Germany have also started to cut corporation taxes and taxes on labor. Although most Scandinavians seemed to rest content with their tax burden, elsewhere cuts were definitely in fashion.

Were these manifestations of a genuine "tax revolt," however, as many right-wing commentators in favor of smaller government were swift to claim? For as long as most of us can remember, the total tax take measured as the share of government revenues in GDP has been on an upward trend. This share was ratcheted up by the twentieth- century wars (indeed, the income tax was invented at the end of the eighteenth century to pay for the Napoleonic Wars) but continued to climb into the 1980s. The Reagan and Thatcher governments halted the trend but were unable to reverse it, despite their profound ideological commitment to doing so. The tax burden in the United States and UK stabilized. It remains at a substantially lower level in the United States, although the late 1990s boom actually increased taxes as a share of GDP because government revenues tend to grow faster than the economy without deliberate measures to stop this so-called "fiscal drag." This leveling off in taxation has—perhaps—just begun in Continental Europe. There is obviously no natural level for the government share of the economy, as the proportion varies widely among the OECD countries, from just over 30 percent in the United States to as high as 60 percent in Scandinavia; these variations reflect political preferences. Nor is it linked in any simple way to how well an economy performs. Fundamental indicators like income per head or mortality rates differ very little between the United States and Sweden, say, although others such as income inequality and poverty do vary (inversely) with the size of government.

There is a very big question mark hanging over the ability of governments to extract more money from their citizens.

However, there is a very big question mark hanging over the ability of governments to extract more money from their citizens. The gas-tax protest in itself is not compelling evidence; after all, many individual taxes have prompted protests in the past. Yet I think it is possible to characterize it as a sort of European version of the Boston Tea Party. The duty came to stand for a much wider set of concerns about government and its power to tax. Doubts about the quality of representation provided by the political elite have been manifested in growing hesitation about paying tax. Britain's Labour Party had arguably only won the election in 1997, forming the first Labour government since 1979, because of a clear pledge not to raise income tax. And when the chancellor subsequently raised business and other individual taxes, he found it had made the government vulnerable to Opposition charges of having raised the tax burden by stealth, no matter that they had done so, too, during the previous administration. Meanwhile, tax cutting had become all the rage amongst politicians elsewhere in Europe, even in high-tax, big-government France. During the twelve months to mid-2000, when finance minister Laurent Fabius announced the biggest reduction in the tax burden in fifty years, opinion polls in France showed a remarkable switch in voter priorities, with the desire for lower taxation knocking the traditional preeminent concern for social solidarity and redistribution off its pedestal.

In an earlier chapter I also pointed to the extraordinary growth in the informal economy in all countries. This is something most economists have ignored, on the grounds of uncertainties about the data. But it is an astonishing phenomenon even if the estimates are off by a long way. Suppose the IMF's estimate of the size of the UK's informal economy is twice as big as the true figure; that still leaves one pound in every fourteen generated in the relatively low-tax UK economy in the informal sector. Informal means, essentially, hidden beyond the reach of government. The evidence is that swaths of people, especially those on low incomes with little to lose, are opting out of the state. Those who work informally are likely to engage in other such economic activities, too, like shopping informally. Increases in tax and regulation must be the principal explanations, although a diminishing ability simply to enforce rules and levy taxes also plays a part.

Some enlightened policy makers have begun to ponder the implications of the New Economy for their ability to raise taxes. For example, Mervyn King, the Deputy Governor of the Bank of England, noted that the increased mobility of capital in particular, but also some highly skilled workers, had already forced governments to trim corporate taxes—or at least not raise them—and reduce the highest rates of income tax.[5] It is hard to recall now that in the 1970s the top marginal rate of income tax in the UK was 98 percent. However, he also pointed out the limits to shifting the burden to indirect taxation such as duties on fuel or sales taxes. Not only might this cause protests, more and more goods on which sales taxes should be levied are being bought online.

To start with, people have a presumption they should not pay tax on these transactions; many jurisdictions have given ecommerce an initial tax holiday to get it off the ground and ensure the technology spreads widely. What's more, with information about online sales moved around the globe in small, individually meaningless packets of information, it is formidably hard for governments to monitor. That implies that sales taxes will depend on either the merchants being willing to calculate the appropriate tax and send it on to the appropriate government—and while Amazon.com might well agree to do that for U.S. state authorities, will it bother for the Italian government?—or to the delivery companies acting as tax collectors. Companies like UPS and Federal Express already collect some customs duties, but sporadically and generating enormous bad will. Customers do not want to hand over a tax payment they already feel aggrieved about to a private company with which they have no relationship and that adds on a chunky administration fee of its own. It is hard, although not impossible, to see this becoming formalized in the way private employers have collected income tax for governments for years.

> Information about online sales, moved around the globe in small, individually meaningless packets of information, is formidably hard for governments to monitor.

These arguments help make taxes like fuel duties, airport tax, and landfill tax seem all the more appealing. After all, you cannot avoid paying duty taxes on fuel because you have to go to the gas station to fill up. But now it looks like there are limits there, too. Ultimately, the people's willingness to hand money to the government is political. As Keith Hart puts it: "The system of taxation depends on citizens' belief in its inevitability."[6] He notes that mid-nineteenth-century governments did not expect to be able to raise much tax revenue. None foresaw the growth of the state the next hundred years would bring.

Martin Feldstein, Professor of Economics at Harvard and the head of President Reagan's Council of Economic Advisers, has been a prominent advocate of the Bush tax cut. He argues that any tax distorts incentives to effort, and tax reductions can end up increasing total revenues if they are designed to restore incentives. Thus the Bush tax plan would boost the share of revenues paid by high earners and reduce the share in the total paid by low-income families, he suggests. Such arguments based on incentives are politically controversial. Democrats respond to the Feldstein argument by pointing out that President Clinton's 1993 tax increases didn't seem to harm the American economy; on the contrary, it embarked on a record boom. Nor does common sense suggest that ambitious professionals really work a lot less hard if the income tax rate goes up a point or two. However, citizens in all the advanced economies have clearly understood that taxation depends on their consent, so there is an electoral limit to increases and probably an electoral reward for tax-cutting pledges.

On the other hand, it would be foolish to predict any imminent shrinkage in the size of government, as measured by the share of taxes and expenditure in GDP. In most countries there remains strong demand for a wide range of government-funded and -provided services. While it was once believed in some political circles that the richest economies could shrink their public sectors to the scale typical of some fast-growing Asian countries such as Singapore, this now seems very questionable. Around a decade of effort showed how hard it is to cut public expenditure significantly, while on the other hand the Asian tigers are rapidly growing their welfare states, revealed to be inadequate for a modern economy by the 1997-98 financial crisis. So we seem to have a paradoxical love-hate relationship with government. Although we value particular services, whether it is public education or Medicare or even farm subsidies, and would like to see them expand, we vote against politicians who fail to propose tax cuts.

The provision of welfare and the basics of education, health, and defense in some shape are irreducible functions of government in a modern economy. But a progressive retreat in the government's role in economic management is inevitable. This remains far greater in scope than many people imagine, despite the undoubted progress of free-market economics since the late 1970s. As economist David Henderson has pointed out, this followed a century of the opposite trend, increasing government interventionism. There is, he argues, no "neo-liberal" (or neo-conservative, or free market) hegemony: "Now as ever liberalism, both as a doctrine and a program of action, occupies ground that is strongly contested."[7]

> We seem to have a paradoxical love-hate relationship with government. Although we value particular services, whether it is public education or Medicare or even farm subsidies, and would like to see them expand, we vote against politicians who fail to propose tax cuts.

The argument that the size of government is at or even beyond its viable limit is often seen as inherently conservative, by people who see taxation and welfare spending as redistributive tools. It is possible for governments to stop people getting rich through heavy taxes, but far from obvious that they thereby do a lot to help the poor. It takes a huge increase in top tax rates on high earners to fund a small reduction in taxes on low earners simply because there are a lot more of the latter than the former.

It is more efficient to redistribute from rich to poor by raising taxes as efficiently as possible and gearing spending programs heavily toward the poorest groups in the population. This is all the more effective if the spending is focused on education and health, where improved outcomes boost individuals' earning power.

A further conservative argument against the role of government challenges welfare spending, another tool political opponents see as playing a vital part in redistribution and a better deal for the poor. However, it is hard to make a compelling case now for the postwar paternalistic welfare state. Whatever its achievements up to the 1970s, its remnants are not serving well now the ethnic-minority inhabitants of inner-city slums or the lone mothers struggling with work and parenting or the low-income elderly and long-term sick. In addition, large-scale fraud and perverse incentives against work have clearly become big problems. On both sides of the Atlantic big experiments in the shape of welfare provision are taking place and the experimentation is likely to continue for some time.

The fundamental economic basis that supported interventionism during the industrial age has been transformed by technology, however. The decentralization of information, the increased ability of individuals to evade government control, the fluidity of production and permeability of borders, the burden of rigid economic management at a time of change all spell the end for public bureaucracy, as indeed they do for private bureaucracies. Intelligent government now requires a retreat on wide fronts and a new focus on creating the conditions for markets to work better. The new role for government is one of facilitation.

The Place of Government in the New Capitalism

What the tax example illustrates is that government is developing into a matter of mutual consent. It has become conventional wisdom to say that multinationals are able to play off one government against another by threatening to remove their investment to a country with lower corporate taxes, and there is indeed evidence that lower-tax countries have successfully attracted more foreign investment, although tax is only part of the story. But can this lesson really apply to individuals, too, at least beyond a wealthy minority of globetrotters who can afford fancy accountants to minimize their tax bill? I believe it can, although the pressure on governments is indirect. Thanks to foreign travel and the media, taxpayers now know whether they pay a lot or a little by international standards. They know how the services provided by their government compare with other countries. It would be fanciful to argue that taxpayers would decide to emigrate because they thought the national tax burden was too high, but they will certainly vote on that basis. And more broadly, it is now widely understood that governments differ in their reach and quality. These are matters on which citizens want to have a choice. We have got to the point where governments do not have automatic authority but rather have to build consent. This is a direct result of the nature of new technologies and the process of globalization they set in train.

This is an extremely healthy development. Governments have for decades got away with abysmally low standards of service, which impinge the most on the poorest, those who depend most heavily on government programs. The typical middle-class taxpayer has little contact with the frustrations of Kafkaesque red tape, bureaucratic catch-22s, with the rudeness of officials who are sometimes dedicated and efficient but often just bored bullies. For many of government's customers, the contact is entirely demeaning. This is certainly part of the explanation for the decision by a sizable and growing proportion of the low-income end of the population to opt out of the state into the informal economy. Although I'm all in favor of tax and spending being redistributive rather than not, and of governments ensuring a minimum standard of living for all citizens, it really is about time the public sector raised its game. The time has come to drive a stake through the heart of public-sector paternalism.

Yet although governments are, thankfully, not "in charge" anymore, there is still an absolutely crucial role for them in the New Capitalism. It is essentially a role coordinating the preferences of citizens in order to sustain and build social capital. As earlier chapters have emphasized, the quality and ease of interactions among people is more important in the New Capitalism than the old because the exchange of ideas and quality of service is so important in leading-edge, high-value industries. A high level of trust and low level of division and conflict is more important than ever for building prosperity. Governments need to ensure they can guarantee these characteristics, at the same time as learning that their former command-and-control capabilities are evaporating. It sounds no easy task. However, as trust or high social capital cannot be implanted from above, and both are essentially organic, bottom-up qualities, there is no reason to be too pessimistic about the future of government.

> We have got to the point where governments do not have automatic authority but rather have to build consent.

The grassroots nature of the challenge is also why post-bureaucratic government will be better for the poorest. Bureaucratic government has been rule by the middle classes for the middle classes. Unless it becomes less ostentatiously self-serving, it will fail to enrich the network of activities and connections that add up to social capital.

War in the New Economy

The second issue in the breakdown of bureaucracy concerns the future of war. Benjamin Franklin famously observed that nothing is inevitable but death and taxes. But just as governments are losing their power to command taxes at will, so they are finding it harder to persuade their citizens to die for them. One of the few institutions in modern economies that remains as centralized and hierarchical as ever is the army. Old communications technologies played a large part in sculpting armies in this bureaucratic ideal. In his book *The Victorian Internet* Tom Standage explains that the telegraph was perfect for centralized control in hierarchical organization. From the 1870s onward organizations could lease private telegraph lines for internal communication between different sites. Significantly, the British Empire had its own telegraph system. The Internet, by contrast, is ideal for decentralized and out-of-control organizational structures. Does it spell doom for the conventional army?

That the technology will change the warmongering seems inevitable. Ray Kurzweil notes: "Technology and knowledge are very similar—technology can be expressed as knowledge. And technology clearly constitutes power over otherwise chaotic forces. Since war is a struggle for power, it is not surprising that technology and war are linked."[8] And the apocalyptic Bill Joy worries specifically about the lack of centralized military control over GNR technologies, in contrast to the situation in the twentieth century when new technologies emerged as civilian spillovers from military projects. New military technologies are spillovers from commercial research. It is his specific fear that there is no one in control now.

The concept of information war, or the vulnerability of networks and even public opinion in advanced economies to attack through the use of information technologies, which greatly exercises defense experts, plays directly to the incapacity of the government and military establishment to respond to a dispersed threat. Information war is utterly unstructured; it can in theory be waged, by crashing Web sites, causing power cuts or traffic chaos, or influencing viewers of a CNN report, from anywhere by anyone with a computer and some media savvy. Crude propaganda tools like the Nazi Lord Haw Haw broadcasts or airdrops of leaflets during the Second World War now look quaint by comparison; info-war half a century ago did not, unlike conventional warfare, spill over from the military to the civilian infrastructure. There is plenty of information on the Internet for would-be information warriors, and it has already been used effectively by groups ranging from the coordinators of the Chiapas uprising in Mexico in 1994, to neo-fascist and militia groups, to terrorist networks and drugs barons. To take just one alarming example, Osama Bin Laden's group used encrypted pornography sites to exchange information in planning its attacks.

Perhaps the greater part of the threat, or the hardest to respond to, is the prospect of psychological warfare, from the use of the Internet and modern media to manipulate opinion and create opposition to national diplomatic and military policies, in a powerful version of conventional propaganda, to the sowing of panics about the stock market or epidemics. It is a very real threat. One Chinese Army summary said: "Under today's technological conditions, the 'all conquering stratagems' of Sun Tzu more than two millennia ago—'vanquishing the enemy without fighting' and subduing the enemy by 'soft strike;' or 'soft destruction'—could finally be truly realized." As Pentagon adviser John Arquilla put it in one interview: "It's sometimes quite hard to call it war anymore. . . . Smugglers, pirates, other forms of criminals, revolutionaries and terrorists have always organized along network lines. Now they are marrying up with the information revolution and it's giving them vast new capabilities."[9] Hierarchy is an inappropriate response, he goes on. Mass armies are unnecessary. "We must decentralize our military for the same reasons that businesses are decentralizing." In a survey for *The Economist*, Charles Grant came to the same conclusion: "Soldiers who have some leeway to take initiatives will be more effective. The organigrams of today's forces are as pyramidal as in the 1950s; they must surely follow companies in delayering and becoming less hierarchical."

However, other defense experts give different explanations for the imperative to decentralize and flatten the military hierarchy. Robert Fox argues: "The era of industrialized warfare, which reached its height when Hitler launched an army of a million at Russia in June 1941, is all but over." Just as there is no more factory fodder in the workforce, there is

Any remaining traces of sacrificing self to nation are evaporating.

no more cannon fodder in the army. He focuses on a particular phenomenon: the "mammista" army. Parents are no longer willing to see their sons killed. Families have fewer children, for one thing. The young soldiers themselves no longer have unquestioning obedience that drives them to risk their lives.

As *Catch-22* reminds us, it would be a mistake to romanticize the war of yesteryear:

> "They're trying to kill me," Yossarian told him calmly.
>
> "No one's trying to kill you," Clevinger cried.
>
> "Then why are they shooting at me?" Yossarian asked.
>
> "They're shooting at everyone," Clevinger answered. "They're trying to kill everyone."
>
> "And what difference does that make?"

The First World War had fatally wounded the typical soldier's idealism about patriotism and self-sacrifice. According to Paul Fussell: "Every war is ironic because every war is worse than expected." But the Great War was the most ironic of all, slaughtering 8 million for no purpose and destroying the Victorian confidence in progress.[10] Out of that irony emerged its great poetry and literature.

Still, any remaining traces of sacrificing self to nation are evaporating. To give just one example, the signing of the Dayton Accord saw U.S. ground troops enter Bosnia as part of the peacekeeping force. But the American soldiers in Tuzla were not allowed out at night; it was too dangerous. One of my colleagues who covered the later conflict in Kosovo described the hilarious contrast between the French and American soldiers jointly guarding a quiet checkpoint, the one a Foreign Legionnaire in shirtsleeves, bored, smoking, and reading a magazine, the other twitching nervously in full Darth Vader–style body armor and mask. "This has made the ground troops of the greatest military power virtually unusable. . . . One consequence is dubious military practice, such as ordering the bombing of Serbia from 150,000 feet," Fox writes. He adds that the European

Human Rights Act will mean soldiers can have legal representation if they refuse an order; the summary court martial for disobedience is history, the execution without trial of young First World War deserters from the killing fields of the Somme a distant nightmare. Those shot in 1914–18 were mostly working-class boys from the ranks; today's soldiers from low-income and minority groups are far more empowered by comparison with that previous cannon-fodder generation.

The reason for the change is the disintegration of the centralized state's ability to mandate violence. John Keane, director of the Centre for the Study of Democracy, notes that the internal order brought about by the emergence of nation states from the sixteenth century on depended on the state claiming a monopoly of the use of violence. But their use of violence has often created other disorders, whether violence between states or violence directed internally against some groups of citizens. "State violence can and often has destroyed civility. . . . Violent rulers have gutted their respective societies and robbed populations of their capacity for peaceful self-organization."[11]

He suggests that we are now increasingly seeing attempts to democratize state violence. The antinuclear and anti-Vietnam demonstrations of earlier decades were examples of this. Even more spectacular, however, have been the Velvet Revolutions of Central and Eastern Europe in 1989 and, in Serbia, 2000. Adam Michnik, one of the leaders of Solidarity in Poland, put it like this: "Taught by history, we suspect that by using force to storm the Bastilles of old, we shall unwittingly build new ones." Keane concludes: "Democratization depends on cultivating non-violent mechanisms of self-protection."[12]

Yet it is apparent that criminal or terrorist or revolutionary protagonists of violence can easily outwit the top-heavy state hierarchies of the police and army. The breakdown of the old hierarchies and state monopoly of power looks nothing short of catastrophic in some cases. There is no shortage of conflicts organized by cell phone and perpetrated with small arms that look like nothing more than the most appallingly violent anarchies, perpetrating genocide, mass rapes, terrible atrocities. However, there is a glimmer of hope here, for countries embroiled in such conflict are invariably economic disaster zones. Market economies depend more than ever on the healthy functioning of civil society, or on social capital. The fragile networks of institutions, companies, and individuals that make up a successful modern economy cannot exist in a place of anarchic conflict. The New Economy is a high-trust economy precisely because the old hierarchies clearly no longer matter.

"Education, Education, Education"

The third issue of bureaucracy in the New Economy, perhaps the most widely discussed, concerns the future of education. Tony Blair, in the 1997 general election campaign, famously made education his top three priorities. Both candidates Bush and Gore likewise made it their tip-top priority in the 2000 U.S. presidential campaign. Blair was more emphatic than most, but it is at the top of every politician's agendsa, and certainly every parent's. Yet there are no aspects of modern societies less well prepared for the information-age economy than their education systems. While institutional details vary from country to country, including the amounts spent and the split between private and public provision, everywhere the education system is inflexible, bureaucratic, overcentralized, demoralized, and inadequate. Policy makers, teachers, and parents are failing their children, a failure that matters most for those who start out with the fewest advantages. The education system is guilty, amongst other things, of fossilizing emerging inequalities as a result of its failure to adapt to underlying economic change.

This is not to say there are no signs of awareness of the extent of this failure. For example, Japan has one of the world's most rigid and conformist education systems, in which students come under enormous pressure to succeed in just one conventional way. Taichi Sakaiya, Japan's Minister of State for Economic Planning, speaking in Paris at the OECD Forum 2000, explicitly recognized the link between the underlying economic structure and education, a system extraordinarily little changed in its broad outline for a century. "The educational system was built up to foster highly patient and cooperative people with minimal originality and creativity, perfectly suited for working in standardized mass production industries. ... As a result, by the 1980s Japan had achieved the most complete modern industrialized society, based on the mass production of standardized goods, in the entire history of human beings," he said.

> Everywhere the education system is inflexible, bureaucratic, overcentralized, demoralized, and inadequate.

Across the industrialized world, however, the political response to the dawning realization that an education system devised to train workers for the assembly line is failing because of the obsolescence of the mass-production economy, has been to try and patch it up. In a desperate and entirely understandable bid to raise standards in failing schools, politicians and bureaucrats have concentrated massive efforts on delivering incremental improvements in the existing education system and its incremental extension to broader groups of the population. Charles Dickens's Mr. Gradgrind is alive and well in every education ministry. ("Now, what I want is, Facts. teach these boys and girls nothing but Facts. Facts alone are wanted in life. Plant nothing else, and root out everything else."[14]) Absent is any sign of deeper thought about what we should be preparing our children for through their schooling.

Of course it is right to seek to raise standards in response to the past failures of what are usually dismissed as "progressive" educational methods. The failure was a sort of anti-intellectualism, which patronized children by treating the earlier conventional schooling as too hard for the majority. Even so, the absence of serious proposals to combine the need for a less rigid education system with a true respect for intellectual attainment is all the more shocking because the Internet has created a vast new array of resources and made possible new methods of teaching. The technology has cut the cost of extending educational provision, made it possible for the best teachers to extend their reach, and literally put the entire Library of Congress at the fingertips of students.

One of the most thoughtful contributions on what kind of education system the twenty-first-century economy will need has come from Alan Greenspan. In one speech he said: "Skill has taken on a much broader meaning than it had only a decade or two ago. Today's workers must be prepared along many dimensions—not only with technical know-how but also with the ability to create, analyze, and transform information, and with the capacity to interact effectively with others. Moreover they must recognize that the skills they develop today will likely not last a lifetime." Whereas once completing high school was enough learning for a lifetime, that is no longer true, he added.[15] In other words, while it was always true that the most able students, those climbing to the pinnacle of liberal education, not only learned well but also learned how to learn, that meta-skill is now needed by almost everyone. For having only generic attainments that start becoming outdated as soon as they leave school leaves people vulnerable to replacement either by machines or by workers in other, cheaper parts of the world. Castells' description applies to individuals as much as companies: "Competitiveness does not seem to result from 'picking the winners' but from learning how to win."[16]

This need for the constant updating of skills is nowhere more evident than on the frontier of the computer industry. After all, this industry changes so swiftly. Programmers acquire shelves groaning with dusty three-year-old or twelve-month-old user manuals for languages once in huge demand and now defunct. New areas of business balloon unpredictably, creating a job market so tight in some skills that companies literally go to the ends of the earth to hire workers. In her memoir of this manic business, Ellen Ullman writes: "The skill-set changes before the person possibly can, so it's always simpler just to change the person. Take out a component, put in a zippier one. Let the people come and go; plug them in then pull them out."[17]

This kind of turnover in the demand for skills is still the exception in the job market. Even so, it is hard to think of many jobs now where what an employer wants in a worker is a passive repository containing a minimum amount of information and basic literacy and numeracy. Although literacy and numeracy are still essential, of course—making it tricky to argue with the official Gradgrind focused on achieving higher standards in this small area of the necessary skill set—the real need is a robust ability to think independently. Even in the most "ordinary" jobs people increasingly need to be able to take responsibility for decisions. In a factory using teams to build products in a just-in-time system, team members need to decide when to stop the line for quality control, or to think up their own process and product improvements. Nurses in a hospital are no longer the bottom layers of the medical hierarchy, humbly carrying out doctors' decisions, but have taken on parallel responsibilities. PAs in an office are no longer just typists and tea makers but have significant administrative responsibilities. Passivity and conformity at work is on its way out. Yet our education system expects passivity at school for fourteen or more years to be an adequate preparation for work.

> The real need is a robust ability to think independently. Even in the most "ordinary" jobs people increasingly need to be able to take responsibility for decisions.

The Measure of Failure

If there is a single sign of the inadequacy of education for the majority of children, it is the increasing inequality in earnings apparent in all OECD economies, but particularly in the United States and UK with their more flexible job markets. By the mid-1990s the degree of inequality had reached its most pronounced level than any time in the past sixty years and probably longer. In particular, the economic return to education and computer skills rose dramatically. Between 1979 and 1995 the earnings of new college graduates in the United States rose 33 percent relative to those of high-school graduates. In real, inflation-adjusted terms the pay of the least educated workers actually fell during those two decades.

Economists have tested several possible explanations for increased inequality. For a while one favored suggestion was that increased competition from low-cost foreign workers was to blame, but that was clearly rejected by the available evidence in a number of studies. Such trade is too small-scale to explain the trend in incomes, nor can it account for increased earnings inequality within specific industries and companies.[18] Instead, the problem seems to be a vastly increased demand for some types of skill combined with too small an increase in the supply of such workers.[19] To give an indication of the demand shift, the proportion of the U.S. workforce using a computer at work climbed from 24.4 percent of all workers in 1984 to 50.6 percent in 1997. And in 1997 the proportions ranged between 11.7 percent for high school dropouts to 75.9 percent for college graduates. The data show a substantial wage premium for use of a computer at work, one above and beyond the higher pay you would expect for a higher level of education. One summary concludes: "Increases in the growth of the demand for more educated workers are concentrated in the most computer-intensive sectors of the economy over the past two decades." This is not conclusive proof that computerization is behind the pattern of demand for labor, but it is certainly suggestive. It indicates that technical progress has been biased toward using certain kinds of new skills and against traditional skills. The modern job market needs a different kind of worker. The pattern of skill demands is similar in other OECD nations, although labor-market institutions mean the outcomes in terms of wages and employment levels vary widely, with less inequality but also lower employment in countries with a high degree of social protection.

When asked, human-resource managers in U.S. companies said big investments in information technology had led to organizational changes. They had decentralized decision making and given workers more autonomy, and they wanted employees with a higher level of educational attainment.[20] This suggests a need for independence or self-reliance, basic intelligence and common sense, and probably more cooperation or consultation with coworkers, less instruction from above—all characteristics exactly opposite to those valued by a manager trying to run a smooth, centralized assembly line.

Obviously computers have been able to substitute directly for many repetitive tasks, whether in the factory or in services like banking. Yet while the microprocessor can substitute for some kinds of labor, it complements others. What computers need humans for is doing all the things they can't manage. In short, they need people skills. These range from raw intellect to creativity and imagination through to friendliness and a cheerful smile. This is exactly consistent with the observed patterns of jobs growth, tracked each year, for example, by the U.S. Bureau of Labor Statistics or Warwick University's Institute for Employment Research.

The evidence of history also supports the argument that all technological revolutions increase the rewards to "skill" over a transitional period. It is no accident that on some measures earnings inequality is greater now than at any time since the late nineteenth century and early twentieth century. For example, Claudia Goldin and Lawrence Katz found that during the period of factory electrification in 1909–29, industries with higher capital ratios and more intensive electricity use employed more highly educated workers and paid them more. This was a contrast to the earlier period when initially mechanization had been de-skilling, requiring only factory fodder. The new system of batch production raised the need for skills once again. However, the pay gap between the skilled and unskilled narrowed again later, for two reasons. One is that the new technologies became more familiar and user-friendly, reducing the comparative advantage of the skilled.

A second reason, however, lies in the response of the education system. That was also the period when the U.S. public school system was created and the provision of education to a standardized level spread throughout the country to a large proportion of the population. In other industrialized nations the same period also saw the mass state provision of education, standardization of the curriculum, and successive increases in the school leaving age. Ever since, the tendency has been toward further centralized direction of education and training by governments, even in countries where there is also private schooling. Teachers are bureaucrats required to furnish their pupils with a prescribed set of information at given times and achieve measurable standards on various tightly defined metrics. It doesn't sound like a good system for the network age, and it isn't.

The evidence of history also supports the argument that all technological revolutions increase the rewards to "skill" over a transitional period.

Education for the New Century

Of course, it is a lot easier to criticize the existing system than to suggest a better one. For a start it is not obvious that improving economic growth ought to be the purpose of the education system. Even if you accept the needs of the economy as a valid framework of reference, the problem is that economists do not understand the links between education and growth. We know that the flow of ideas is the most important factor in long-run growth but not how it works. As the Harvard economist Ed Glaeser puts it: "The critical theoreti-

cal insight of growth theory has almost no solid empirical foundations." The sensible response is to experiment with a range of reforms rather than making an instant commitment to a new model
approved by a central government department.

There may be some clues in looking at the kinds of people who
have succeeded in the ur–New Economy industry itself, computers.
Two researchers from the extraordinarily innovative Xerox PARC
note that successful software and hardware innovators are anything
but conventional. John Seely Brown and Paul Duguid write: "Much
digital innovation has come from people who spent their time on
campus wandering around in the arts, theatre, psychology and the
humanities—areas not well supported in the unplug-and-pay model
of education."

It is also noteworthy that almost the only world-class universities
in almost all subjects, attracting the best students from many countries, are the private U.S. universities. These have two features that
distinguish them from universities in other countries. One is the
freedom available to students in the curriculum. The range of subjects studied by undergraduates is far wider than in other countries,
providing a much greater choice and variety and educating students
more broadly. They have stayed closer to the classic educational
ideal of forming well-rounded graduates, leaving narrower professional or vocational skills to postgraduate training. At an earlier stage
it does not matter what they have learned specifically, only that they
have learned something and can therefore do it again.

The second feature is the weight placed on having to attract the
paying customer, tapping into the great merit of markets, that they
convey unparalleled information about what people want. At present in most countries outside the United States, public funding is
committed to the institution rather than the individual. Students can
in many cases shop around in the sense that they can choose their
university or college but, within limits, their choices have little impact on the institutions and there is no price mechanism to signal
preferences. In hiring academics, too, only the United States has

anything like a market creating incentives to excel and attract students. Professors have to compete to attract students to their courses, and universities have to compete for the best teachers and researchers. Elsewhere, universities are stuffed with undistinguished workhorses who put up with declining relative pay and status in return for a quiet life.

In their book Seely Brown and Duguid, writing about the United States, suggest a refined university model, one that takes advantage of the new technologies. Universities would continue to exist as research centers and degree-granting bodies, but a student's education could be more fluid in time and place. "Essentially a student's university career in such a system would no longer be through a particular place, time or pre-selected body of academics, but through a network principally of their own making yet shaped by a degree granting body and its faculty," they write.[21] Students could stay home or travel, work online or meet their teachers face-to-face, work with a class or with mentors, and learn continuously rather than for a fixed period. Such changes seem inevitable. Indeed, many universities are already experimenting with more flexible schemes. Harvard and Oxford are collaborating on a scheme to provide online learning to their alumni, allowing them to refresh and update their education. MIT has upped the stakes with the announcement of a plan to make its course material freely available online. Distance learning is well-established—Britain's pioneering Open University was founded in 1969—and much improved through use of the Internet.

Although extending access to higher education and exploiting new technologies effectively will be challenging, especially in the highly bureaucratic and centralized tertiary education systems outside the United States, reshaping primary and secondary education will be far more difficult. Inevitably, the economic and social costs of a failed experiment at this stage of children's lives are far higher. Still, some of the necessary features of an education system that goes beyond the mass production of standardized workers are clear.

For example, the content of many school lessons is of no use in adult life. This has been true at least since I was a child, making education a process of jumping required hurdles and then, mercifully, forgetting whatever it was that got you over them. But that is no excuse for it to go on. Ministries of education ought to stop wasting time prescribing the detailed content of lessons in specialized subjects at every stage of a pupil's school career. They are perpetrating an intellectual fraud, one whose biggest victims are those children who are least able in the conventional academic sense. It condemns them unnecessarily to failure, both financially and in the more important personal sense.

Even somebody who is going to become an academic will acquire the necessary content matter in her undergraduate and postgraduate courses. After all, that material has never been more easily and cheaply available than it is now. What children need to learn at school is some general "how-tos" rather than "whats." English literature should deliver the ability to read "difficult" books and poems and teach empathy and stretch the imagination; chemistry an ability to frame an experiment and assess the evidence rather than memorizing the order of the elements in the periodic table. Reading and writing and numeracy, obviously, are the basic building blocks for acquiring and processing information. But also needed are skills of logic and powers of argument, and, in an age when we are saturated with images, visual skills. The low-status lessons in citizenship and society may be more useful than some conventional academic subjects.

> What children need to learn at school is some general "how-tos" rather than "whats." . . . The New Economy is not about what you know but how you know, and knowledge is a process or experience.

Subjects that have come to be seen, Gradgrind-fashion, as frivolous such as music and drama are almost certainly more useful for both the pupil and the economy as a whole than the narrowly academic, core curriculum subjects edging them out. Experiments in some inner cities demonstrate that a drama or arts program can have an enormous impact on the self-esteem and conventional success of some of the most deprived children in our societies. They indicate that there would be positive, if less spectacular results for all children. Charitable schemes in New York and London focus on giving young people written off as no-hopers at the end of their school careers, who are long-term unemployed, key life skills they should have learned in school if not at home. As well as punctuality and politeness, for instance, these include presentation, speaking confidently and clearly, good posture—all skills a drama teacher could have offered.

At a time when in so many subject areas there is obviously no such thing as a static body of knowledge, it seems madness to imagine we should nevertheless be instilling such a set of information into the minds of young people. The New Capitalism is not about what you know but how you know, and knowledge is a process or experience.

To focus on incremental improvements in redundant skills is all the more damaging given the importance of values and intangible social capital in modern economies. Children know when their education is useless, and in many schools—especially amongst boys—there is tremendous peer pressure to shun conventional academic success even though it clearly can offer a path to other and better opportunities. Given that lack of respect for conventional schooling, and given the need for alternative role models or sets of values, it beggars belief that the principal policy solution offered is to push even harder down the conventional route. It obviously will not work. It will not attain the results, and it won't do the children any good, either. They know getting a grade C rather than a D in history doesn't matter.

There is a compelling case for decentralization in primary and secondary education, not so much in the administrative sense as the intellectual. Who pays for the education system, or what the lines of organizational accountability should be, are secondary questions in this context, although there is of course an active debate about such organizational questions. One suggestion in the United States is the autonomous "charter" school, publicly funded and locally run. In a number of countries the idea of education vouchers, which give parents the freedom to shop around for schools using public funding, is popular. There is a left-right cast to the debate, with conservative parties keener on such experimentation and parental choice, and liberal or social democratic parties suspicious that choice is a vehicle for unfairness and placing more emphasis on consistency of access and standards.

High standards for all pupils are best achieved by ensuring their teachers are high quality, and while relatively low pay plays a big part in having creamed off some of the best teachers into other occupations in recent years, the diminishing responsibility and freedom accorded to individual teachers are also culprits.

The bureaucratization and centralization of school systems have tried to turn teachers into machines. Now that they can, let the machines do all the boring business of churning out facts and marking homework. Most of the material is already there online somewhere: a motivated child could pass through high school right now with the BBC Online and similar Web sites. Free all the teachers to instill a sense of curiosity and intellectual excitement, self-respect and fun, personal discipline and logical thought. Some will be good at it, some bad; after all, many are natural bureaucrats rather than born teachers. But the overall standard of education will without any doubt improve.

Increasing standardization has also served children, in all their variety, very badly. It has been standardization of the education process without achieving uniformly high outcomes for all pupils. The latter is certainly desirable. As the bipartisan emphasis in the United States on the need to use federal funds to ensure all schools deliver good results recognizes, standards in educational outcomes are a top priority. The focus on academic success alone, however, and success attained by a uniform method, means education systems inevitably produce first- and second-class citizens. Decentralization would also permit more diversity and recognize that success takes many shapes. Most people are not stupid, but relatively few are academically able. As it is impossible to predict exactly what workplace skills will be needed in even five or ten years' time, it is dangerously obsessive to insist on a single and clearly already slightly archaic set of achievements.

> Free all the teachers to instill a sense of curiosity and intellectual excitement, self-respect and fun, personal discipline and logical thought.

The financial markets provide a wonderful example of the sudden mushrooming of demand for an unexpected set of skills. The explosive growth of the derivatives markets from the late 1980s on created an insatiable demand for traders with a particular set of mental arithmetic skills. It was not academically high-level stuff—they didn't need a PhD in mathematics, although the banks did want people with those, too. Rather, on the trading floor, they needed the ability to add up and multiply very fast, to be thoroughly at home with certain simple mental arithmetic skills. The City of London sucked in tens of thousands of young men and women working in another kind of market, street markets, or perhaps in bank branches as tellers, people who might or might not have left high school with a paper qualification in mathematics but could do the business. Now, nearly twenty years later, the demand for such people is tailing off as more trading is computerized. In the next decade there will be a demand for another, unexpected skill.

Existing education systems are heavily geared toward perpetuating the economic success of those who are already successful. Nearly half of U.S. college graduates come from high-income families, only 7 percent from low-income families. In the UK and elsewhere in Europe the skew is just as pronounced. The bias is manifested in many ways, one of which is the fact that only purely academic skills are valued. This means there is a rigid hierarchy of educational attainment with certain schools and universities at its pinnacle. A more diverse system would clearly value a variety of types of attainment. The fragmentation of ambition would chip away at the monopoly that the better-off currently hold over the issuance of passports to success. It might even turn out that a lot more of the poor kids from the wrong side of the tracks could excel in conventional academic terms if there were more than one route out of where they start from.

A lot more of the poor kids from the wrong side of the tracks could excel in conventional academic terms if there were more than one route out of where they start from.

What policy makers hate about this kind of prescription is the thought of giving up control. Even if they can accept the case for decentralization intellectually, and a minority can, they hate the idea of not being able to spell out exactly what it is supposed to achieve. In this, they are no different from the top executives in many big companies who talk of empowering the workforce or decentralizing decision making to business units, but in the end cannot bring themselves to do it. Instead they use new technologies to control the units even more tightly or monitor every keystroke made by an employee. However, at a time of rapid and tumultuous economic change, it is impossible to predict what workforce skills employers will need. For bureaucrats to pretend they can spell out an appropriate curriculum and standards in every detail is both dishonest and an appalling failure of their responsibilities to the public. Bureaucratic planning failed as an economic system under Soviet Communism and now it is failing under Western capitalism, too. Yet it clings on grimly in ministries of education the world over, at the expense of our children.

The Democratic Politics of the New Economy

There is an important lesson here about the nature of government. Economists have long shied away from politics, the subject becoming studiously technocratic. However, the increased importance of civil order and political structures in today's changing economic circumstances has made it plain that politics matters for economies. In short, any country that cannot build the classic institutions of liberal democracy is condemned to poverty. A mass of evidence has been collected by the World Bank, evidence that has shifted the organization's emphasis onto political and institutional structures in its efforts to reduce poverty.

Clearly, the poor are different from the rest of us; they have less money. This simple fact explains why for many years the focus of economists, and organizations such as the World Bank, has stayed firmly on boosting GDP growth rates in the developing world. If 2.4 billion people in the world live on less than two dollars a day, getting some more dollars into their pockets is a clear priority. But is it enough? One World Bank report paints a far more complex picture.[22] Countries with the same growth rates can end up with very different numbers of people living in poverty, and the same sorts of economic reforms can end up having very varied outcomes in different places. Economic progress requires more than money. Clean air and water, freedom from disease, access to education, and security from natural and financial disasters all matter to people as much as having the cash to buy food and goods. While these other aspects depend on GDP growth, the recipe is subtler than going for growth.

It is typical of economists, a cynic might say, to lift up their noses from dusty tables of figures at last and notice the obvious. Maybe so, but the economists triumph in their collection of detailed evidence on the links between all these good things. It's easy enough to generalize about the importance of good institutions or better education for economic development, but, if true, then we need to understand the specifics, too. For example, extensive corruption is strongly linked to increased infant mortality, with a mortality rate four times higher than in low-corruption countries. The study estimates that if the most corrupt countries adopted the standards of the least corrupt, they could treble GDP per head. It would be easy to dismiss the conclusion that corruption hinders growth as a platitude, but this is an extraordinarily powerful result.

The same holds for other seemingly obvious links such as the fact that a reduced burden of regulation is good for growth. There are less obvious findings, too, like the economic payoff from improvements in civil liberties. The evidence clearly overturns the once-fashionable notion that authoritarian regimes might even be better for growth because they could get things done. Good government is decisively more important than firm government. There are clear and possibly controversial policy implications, however. For what the evidence ends up saying is: if the poor want to be more like the rich in terms of money, they have to be more like the rich in other ways, too. These include a liberal political regime, a commitment to more equality for women and members of ethnic minorities, and a concern for the environment. So, for example, the education of girls from poor families is one of the clearest correlates with economic development. It increases the skill pool in the workforce and reinforces this process in future generations, because educated mothers can better teach their children. It lowers the typical number of children a woman has, and a lower birthrate reduces unsustainable pressure on the local environment. It encourages more women to work and raises family incomes. Yet treating girls and boys as equals in their access to education is still a new cultural departure in many developing countries.

Similarly, there is a link between the institutions of liberal democracy and faster average growth rates. The economist Dani Rodrik explains it as the route to success in managing conflicts between different groups. In a divided society it is better for the smooth operation of the economy to be able to settle disputes in the courts or at the ballot than with guns or knives.

Put too crudely, this can look like American triumphalism. This was certainly the flavor of Thomas Friedman's book *The Lexus and the Olive Tree*. The eminent *New York Times* journalist made it plain he thought the rest of the world had to become more like the United States. A wittier and subtler version came from P. J. O'Rourke in *Eat the Rich*, in which he concludes that the classic democratic freedoms and rights are essential; otherwise you have to wonder: "Can men who have guns restrain themselves from interfering in the affairs of men who have nothing but checkbooks?" But of course America has no monopoly on liberal democracy, which comes in many varieties. Key to all are certain basic conditions, however, like the rule of law, basic political freedoms including freedom of expression and association, and an absence of pervasive corruption.

James Morgan, who reported for the BBC on a lavish G7 summit at Versailles in 1982, recounts that François Mitterrand, the French president, was asked how the vast amount spent on banquets and entertainment could be consistent with the ideals of the French Republic, liberté, egalité, and fraternité. He replied: "It is because of those ideals that we can afford it." Morgan writes: "At that moment it was hard not to admire that awful man."

If the poor want to be more like the rich in terms of money, they have to be more like the rich in other ways, too. These include a liberal political regime, a commitment to more equality for women and members of ethnic minorities, and a concern for the environment.

These are ideals worth crusading for, and, corrupt and cynical as the old Frenchman turned out to have been, he was right to say they were foundation stones for building prosperity. Indeed, the classic values of liberal democracy are more closely intertwined with prosperity than ever in the New Capitalism. The traditional state monopolies—taxation, violence, even money—are no longer the preserve of a self-selected and unaccountable bureaucracy. We now have a patchwork of public spheres, not least the Internet, replacing the old centralized, often state-run structures of broadcasting and big-circulation newspapers. There is more capacity for public scrutiny and controversy to monitor the exercise of power and limit it. Behavior that politicians in all democracies evidently used to regard as normal, such as slipshod fund-raising, accepting presents and trips, and giving jobs to friends, is no longer acceptable to the public. It is now exposed and criticized. The new politics and New Economy are mutually reinforcing, with liberal values helping sustain growth and the technologically driven prosperity helping boost political accountability and disperse power.

There are intellectual fashions amongst economists and other academics when it comes to the question of whether democracy and growth go hand in hand. Recently the economist Deepak Lal and historian Niall Ferguson have concluded that democracy is not essential for prosperity. While the links are obviously complex, I disagree with their conclusions. In the past authoritarian governments could preside over rapid growth as long as they were competent and got their policies right. In the New Capitalism I believe democracy will prove crucial, because the sources of economic growth are dispersed. No longer does any increase in prosperity depend on the accumulation of land or capital and the disposal of unthinking labor. It depends increasingly on the individual contribution of all the people who make up an economy.

> The classic values of liberal democracy are more closely intertwined with prosperity than ever in the New Capitalism.

The End for Men in Suits

In the tense and unnaturally quiet atmosphere in Prague ahead of the 2000 annual meetings of the International Monetary Fund, one of the stranger aspects of Franz Kafka's hometown was the presence of hundreds of bankers. Amongst the tourists and inhabitants, and the occasional scruffy anarchist, and against the fairy-tale background of the city's beautiful and historic center, these men (almost all of them are men) stood out. They always walked in pairs, all wore expensive navy or gray suits and sober ties, all carried briefcases even while sightseeing. Their conformity, being voluntary, was striking. They stood out far more than the eleven thousand armed police on duty ahead of the expected riots, looking like members of an alien race beamed secretly onto the surface of the earth, Stopford bankers, inhuman in their lack of individuality. These conformists face serious charges. Keith Hart writes: "A bureaucratic elite, distinguished by its uniform ('the men in suits') and divided in principle between government and commerce, has supervised one of the most unequal systems of rule seen in history, state capitalism."[23]

It is this system that is drawing to a close. Its death warrant was signed in 1989 with the end of the Cold War. That was a war not between the USSR and the USA, between Communism and capitalism, so much as a war between the bureaucratic elite and the people. The postindustrial economies are in a period of transition and political struggle, just as the industrial economies were in Karl Marx's day. Marx is too rarely valued for his optimism. He wrote: "Mankind always sets itself only such problems as it can solve; since, looking at the matter more closely, it will always be found that the task itself arises only when the material conditions for its solution already exist or are at least in the process of formation."

Hart continues: "There is no popular government anywhere, and most people have forgotten when they last took an active interest in such a possibility." There was much hand-wringing by pompous pundits when more people in the UK voted on which participant to eject next from the house in the tacky TV show *Big Brother* in the summer of 2000 than had voted in the previous year's European Parliament elections. The relative popularity of the mock TV referendum should have come as no surprise, however. Voter turnout has been dropping in all democracies for at least a couple of decades. It fell to two-thirds from a more typical three-quarters in a French constitutional referendum in 2000. That year's U.S. presidential election saw a turnout of just 51.2 percent of the voting-age population, only a shade better, in a close race, than the low of 49.1 percent in 1996. Politicians join journalists in plumbing the depths of popular esteem.

The voting patterns say government as it stands today is irrelevant. If politicians want to be relevant, their task is to resign themselves to this redundancy and fill the vacuum left by the end of bureaucracy. The struggle is now on for the distribution of the benefits that will be generated by a surge in prosperity thanks to economic growth driven by the new technologies. Who will win? A new cosmopolitan elite as the emerging economic inequalities are cemented into place? Criminal networks? Old hierarchies beating back the tide of technical change, like the Chinese mandarinate? Perhaps. The people have won the war. They have yet to win the peace.

> The struggle is now on for the distribution of the benefits that will be generated by a surge in prosperity thanks to economic growth driven by the new technologies.

They will. Certainly the New Capitalism tilts the balance of power toward people, all people, including the poorest, and against powerful elites. And if economic gains are not shared, the promise of greater prosperity will certainly not reach its fullest potential. However, it is not yet in the bag, which makes the first decade or so of this century a turning point in history. The time has come to write the next chapter in that never-ending story.

8

The Corporate Dinosaurs

In March of 1990 I was one of a small group of financial journalists
invited to visit one of Hungary's giant state-owned enterprises. No
sooner had the Wall fallen than some pioneers started thinking
about the inevitable process of privatization in the planned
economies, and Hungary had long been about the most liberal of
these. Ganz Electric occupied a huge site on the outskirts of Bu-
dapest. The group manufactured trains, trams, and buses, and also
pretty much everything needed in turn to make them. Steel that
went in at one end rode out as a new train at the other. It was in
many ways fascinating, but one of the most revealing aspects of the
factory tour was the executive lavatory. The managing director's secretary kept the key, escorted the slightly sheepish user at all times,
and also had a separate key to the cupboard in which the toilet paper
was locked. She doled it out a few sheets at a time. Not only did the
boss class have its own facilities, which was no surprise, but even the
executives couldn't be trusted not to steal toilet rolls.

Some things are different under capitalism, of course. Our executives have always been at liberty to take home as much toilet paper

as they needed. But otherwise the privilege of executive rest rooms or dining rooms or flashy cars or golf-club memberships was the same under corporate capitalism as under Communism. So urgent is the desire for the badges of status that I know one entrepreneur who drove a ten-year-old boring mid-market sedan just to stop the managers he was hiring from clamoring for BMWs. And I lost all respect for the executives running British Airways about a decade ago when I was assigned to go to the headquarters at Heathrow Airport to look at their contracts to check on that year's pay rise; I found that each had the type of luxury limousine he was entitled to spelled out there in detail, right down to the exact engine size and the number of hours the chauffeur would work. It cast a halogen light on their real priorities. But the corporate status symbol is heading for the dustbin of history just as surely as is Eastern Europe's inability to manufacture enough small squares of absorbent paper to satisfy consumer demand.

Take the example of Britain's Marks & Spencer. It was the flagship of the British main street for as long as I can remember. Everybody shopped there for at least their underwear but usually for much more, too. The company was a phenomenal success and one of the key blue-chip shares for any investor to hold in their portfolio. Then, in 1998, the M&S share price tumbled as sales started to fall catastrophically and the company issued one profit warning after another. The long-serving chairman and chief executive stood down. His replacement lasted less than a year. It was his replacement in turn, Luc Vandervelde, who took the crucial step. In November 2000, he tore up all the executive carpets and decreed that everybody at head office would henceforth have a carpet with the same depth of pile.

Like many a big, bureaucratic company, M&S had been slow to respond to changes in its market. Retailing, especially in clothing, had become far more competitive during the 1990s. Cheap imports posed a threat to a company that had always made buying British part of its brand image, and there were also many more retail chains offering different images for customers to buy into. The market became more fragmented. And besides, tastes changed. Middle-aged, middle-class women, the key M&S customers, had mostly stopped buying respectable "classic" clothes when they hit their forties and instead opted to try to stay feeling young. They wanted leather jeans or designer looks, not A-line, kneelength tweed skirts. Aging male executives whose only dilemma at the door of their wardrobe each morning was which tie to wear with the gray suit, and whose fashion information had to filter its way up through a hierarchical organization, were not best placed to spot this new trend.

Other companies have made similar mistakes. IBM's failure to spot the importance of the PC is a classic example. Up until the mid-1980s, and especially under Thomas Watson, its culture had been paternalistic and hierarchical in the extreme. The old company song said it all: "With Mr. Watson leading, to greater heights we'll rise, and keep our IBM, respected in all eyes." But I single out the British retailer as an example instead because it had remained such a pure instance of bureaucratic business right through the 1990s, right down to the different thicknesses of carpet for different ranks of executive. On the upside, perhaps, it was famous as a hugely paternalistic employer, getting dentists and hairdressers, for example, to visit its stores and guaranteeing employees a lifetime career structure as long as they wanted it.

The Demise of the Paternalistic Employer

While there are relatively few companies in the UK and United States offering such a contract, security, and comfort in return for loyalty and effort, the pattern was of course widespread in other countries. In Continental Europe employment legislation has enforced arrangements like the compulsory provision of a hot meal for staff at lunchtime, long paid holidays, job security. In Japan and Korea the corporate existence has been even more all-embracing, with many workers—core, male workers—guaranteed a job for life.

But these days have gone, just as decisively extinct as Ganz Electric or any other Eastern European combine in its precapitalist form. For some commentators this is a cause for regret. They would interpret the disintegration of the corporate social contract, and the withdrawal of political support for protective employment legislation in the name of increased job market flexibility, as a move toward the more thorough exploitation of workers by greedy bosses. There are such bosses, for sure, and there are politicians who see flexibility purely in terms of sectional interests.

Yet the stability provided by big corporations only ever protected a minority of the workforce, although a large minority. Most employees work in companies with fewer than fifty staff members. Those under the secure wing of big companies have tended to be male and white, with female and ethnic minority workers more likely to be in the job market "periphery." The corporate embrace also had its costs as well as benefits: security in return for conformity, long hours, a willingness to belong body and soul to the organization. It is hardly surprising there is such a strong tradition of the browbeaten middle manager rebelling against the roles prescribed him by job, family, community, culminating in the notorious midlife crisis. No need for such a crisis, definitely a middle-class, middle-management problem, if life has been more or less satisfying. Luckily, the hide-bound corporate roles are disappearing along with pyramidal career structure.

> The stability provided by big corporations only ever protected a minority of the workforce, although a large minority.

Any company faces certain obvious challenges. The growth in international trade and investment ensures that almost any market can be global in scope, meaning you could wake up one day to find you have a serious competitor you've never heard of before. Technology means the boundaries between what used to be different markets are more fluid, so your new competitor might be from a business you used to think of as entirely different from yours. It is even getting harder and harder to hire staff. For one thing, full employment has returned, for now, in some countries where ten years ago it seemed a forlorn hope. In cities in the United States and UK, and increasingly in the rest of Europe, you see "help wanted" signs in the windows of shops and restaurants. These are desperate employers, saying to passersby, I don't know who you are but come and work here! "Jobs galore," as the sign I saw outside one employment agency in outer London put it. "Come in and get one!"

More seriously, the advanced economies are running short of people of prime working age. The "dependency ratio" of retired people to workers is rising in all the advanced economies, the pressure exacerbated by early retirement. Before long we will have to put our pensioners back to work and nudge back the normal retirement age from the current sixty-five or sixty or even fifty-five. Many employers prefer to hire younger workers, who are cheaper, more adaptable, and have more up-to-date skills, but equally are well aware of the chronic shortage of the highly skilled young. This is why Silicon Valley has already imported them (mainly from Asia) in such huge numbers.

Such pressures mean that many companies, because there's money at stake in obvious ways, have been much faster than politicians or officials to understand that fundamental organizational change is needed. There has been a massive twenty-year boom in management advice geared to answering the question as to what organizational form will replace the hierarchical corporation and the assembly-line method of production. A lot of it is, of course, complete twaddle, empty intellectual calories pandering to the hunger for advice of managers aware of the pressures for change. A lot of incompetent and cynical executives have awarded themselves obscene paychecks and share options under the pretext of creating a better structure of incentives, and using the excuse of "market forces." The stupidity and excess of such responses does not, however, make the basic argument untrue. Corporate structure is changing, and in the successful corporations of the twenty-first century the relationship between company and workers will be transformed.

Doing Business on a Global Scale

One of the most striking changes concerns the size of companies. They are getting bigger. Or smaller. In between is a bad place to be. It combines lack of flexibility and speed with lack of economies of scale. In many markets the potential economies of scale are increasing, and network and winner-take-all effects mean one or two companies come to dominate. At the same time these are often the markets with the highest degree of product innovation. Bill Gates is, with any luck, right to be paranoid about Microsoft's ability to hang on to its dominant status. Against the desirability of economies of scale has to be set nimbleness and responsiveness. Small companies don't take two weeks to find a time slot in everybody's diary when all the parties to a decision can meet.

It is hard to obtain comparable figures across all the industrial economies. However, the OECD estimates from different national data sources that the average size of company has shrunk almost everywhere. The number of very large businesses, with over five hundred employees, has declined in most countries since the early 1990s, whereas the number of very small businesses, with up to ten or forty-nine employees depending on data source, has rocketed. Japan is the most noticeable exception, where mergers have created more very big companies in some industries. One or two Continental European countries lost firms at all scales during the recession of the early 1990s. Nevertheless, the broad trend is clear.

At the same time, there has been a ten-year-long merger boom.

Companies are getting bigger. Or smaller. In between is a bad place to be.

The value of corporate mergers worldwide exceeded $720 billion in 1999 a third higher than the previous year, according to UN figures. The extent of the management time, upheaval, and bankers' and lawyers' fees implied by that figure suggests the perceived economic benefits must be very large indeed. So big firms are getting ever bigger, and at the same time there are more and more small ones. What is driving this shifting pattern of industrial organization, where the mini and the mega are squeezing out the midi? A number of explanations are plausible. One is that it is easier to start up new companies because barriers to entry in the form of the availability of finance, cost of necessary equipment, burden of red tape, and so on are lower than in the past. It is definitely cheaper to set up a company programming video games, say, than a steel mill. This factor certainly seems to be important in some industries, especially those on the fringes of high technology such as media or software.

At the other end of the scale, it is obvious that globalization has extended the markets for many goods and services and led many companies to rearrange their production and marketing on a worldwide basis. This has increased the potential economies of scale in many cases, favoring giant companies. These scale economies can take several forms, whether high setup costs in manufacturing or the marketing benefits of having a global brand like Coca-Cola or Nike. Another popular explanation is that network effects favor the biggest company in any market, the classic example being Microsoft in the market for desktop computer operating systems. Compatibility is so important that Microsoft has achieved dominance, and it would be a brave entrepreneur who decides to bring a competing operating system to market now. Gates-o-phobes are fans of the competing Apple system and are cheering on the progress of Linux, the open-source operating system, but it is not yet clear if, like Apple, it can do more than carve a viable niche.

Such arguments are true and interesting. But there is a lot of mileage in going back to the most basic question in industrial economics. Why do companies exist when markets are supposed to be such powerful mechanisms for allocating resources? Since posed in this way by Ronald Coase in 1937, the answer has hinged on the understanding that the transactions costs of market exchanges can make it more efficient to bring some transactions inside one organization. The favorite example in the economics literature is the "holdup" problem: a supplier has to invest in a piece of equipment to make a car part, say. Once it has spent the money, it is vulnerable to demands from the car maker to cut prices on no matter what pretext, because the equipment is useless if not used for making that one type of part. In such cases where it is impossible to write out a legally binding contract covering all possibilities, it can be more efficient for the manufacturer to take over the supplier of the parts.

However, there are many other types of cost involved in transactions that can shift the desirable boundaries of the firm. After all, patterns of subcontracting and relationships with suppliers differ widely between countries—contrast American and Japanese corporations, for example—so it is clear that other influences play a part. Among them are the difficulties involved in transferring knowledge and the question of the ownership of assets, including intellectual property. One explanation for Japan's *keiretsu* organization, the long-standing networks of supply relationships between a dominant firm and a small number of suppliers, is that they are information-sharing relationships. That they are long-term means the repeat business makes reputation important; neither party tries to rip off the other. Yet to make monitoring of the goods and services provided, and the price paid and volumes ordered, easier, the numbers of companies in the network cannot be too large, either.

As both knowledge transfer and intellectual property are pretty crucial in modern economies, it should be no surprise that there is such upheaval now in corporate structure and ownership. The new technologies have reduced the costs of transferring information and at the same time raised the economic return to some types of knowledge. There is an increase in value here well worth contesting. Existing companies, their managers and shareholders, cannot assume it will belong to them. Economists Bengt Holmstrom and John Roberts suggest that companies do not seek control over physical assets so much as "contractual assets" such as licensing agreements or exclusive dealing contracts or franchises.[1]

There are many examples of companies offering complex products not by developing everything themselves, on the industrial-age model, but by negotiating a network of contracts with other suppliers. These are the "virtual" or "hollow" corporations. For instance, BSkyB owns almost none of the physical assets needed for satellite broadcasting. Instead, it puts together an alliance involving transmission, home reception, encryption, and program making. Nike famously does not manufacture sneakers, relying on outsourcing. Its main asset is the brand, not the manufacturing equipment. One $100 million turnover company selling hair clips and combs, Topsy Tail, has three employees, and develops, manufactures, and sells the products through its contractual network. Microsoft's stock-market valuation reflects almost entirely the worth investors put on its intangible assets, the chief of which is the company's ability to leverage its control of software standards through a huge network of relationships in the computer industry. Networks of the Microsoft or BSkyB kind are common in other knowledge-intensive industries like biotechnology, the media, and, increasingly, professional services and finance.

These types of network business could not exist without the new technologies. Since the late 1980s, almost every corporation has started outsourcing some of its business, and while the motive was often simply crude cost-cutting, managing the process would not have been possible without the improved availability of information and ease of communication enabled by technology. From those beginnings, all businesses have now become extremely dependent on a sophisticated flow of information around a network, from supply of materials at one end to delivery logistics at the other. Even companies in the heaviest of Old Economy industries are beginning to seek a different kind of network leverage, establishing "business-to-business" electronic exchanges. The

There are many examples of companies offering complex products not by developing everything themselves, on the industrial-age model, but by negotiating a network of contracts with other suppliers.

auto industry was in the vanguard, migrating its supply chain online, starting with sixteen suppliers. The auto industry Internet-based exchange, Covisint, involving Ford, GM, DaimlerChrysler, and Renault/Nissan will incorporate tens of thousands of suppliers. Even cement has got in on the act with the launch at the end of 2000 by Blue Circle of eCement for the global procurement of highly specialized equipment. According to market researchers at IDC, the value of business through such exchanges will grow from $2.5 billion in 1999 to $15 billion by 2004. Economists at Goldman Sachs have estimated that business-to-business exchanges could cut industry's costs by as much as a third and boost GDP by 5 percent. Clearly the potential scale of such trading exchanges is huge.

The emerging pattern is one of whales and minnows.

Economist John Kay has compiled a list of the top twenty U.S. corporations (by stock-market value) at the beginning and end of the twentieth century. A few figure on both lists—Exxon, GE, and Shell. Companies such as Pullman, maker of railroad coaches, Anaconda, and Singer, the sewing-machine manufacturer, have disappeared. Their replacements include modern titans such as Microsoft, Intel, Merck, and Novartis. The changes illustrate the weightlessness of the modern economy. Things big enough to climb into have been replaced by things you can put in your pocket. Beyond that, what are the lessons for corporate success? Several pieces of received wisdom are just wrong, Kay argues. Success does not depend on being in the right industry: there is one tobacco manufacturer, although a different one, on the beginning-of-century and end-of-century lists. It does not depend on grabbing the first-mover advantage: there are many examples of the innovator being elbowed out by a bigger, more established business that takes a fancy to the new market. Nor does he believe that network effects are decisive. If they were, there would be one global telephone monopoly, but this is actually a rather competitive industry.

In other words, competitive advantage does not depend on any of the technical givens about the industry structure of the market, but rather on the distinctive characteristics of particular firms. As Kay puts it: "Whoever has run GE has always been the most admired businessman in the United States. It's to do with GE, not Jack Welch." What's distinctive about GE is a reputation and corporate culture that makes the company attractive to the best managers in the U.S. job market. Other sorts of distinctive advantages certainly include success in managing long-term relationships with customers through branding and marketing, the creation of an aspirational image so much abhorred by some critics of modern capitalism. Another route to success is the skilled coordination of complex manufacturing and distribution processes. "Hollow" corporations that focus on the parts of the production chain adding most value—definitely not the manufacture but rather the design, marketing, and distribution—choose this route. Examples include the newcomers to Kay's list, companies such as Intel or Merck.

What all have in common, he suggests, is the ability to manage information well, much of it tacit information embedded in the relationships among corporations, customers, and suppliers. Tacit information is that which cannot be codified and written down, and is therefore hard to pass from person to person or organization to organization. It depends essentially on shared experience, having to be passed from person to person in real time.

> Competitive advantage does not depend on any of the technical givens about the industry structure of the market, but rather on the distinctive characteristics of particular firms.

Holmstrom and Roberts write: "Information and knowledge are at the heart of organizational design." Sharing ideas is key to economic growth, and the more so the more weightless the economy becomes, but it is difficult to work out and enforce a fair price for the trade because of the very nature of information. "Until the new ideas have been shown to work, the potential buyer is unlikely to want to pay a lot. Establishing the ideas' value, however, may require giving away most of the relevant information for free." It's a perfect catch-22. They believe the search for better ways to transfer knowledge, given the background of new information technologies that make this cheaper and more valuable at the same time, is driving the current merger wave. For one way round the problem is to bring the parties trying to exchange ideas into the same organization.

However, this is only part of the story. For it is not at all obvious that big companies are good at generating ideas in the first place. Creative mavericks sit uneasily in large organizations, which necessarily have rules and systems. In addition, it is unclear that the people able to generate new ideas will want this asset to belong to an employer rather than themselves. The value of intellectual property makes it a prize worth hanging onto, perhaps through creating a start-up company, rather than allowing an employer to claim it.

The Creative Company

One striking example of the difficulty of generating increasingly weightless economic activity is provided by the highly research-and-development intensive pharmaceutical industry. Drug companies spend a fortune on trying to create new products, and some tempting rewards await their success, the potential to cure or treat cancers or dementia, for example, in a rapidly aging and increasingly wealthy population. Yet the pace of pharmaceutical innovation is disappointing. The evidence suggests a decreasing number of new products per $150 million spent on R&D. This disappointment is one of the main factors driving the pharmaceuticals companies into ever bigger mergers. For to keep the industry growing at its past average rate, each company needs to introduce one new product a year that will achieve $450 million worth of sales each year. The number of big-enough discoveries was eighty to a hundred a year in the 1960s, and is now running at thirty to forty a year. Investment analysts have grown increasingly concerned about the future growth prospects of this huge industry; the *Wall Street Journal*, not prone to hyperbole, said the $350 billion a year industry was "soul-searching."[2]

Why the decline in creativity in the industry that depends utterly on human inventiveness? One reason is the need for nimbleness and change in the New Capitalism, a characteristic that is easily undermined by growth and profitability. After all, executives are understandably reluctant to alter what has been a winning formula for them. But that makes their business sclerotic. Paradoxically, success can contain the seeds of its own destruction, and innovation often comes from those who have not succeeded yet. Small companies are in many industries by far the most innovative even though the amount they can spend on R&D is substantially lower than the big company budgets. The big pharmaceuticals corporations rely on market research for guidance about where to direct their research efforts. There will be no investment in potential drugs if the market research indicates the likely sales are too low. But there are many examples of blockbuster drugs (such as beta-blockers and SSRI antidepressants) that were nearly killed off by market research. It is true in many industries that market research is a misleading guide to what consumers will buy, for the research only poses questions with limited horizons: asking what features would make this coffee percolator work better (speeding up the brewing? filtering the water? changing the shape of the spout?) rules out the answer that an entirely different type of coffee-making machine would sweep the market.

Shaping the answers by setting the questions rules out serendipity, by far the most fruitful source of genuine innovation and fresh thinking. The increased cost of gaining regulatory approval for a new drug has made the companies more averse to taking a risk on a new drug that might not sell enough to cover the development

> Paradoxically, success can contain the seeds of its own destruction, and innovation often comes from those who have not succeeded yet. Small companies are in many industries by far the most innovative.

costs, so they seek the reassurance of high sales from market re-search. In effect, the costly process of regulatory approval raises bar-riers to entry in the pharmaceuticals industry. The U.S. FDA's rules are much more stringent than those elsewhere but are in fact the world standard because every successful product must sell in the huge American market. The regulatory barriers act to protect the big American pharmaceuticals companies at the expense of new en-trants anywhere else in the world.

The forces for concentration in the industry bring an even deeper problem, however. According to one critic of the industry's management of the innovation process: "The merger activity is a sign that R&D is failing. Why should this be when so many clever people are throwing so much money at it? . . . The management is-sues relate to the fact that, despite all the guru-speak, discovery is an individual and not a team effort. Large corporations are inimical to creative genius and have in place elaborate structures to stop it."[3] They try to systematize research when creativity is a product of di-versity. Financial experts, market strategists, and sales directors have no role in the development of new ideas but most corporations, and not just in this one industry, fence in creativity with precisely such guardians of convention and safety. Voltaire could have told them it wouldn't work: "God is on the side not of the heavy battalions, but of the best shots." The British public seems to agree; "serendipity" was voted the nation's favorite word in the first year of the twenty-first century.

So alarmed had some leading oncologists become about the fail-ure of past efforts in cancer research, including the vast R&D effort of the drug companies, that in December of 2000 they held a "blue-skying" conference in Cambridge, England. The point of the blue-sky technique is to liberate experts from prefabricated patterns of thought, from old paradigms, by bringing together a cross section of people with completely different sorts of expertise. They will apply to the issue at stake the metaphors and ways of thinking they use in their own fields. The hope is that the exposure stimulates fresh bursts of creativity into a moribund subject. In his introduction to the Cambridge meeting Professor Michael Baum noted that the decoding of the human genome and developments in proteonics offered much new hope for cancer therapies. But he said: "Yet we believe that the opportunity could be lost for a hundred years if we continue with the rigid mindsets and vertical thinking which has inhibited progress in the past. We wish to encourage thinking outside the box of our conceptual frameworks."

The hope is entirely in line with the suggestion, in the work on recombinant growth by Martin Weitzman and others, that new ideas formed from combining old ideas are more valuable the more far apart, in some sense, the original ones were. It is the unexpected concatenation of thoughts that brings true insight. Like any idea, this is not a new one. Thomas Aquinas said: "The essence of the human being is to take two concepts which are themselves abstract, then put them together to form a new abstract concept which is unlike the two original concepts." It is just that in an economy that depends more and more on human beings fulfilling their nature, creating the conditions for creativity is vitally important. The industry's current approach to cancer research, however, is based on number-crunching the results of the human genome product, the industrialization of drug design, and abandonment of serendipity. The detailed study of a particular gene suggests targets for the treatment of certain diseases. The researchers prepare an "assay" and test systematically hundreds of thousands of chemical compounds to see whether they have any effect on the target. One leading company in the field, Pharmacia, spends $7,500 million a year on such assembly-line research. Others, like Glaxo Wellcome, have pulled out of the cancer field because of the high cost of this approach. Seeking a middle way, Novartis spends a quarter of its research budget on collaborations with small biotech companies. In addition, in December 2000 it launched a three-year Euro66 million experiment to create an independent gene therapy "incubator" that is to operate at arm's length from its main internal research labs. The Novartis incubator will take an alternative approach involving biologists investigating the action of genes, and will also introduce artificial intelligence systems to keep track of experimental data, including failures, useful information that is normally thrown away.

The history of serendipity in medical advance gives good grounds for being skeptical about any systematic research approach. We still know too little about the complexity of the human body. Tilli Tansey, historian of modern medical science at the Wellcome Trust Centre for the History of Medicine, oversees the Trust's annual award to encourage "blue sky" research. She says: "Science is easily as creative as the arts. It is a dynamic, kinetic activity dependent on a synthesis of old, new, completed, and random ideas."[5] Amongst the many examples of the accidental fruits of research: Viagra started life as a treatment for angina, and its side effects were concealed by prudish researchers as long ago as the 1960s; antismoking drug Zyban was tested originally as an antidepressant; and Thalidomide might turn out to be an effective anticancer treatment as it blocks the development of blood vessels on which tumors depend to grow.

It is not that the dissident oncologists at the Cambridge conference were unexcited by the latest developments in molecular biology and proteonics and thought the heavy battalions were a waste of time. Rather, they regretted the way this had squeezed out any other approach. Thomas Edison famously described genius as 99 percent perspiration, but the 1 percent inspiration is essential, too. The burst of creativity in the computer industry in the 1980s and 1990s had both the massive firepower of big companies and the scattergun shots of start-ups to fuel it.

It is apparent that the titans of an extraordinarily innovative industry need to look outside for new ideas.

Indeed, the big corporations in the computer industry have also been on the prowl for ideas, despite its incredible record of innovation. Unlike the heavily regulated pharmaceuticals industry, where the high hurdle of FDA approval and the regulation of price and sales in many countries give huge multinationals an unmatchable advantage in marketing, there are not the same external pressures on computer companies to be big. Nevertheless, those that have simply grown huge through success are hunting in a variety of ways for a creativity transfusion. Buying start-ups has been one pattern, a route used by Cisco and Microsoft. Many are now trying corporate venturing while 2001 brought budget cuts, taking small stakes in start-ups, partly for the investment returns but mainly for the access to creativity. Corporate venture-capital spending in the United States climbed to $15.7 billion in the first three quarters of 2000, up from a total of $9.5 billion in 1999 and just $1.5 billion in 1998. Companies like IBM, Intel, and Lucent are heavily involved in such venturing. Lee Dayton, IBM's head of corporate development, explained: "It has improved our technology headlights. This is all about developing more intellectual property."[6] IBM said it had invested about $300 million in a thousand companies, Lucent has a $250 million venture fund, Adobe $172 million, and so on. In the case of Intel the figure had tripled from $330 million in 1997 to a staggering $1.2 billion in 1999, involving direct investments in more than five hundred small companies. The decline in technology share valuations through 2000 had clearly started to slow down the pace of corporate venturing, as big companies do not want to take capital losses on their investments. Nevertheless, it is apparent that the titans of an extraordinarily innovative industry need to look outside for new ideas.

Corporate Social Capital

In short, the mavericks, subversives, and crazy people are about to have their day. Bosses don't like them and they don't think much of bosses. Here is the mission statement of Actis Technology, based near Glasgow, an innovative Internet company whose founder, Stephen Whitelaw, describes what they do as "mapping the dark side of the Internet":

Here's to the crazy ones, the misfits, the rebels, the troublemakers, the round pegs in square holes, the ones who see things differently. They're not fond of rules and they have no respect for the status quo. You can quote them, disagree with them, glorify or vilify them. About the only thing you cannot do is ignore them, because they change things. They invent. They imagine. They heal. They explore. They create. They inspire. They push the human race forward. Maybe they have to be crazy. How else can you stare at an empty canvas and see a work of art? Or sit in silence and hear a song that's never been written? Or gaze at a red planet and see a laboratory on wheels? They push the human race forward, and while some may see them as crazy ones, we see genius, because the people who are crazy enough to think they can change the world are the ones who'll do it.[7]

Actis Technology is new, relatively small, and innovation driven. Its executives understand that this is the kind of employee they need and so value the rebels and subversives. After all, that's the kind of person they are themselves. However, having to embrace trouble-making is a nightmare for managers in companies where value added is coming from inside the minds of the workforce. Much has been written about the "knowledge management" problem. I read the advice some gurus give about how to ensure that key workers share their knowledge fully with the rest of the organization with wry amusement. Who do they think they're kidding? Each bolshie employee can, if he wishes, go on strike without any visible sign of not working as hard as ever. It is as if Victorian mill owners had had to get the looms to cooperate. Managers in today's corporations are like the hapless adult in a children's tale where the machinery comes to life and rebels. Except it's worse. They can't even be sure when there is a rebellion going on. Necessity will compel managers to ditch the old paternalistic attitude to employees. Instead, they will need to build high-quality social capital within the company in order to draw the best out of the people who work in it. The social fabric of the business is becoming a key part of business success.

In many weightless industries, and especially in activities like R&D, tacit knowledge, impossible to codify and pass on through a textbook or formal training, is likely to be crucial. It stands in contrast to the codified, mass-production knowledge that used to have a greater importance in the economy. Similarly, the provision of products or services whose characteristics can be written down in detail and easily verified, and therefore enforced by contracts, are decreasingly important. Instead, a bigger share of activity is accounted for by non-verifiable goods and services. It is much easier to assess the product of the assembly line than a more typical piece of modern economic output such as a computer program, a financial service, or even a book.

What's more, the same argument applies to almost any type of business in the New Capitalism. It is not just a question of brainy knowledge-workers in high-tech companies. Any service business will need the same strong social fabric and mutual respect inside the company in order to ensure that frontline workers like shop assistants or call-center operators are indeed delivering a high-quality service to customers. It is easy, as a customer, to tell which kind of business you're dealing with from the attitude of the staff. Attaining a high level of quality matters just as much in everyday services like shops and restaurants as it does in financial services or industry. Profit margins are entirely driven by quality of service. Similarly, in modern manufacturing with team working and just-in-time manufacturing, the contribution of every individual worker matters, and managers have to relate to employees in a manner that draws from them high-quality work. Zero-fault, high-productivity production is not possible without robust social capital inside the company.

Japanese corporations understood this three decades ago, and it was an attitude that sat happily with the country's social norms and "stakeholder" approach to business. The contrasting emphasis on shareholder value alone in Anglo-American companies has led some commentators, such as Will Hutton in the UK and Jeremy Rifkin in the United States, to be very pessimistic about the New Capitalism, assuming that hard-nosed profit seeking for the sake of

It is not just a question of brainy knowledge-workers in high-tech companies. Any service business will need the same strong social fabric and mutual respect inside the company in order to ensure that frontline workers like shop assistants or call-center operators are indeed delivering a high-quality service to customers.

the dividends and share price will drive out any longer-term efforts to build companies around mutual respect and social responsibilities. But this is overly gloomy. The most successful companies will turn out to be those with the strongest social networks and the most empowered employees. Exploitation will harm the bottom line.

According to Nick Crafts of the London School of Economics: "If we're starting to see more activities in which it's not altogether easy to control bad behaviour through formal legal institutions, that's to say through going to the courts or something like that, then informal social institutions matter." Business is becoming more vulnerable to opportunistic behavior, he argues. "If we think about ways of dealing with opportunism, some of them are formally legal. They might involve writing a contract, they might involve enforcement through the courts. Others are essentially situations where it's impossible to write a good contract and good behaviour is informed more by continual interaction and by close social proximity so that someone who steps out of line can in effect be effectively excluded." Just as an author tends to try and deliver a manuscript that will keep the publisher happy out of concern to maintain her good reputation, he adds: "I think rather similar things occur in R&D where after all it's very hard to know whether the scientific breakthrough just wasn't feasible or whether actually with some more effort and application, you would have made the expected pay-offs that you'd hoped for originally. So I think we're talking here about situations in which people invest in acquiring a reputation.

"When we're trying to commission things like new ideas, then the verifiability issue becomes much larger. . . . This is likely to be a bit more important in a knowledge-intensive economy than one which is trying to produce relatively homogeneous commodities like cars."[8]

Reputation is necessarily taking the place of legal remedies because it is impossible to write complete contracts. There are three reasons for this. One is that it is impossible to foresee all or even most of the likely contingencies in today's subtle and intangible economic transactions. Another is that it is hard to verify the outcomes. And thirdly, there are inadequate legal mechanisms to enforce a decision on whether or not the contract has been fulfilled. Whereas complete contracts were feasible in much economic activity in the industrial era, they are hard to contemplate in most knowledge-intensive businesses.

The issue for companies is how best to organize these repeated human interactions and reputation building, and how to retain the human capital of employees who have successfully built their own personal reputation, a reputation that has economic value. This is all the harder because information technology is forging new internal structures in big companies and dispersing more widely information about the organization, revealing conflicts and controversies. Secrets, once a great source of hierarchical power, are now extraordinarily hard to keep. IT is making more employees aware of what's at stake and better able to talk back. The more they see of the inner workings of the corporation, the more they understand the executive emperors are wearing no clothes.

There is a tension for the top managers between monitoring people's work through continuous personal contact, which might be best done inside a firm rather than through market trans-

> The issue for companies is how best to organize these repeated human interactions and reputation building, and how to retain the human capital of employees who have successfully built their own personal reputation, a reputation that has economic value.

actions, and the desire of employees who build up such expertise and reputation to gain the full benefits of their own human capital by leaving to launch a start-up or quitting for an employer who will pay a higher salary. Why should they hand over valuable information to their boss, especially considering the battalions of mediocrities who still get promoted to middle-management positions. Just think Dilbert: the fact that it's true is what makes it so funny.

For instance, it has become a bit of a platitude to talk about the need for networking and cooperation in business. The fluid flow of knowledge across barriers is essential. The reason is that as the range of technologies has expanded, and they have become more complex, even the biggest business can no longer generate all it needs to know internally. The need for a wide range of commercial and technical knowledge, and the desire to share risks and reduce uncertainty in bringing new products and services to markets, has made alliances essential. Collaboration has in fact become more common everywhere, in the academic world as well as business. Even so, there is still a lot of resistance to the necessary fluidity and openness. A lot of executives like to imagine they can still be masters of their own corporate destinies.

One very visible symbol of the demise of corporate man, the epitome of the Old Economy, is the disappearance of corporate uniform. This is the uniform formerly known as the business suit. Thanks to the explosive impact of Silicon Valley culture on the entire world of business, the new conformity is dressing down. It started with Fridays and before long spread to Monday to Thursday, too. Of course, being told by your senior executives that there is an official casual dress code does not amount to a genuine flowering of individualism in the corporation. On the contrary, it sent most office workers scurrying to the closest Gap branch for the standard pair of chinos in place of the standard gray or navy suit. But even if the casual dress code does not correspond to any meaningful relaxation of the old structures of corporate control, it certainly shows an awareness that there is something desirable about breaking out of the old tramlines.

So do innovations like comfortable rooms or coffee bars at work, where colleagues are encouraged to sit and chew over ideas with each other, a recognition of the importance of creativity. It is still a bit forced, and overeagerly trendy, even in companies genuinely experimenting with new structures. Some management fads are plain daft, nonsense hiding behind a veil of teeth-grindingly awful jargon. But there are nevertheless important symbolic changes within many companies that will become ever more genuine.

The journalist Michael Lewis noted one consequence of the widespread admiration of the new and the experimental in the world of business: "If you celebrate innovation, you call into question the status quo. If you glorify the entrepreneur, you denigrate Organization Man."[13] The catch is that lots of people in the workplace still prefer life as Organization Man. Reshaping those complex social institutions we call businesses might not actually be complete until there has been a generation change.

Lewis went on: "Capitalism is eating the capitalists."

As in almost every other area of life, the traditional authority of corporate executives has simply evaporated. For workers at the bottom of the food chain doing routine jobs, that translates into a straightforward loss of respect. The higher up the economic value ladder you look, the more likely it is that workers will have a strong sense of their personal ownership of the ideas or creativity that generate profit.

One very visible symbol of the demise of corporate man, the epitome of the Old Economy, is the disappearance of corporate uniform.

Ownership of Ideas

The ownership of intellectual property is shaping up as one of the most contentious issues in the weightless economy. If the value of a product or service lies in intangible ideas and creativity rather than the stuff, then the greatest reward now attaches both to the part that is cheapest to produce and easiest to copy. No wonder it looks as though the winners will be the lawyers, with cracking down on "piracy" a big business in its own right. In one of the highest-profile recent intellectual-property cases, titans of the music industry sued Napster over the provision of the facility for rightful buyers of music to exchange songs online. However, the number of other cases is soaring. One of my favorites concerned the squeezy plastic lemon-shaped juice dispensers, which indeed upheld a patent on the plastic lemon shape. U.S. courts have also upheld patents covering business processes, including, notoriously, Amazon's "one-click" online ordering system. Even more controversial have been patents granted for uses of traditional medicines and plants for developing countries. One covering the use of turmeric as an antiseptic was overturned thanks to ancient Sanskrit documents showing this was a traditional use and therefore not a new discovery. However, the courts require documentation to overturn a patent. Others covering, for instance, strains of basmati rice granted to an American company still stand.

The traditional, and valid, defense of patents and copyright is that without the granting of a temporary monopoly there would be no incentive to innovate in the first place. The development of a new product takes an investment of time and money, and innovators must be allowed to recoup these and make a reasonable return, or they wouldn't bother to get out of bed in the morning. However, the nature of innovation has changed. A new piece of software is not like a new type of steam engine. In the famous passage quoted earlier in this book, Thomas Jefferson concludes: "Inventions then cannot, in nature, be a subject of property." As the exchange of ideas enriches both parties, to treat an idea as a type of property whose use can be reserved for some people and not others does require a system of vigorous enforcement.

Lawrence Lessig, a professor at Harvard Law School, has argued vigorously that the ever increasing efforts to defend intellectual property—in effect a contradiction in terms—represents the defeat of the open, liberal society. "We are at a critical moment in the history of our future because we are now witnessing the defeat of what 2000 years had built, the defeat of the open society, the triumph of the closed society," he writes.[9] The closing is being done in the name of the defense of property rights, and done through the use of government regulation, particularly the U.S. 1998 Digital Millennium Copyright Act, which is applied extraterritorially by American courts and U.S. patent approvals.

Lessig argues in favor of restoring an intellectual commons to combat the harmful extension of private property rights over the terrain of ideas and creativity. Since the end of the Cold War, the balance has become distorted away from the commons and toward private property, in his view. Ideas can't be stolen, only shared, with varying degrees of voluntariness. Many producers of ideas instinctively agree, and even those who do not certainly do not want a corporate employer claiming property rights over something that the corporation has not created and cannot actually appropriate from the mind of the originator.

It is hardly surprising, then, that so many creative people want to become their own companies; or even develop themselves as a brand, in line with one of the recent fads in management literature. It marks their ownership or at least origination of an idea. It sets up the presumption that anybody who wants to share and use the idea will have to reward them for it. There will have to be negotiations, a contract, some formal recognition that they have produced something of value. This genie is well out of the bottle. It is going to remain hugely unattractive for the most creative people to want to work for big companies, and those who seek corporate jobs will probably not be the most creative. The fact that it is what is weightless that's valuable is great news for creatives and entrepreneurial types. It is a huge problem for corporations.

There is intense interest in the few companies that have experimented with radical approaches. The same examples are featured over and over again in the business press. Often they are in overtly creative industries, like London's well-known St. Luke's advertising agency. Other prominent examples include big companies that rearrange their offices to incorporate café-style spaces or relaxation areas, although these efforts are often faintly embarrassing, like a parent intruding on a teenage party, saying, Get with it, hipsters! In a different sort of effort to capture a little creativity, a number of big consultancies such as PricewaterhouseCoopers and Accenture have created their own in-house business "incubators" to allow staff to form start-up companies without losing all the human capital involved.

However, the more typical response is to devise ways of reasserting control. For instance, legislatures can be persuaded to pass laws allowing employers to monitor email and Web use. Some companies bother to keep tabs on every keystroke without pausing to think that if they have to do this in order to extract effort there might be something deeply wrong with their approach to management. Moral pressure is exerted in order to boost loyalty. Little perks help, too, like gym membership, parties during the festive holiday season, and stress counseling or massage. More radical are arrangements that cede control in some areas in order to keep it in others. Flexible working arrangements that allow employees to work from home or reduce their total hours are one example, grudgingly granted by more and more employers especially while the job market is so tight. Grudgingly, because the typical boss hates to let staff out of his or her sight. The resurgence of long-hours culture and presenteeism in recent years is a gut executive-class reaction to the sneaking realization that the balance of power in the workplace has swung irrevocably against them. Their aim is not boosting productivity and profit; this is a raw power struggle, a contest to appropriate economic value. Many employees have the only sensible response: Eat my shorts!

Of course, not all workers are equally powerful. Not all have a high level of that dangerously portable human capital. So for the cleaner or security guard this argument might seem irrelevant. But, although it applies more immediately to the professional and managerial classes, it does work more broadly. There are several reasons. One is that the content of once-routine jobs is becoming more demanding and important. For example, thanks to the way technology has reduced the number of administrative jobs and altered their content, the secretary of today plays a vital organizational role compared to the typists of twenty years ago. In almost every type of work, more responsibility rests on the individual now than in the past and the jobs have been up-skilled.

A second reason is that quality is visible throughout an organization, and key workers don't really want to stay with companies where the lavatories are always dirty because the cleaning is contracted out on the cheap to a supplier who underpays illegal immigrants to do the job. It's the little details that are the best signal of high quality. Finally, and perhaps most immediately, the Western countries are running out of people to do any jobs but especially the mundane ones. When something is in short supply, its price rises. So having a lot of human capital is giving a boost to employees, but being human is a good start. It is not capital that is scarce in the New Capitalism, but people.

> The Western countries are running out of people to do any jobs but especially the mundane ones. When something is in short supply, its price rises.

Bogus Buzzwords

The old joke puts it in a nutshell. How many psychiatrists does it take to change a lightbulb? Only one, but the lightbulb has got to really want to change. Many corporations are in the same position as these dim lightbulbs. Change is the last thing on their wish list.

Managers have a good idea what they should be doing, or ought to. There's no shortage of advice from the business schools and authors of business books. Some of it is unintelligible, but much of it is sensible. Besides, the point of the impenetrable language is probably to hide an unwelcome message: many executives don't want to change. They don't want to admit their fundamental loss of power. Think about some of the key words in management.

"Creativity" is one of the most overused buzzwords in modern management-speak. It is not that creativity is actually undesirable, of course. On the contrary, it lies at the root of the essential ability to innovate. No, the problem is that although it is a desirable characteristic, many managers fear creativity. It strikes at the control and conformity that are the workplace legacy of the bureaucratic era. It is the freethinkers, the dissenters, the eccentrics who are creative. Advertising agencies and other "creative" businesses try to formalize the eccentricity, through casual dress codes and ponytails for men, but there's a troubling internal contradiction in trying to codify creativity in any way. Such businesses only manage to achieve genuine creativity sporadically. Others, paying less lip service to the importance of creativity, manage to achieve it hardly at all. No wonder it took a genuine surge in innovation by strange and colorful individuals, in the dot.com share bubble, to get large numbers of people interested in business at all. Most established business executives are overwhelmingly, anesthetically dull.

A similarly hypocritical nugget of management jargon is "empowerment." The kinds of managers who proudly say that theirs is a people business, and they are empowering their people to take decisions themselves, thereby reveal that they have had to think very hard about this process. It has been a conscious strategy based on business school and management theory, not one that comes naturally. They are exactly the managers who will find it hardest to give up control in practice. As almost anyone who has ever held a job will know, giving up control is something most managers truly hate.

This is one of the great motives for entrepreneurs. They in turn truly hate being controlled. Being your own boss is, however, easier than ever. It's easiest in the United States, where it is cheap and simple to set up a company. There's scant administrative or legal difficulty compared to anywhere else. At the other extreme, emerging economies have mummified the entrepreneurial spirit in red tape, forcing most small businesses into the illegal sector. Many gov-

Many managers fear creativity. It strikes at the control and conformity that are the workplace legacy of the bureaucratic era.

ernments outside the United States are now getting the idea, however, although not rushing to put it into practice. It is also becoming culturally more acceptable to try and fail. This is another very beneficial result of the dot.com boom. For example, the UK has a new bankruptcy law similar to America's Chapter 11 rules, which allow companies to trade insolvently under certain circumstances, in the hope of bringing them through the crisis as ongoing concerns. Aside from the legal position, it's rather fashionable to have run a failed start-up. The fashion might ebb, but it is hard to see honest business failure ever regaining the stigma it once used to carry.

Aside from legal and cultural changes, however, there are fewer financial and practical obstacles to setting up a company. Start-up costs are very low in some areas, such as business services, software, publishing, and ecommerce. The main barrier to entry is drumming up enough money for a marketing drive. Although the bursting of the Internet share price bubble has certainly turned off the tap of freely flowing start-up capital for now, it has not shut it off for good. As such finance barely existed outside the United States until recently, this is another lasting legacy.

Improved communications technologies have made outsourcing a cheap and practical alternative to hiring a big staff, for start-ups as much as large, cost-cutting corporations. The proverbial computer geeks setting up a business in the garage can buy in virtually all the other services they might need, from legal and accountancy work to pizza delivery instead of a canteen. If you have a business idea, it's hard to think of an objection to the so-called Nike strategy: just do it.

Teamwork is another management obsession. Richard Sennett

rants, rightly, that this is yet another piece of hypocrisy. It creates a false impression of equality of power and status. Although he admits that the old work ethic made people put enormous burdens on themselves, it nevertheless left them dignity and character. In contrast: "The modern work ethic focuses on teamwork. It celebrates sensitivity to others; it requires such 'soft skills' as being a good listener and being cooperative; most of all teamwork emphasizes team adaptability to circumstances."

If you have a business idea, it's hard to think of an objection to the Nike strategy: just do it.

He concludes: "Teamwork is the group practice of demeaning superficiality."[10]

However, although he argues that teamwork is the ethic best suited to the flexible new political economy, I'm not sure this is true, much as some management gurus would like to persuade us of it. As the example of the pharmaceuticals industry suggests, it might just be a recipe for the lowest common denominator, for bland conformity. Teamwork looks more like a management-centerd reinterpretation of old hierarchical structures that leaves the top dogs in control and gets the underdogs monitoring each other. Worse, it is short for "getting key employees to hand over valuable knowledge to the company." Whether it is the best organization of effort for innovation in particular and productivity in general seems highly doubtful.

It is more likely to be the case that different organizations and work ethics will be needed in different industries or different functions. Here, as elsewhere in analyzing the weightless world, one of the lessons is the danger of bogus generalization about a fragmenting reality.

So the hastiest of glances along a shelf of business best-sellers will reveal that the most popular themes are almost all revered in theory and shunned in practice in big companies. Executives do not want to empower their staff, do not want them to take charge of their own working time in order to find the right work-life balance, do not like unpredictable creatives, don't fancy devolving decision making. On the contrary, they would rather exercise as much control as ever, value presenteeism, and like predictability in the office even if they can no longer guarantee it anywhere else.

Are they, like King Canute, doomed in their efforts to stem the tide of upheaval? The current fluid state of business organization suggests that many companies will indeed bow to reality before the waters close over their heads. Those that don't will drown.

9

The New Politics

I suppose it is the fate of every angst-ridden teenager to wish they had been born in some other place and time, somewhere more exciting. Hanging around a small, depressed mill town during the 1970s, I longed to have been around in Paris or Prague, or at least London or Washington, in the heady spring of 1968. I read De Beauvoir and Sartre, surreptitiously smoked Gitanes, and kept a special notebook in which to list revolutionary ideas. At school we read Wordsworth's *The Prelude*, sighing over its famous line: " 'Bliss it was in that dawn to be alive. . . .' " But I was too late. By the time my parents allowed me out by myself after dark, the glorious dawn of that revolutionary spring had given way to the misery of recession and inflation in the 1970s, which brought everybody worries about jobs and being able to afford to keep up the family living standard; in the UK to strikes that left the rubbish uncollected and the dead unburied; and to the Thatcher and Reagan election victories. The only rebellion left was the nihilism of punk, so those of us who would have been out on the march or levering up cobblestones a decade earlier stayed instead cooped up in darkened rooms listening to The

Clash or the Sex Pistols: "I am an anarchist . . . /Don't know what I want but I know how to get it/I wanna destrooooy. . . ."

There is, of course, always a danger that you will get what you wish for, only in the wrong place and at the wrong time. Thirty-five years on from the events of 1968 and more than a decade after the fall of the Berlin Wall, the Western democracies are shaping up for another dramatic political convulsion. This prediction is not sheer melodrama — or at least, if it is real I'm in good company.

David Landes, the economic historian, wrote in his classic 1969 study of technological progress: "Change is demonic. It creates but it also destroys."[1] Technological change is never automatic. It means the displacement of established methods, damage to vested interests, and serious human dislocations. If it happens nevertheless, it implies that the new techniques are so dramatically superior in economic terms to old ones that the efficiency gains can offset all the adjustment costs. Technological changes that are adopted and put into practice are therefore inherently radical. New evidence of the sheer difficulty and upheaval involved in technological change at the level of the individual company has been furnished by a number of recent studies. According to one: "The three-way complementarity between IT, organization and quality involves very complex changes to the firm. . . . Firms do not simply plug in computers or telecommunications equipment and achieve service quality or efficiency gains. Instead, they go through a lengthy and sometimes difficult process of co-invention."[2]

An appreciation of the difficult process of capturing the economic gains of new technologies, gained from watching it unfold in the American economy during the long boom of the 1990s, means a steadily growing number of economists are warning about the political tensions that are bound to accompany the onward march of the New Capitalism. Economic slowdown over the course of the business cycle, and especially a significant recession, can only exacerbate the tensions caused by fundamental restructuring. According to the unexcitable bureaucrats at the OECD, writing about the interweaving of technical, economic, and cultural changes: "Even though this tapestry has been rewoven on numerous occasions as the world economy has moved through different phases, it has never so far been done without very high costs." Mancur Olsen, who was one of the most creative economists of recent times, suggested there was indeed an internal contradiction in capitalism, "an inherent conflict between the colossal economic and political advantages of peace and stability and the longer-term losses that come from accumulating networks of distributional coalitions that can only survive in stable environments."[3]

It is impossible to be both stable and dynamic, he suggested, even though too much stability ultimately undermines the beneficial conditions it brought about in the first place. A dynamic phase is bound to mean instability and the overturning of vested interests and existing social coalitions in order to build the platform for the next economic and technological leap forward. Robert Rubin, the highly regarded former United States Treasury Secretary, has also emphasized the need for a political response: "As in many turbulent eras gone by, the great challenge before us is not only in moving forward in the intellectual response to complicated substantive issues, but also winning the battle for people's minds in support of good policy." We face, he said in a thoughtful speech looking ahead to a new century, "a true challenge to our political systems."[4]

Ripe for Change

The battle lines are being drawn well away from conventional politics, however. As many commentators have noted, quotidian party politicking generates deep cynicism amongst voters, election turnout is in a nosedive in all democracies, and polls show that professional politicians are amongst the least respected members of society. So successfully does the process turn out bland, lowest-common-denominator lookalikes that Americans voted in almost literally exactly equal numbers for Bush and Gore in November 2000; the result truly might as well have been decided with the toss of a coin. In their panic, most party politicians cling to the security of opinion polls and focus groups, calibrating their policies to produce what ought to be the most popular and vote-winning combination. But voters sense the questions are irrelevant, and the results confine conventional politics to an outdated framework.

Keith Hart put the obvious conclusion especially vigorously: "World society today is at base as rotten as the aristocratic regimes that preceded the modern age. , . .The rule of elites has been restored; state bureaucracy is absolute; and world society is divided into national fragments. There is no popular government anywhere, and most people have forgotten when they last took an active interest in such a possibility."[5]

There is a mass of evidence that politics as usual is indeed rotten, and ripe for revolutionary change. There is the simple fact of the downward trend in electoral turnout in the old democracies, even at a time when many relatively new democracies such as South Africa or the former Soviet bloc countries remind us of the fundamental importance of the right to vote. Even Tony Blair's staggering landslide victory in the UK in 1997, giving Labour the biggest parliamentary majority since 1832, rested on less than 50 percent of the popular vote. George Bush's narrowest of victories in 2000 made him a president for whom only just 50 percent of the scant 50 percent of the electorate that voted (but luckily for him five out of nine Supreme Court justices) had chosen.

Rare is the government that can claim any sort of popular mandate. In many countries other conventional channels of political participation such as trade-union membership or membership of a mass political party have also seen declining numbers. Sociologist Robert

Putnam has traced the diminishing engagement of Americans in a wide range of voluntary associations that involve some kind of formal social engagement with others, from sports clubs to unions.[6] Opinion polls reveal an unusual degree of volatility in voting intentions. They also indicate a profound lack of respect for politicians, along with declining respect for other former authority figures: judges, royal family, doctors, civil servants, and definitely journalists. Instead, the general public would prefer to trust sporting heroes, successful entrepreneurs, or perhaps familiar TV faces like Oprah, people respected as individuals for their achievements or personal qualities rather than simply for their position in society, and people more representative of their broader societies than the ranks of men in gray suits.

Many politicians and technocrats, those traditional governing elites, have a long-standing pessimism about ordinary people and, indeed, about democracy. On the whole they are instinctively against greater democratization. However, many also now have an uneasy feeling that politics as usual cannot continue, when nine out of ten voters say they believe politicians lie and more than half of all young people say they have no interest in politics. In one revealing article, Matthew Taylor, a key New Labour strategist, wrote: "It is hard to ignore the contrast between a market that is dynamic, flexible and creating 100 new choices every day, and a democratic system that is seen as corrupt, incompetent and incapable of articulating let alone delivering real choices."[7] His conclusion was twofold: politicians would have to abandon the command-and-control model (a step that will perhaps prove especially difficult for the New Labour government, often accused of "control freakery"); and would also need to build a persuasive moral case for a different political philosophy, one based on fairness and social cohesion.

Certainly, it will become ever more obvious that command-and-control

> Politics as usual cannot continue, when nine out of ten voters say they believe politicians lie and more than half of all young people say they have no interest in politics.

techniques are technologically redundant. The contrast between market outcomes on the one hand and planned outcomes on the other will become not just hard to ignore but impossible to sustain. Citizens, especially young ones, see no reason at all to do what authority figures tell them. Social disorder and urban violence are one manifestation; on the fringes of society many people have opted out of the formal political and economic system altogether. They can't see what government (in its broadest sense) does for them, and they are perhaps right. But there are many other manifestations, whether it is the many parents in the United States and England who can afford to do so opting to pay for private schooling instead of sending their children to a state school, or the Italians not bothering to vote even though it is supposed to be compulsory, or instead claiming a Padanian passport from the Lega Nord, or a French businessman starting up a company across the Channel in Kent because it is now possible to shop around for governments, or almost everybody in the world avoiding some taxes some of the time. Even when everything is going well and the economy is thriving, governments do not get the credit, as Al Gore discovered to his cost like George Bush Sr. before him, and as Tony Blair started to fear in the approach to the June 2001 UK election. All these are manifestations of the redundancy of politics as usual.

It is starting to change. The Internet era has launched a period of political turmoil, with the "wired" professionals in the vanguard of wide-ranging social and economic change, echoing the role of the middle classes in earlier upheavals. The Western capitalist countries are, with luck, following the former centrally planned countries down the road that leads away from corporatism and centralized bureaucratic control of the economy.

The Wrong Line of Attack

The coming turmoil will bear some resemblance to that earlier episode of revolutionary energy in the late 1960s, as the opposition to the current order is coalescing around an anticapitalist agenda, even though it covers disparate groups ranging from environmental extremists to cultural critics of multinational companies. However, the 1968 movement was fundamentally libertarian and anti-authoritarian, whereas this new millennium movement is in severe danger of becoming the reverse, with a prescriptive agenda for collective action, either led by government or by its own leaders. The profoundly democratic agenda held dear by at least some of that generation of radicals before mine is incomplete. However, today's anticapitalists are already heading for the same mistakes as the now middle-aged leftists who distrusted the democratic urge and opted instead for central control and discipline imposed on others by themselves.

In an article written in 1988, marking the twentieth anniversary of *les évènements*, Anthony Barnett, a prominent British '68er, said: "It was the impulse of modern capitalism itself that had created the conditions which led the young to rebel against their old-fashioned elders. For all our anti-capitalism we were also, if despite ourselves, acting on behalf of the new market forces. We were not the makers but the made."[8] New technologies and the consumerism of an increasingly prosperous society thoroughly undermined the economic planning of the postwar era. It made the young restless and engendered the spirit of '68. After all, it takes either material comfort or sheer desperation to get people out on the streets; run-of-the-mill hard times keep them hard at work instead.

However, the revolutionary spring led the authorities on both sides of the

> Today's anticapitalists are already heading for the same mistakes as the now-middle-aged leftists who distrusted the democratic urge and opted instead for central control and discipline imposed on others by themselves.

Iron Curtain to crack down on those liberalizing forces, at least in the economic if not the social arena, for another twenty years. Paradoxically, it was then Thatcher and Reagan who were able to appropriate them, from the radical right rather than the radical left wing of politics, using the moral case for individual freedom as the basis for economic deregulation, privatization and, tax cuts. And even then they only went partway, confining the liberalization to the economy while sticking to the traditional conservative agenda on social matters.

David Henderson, who used to be the OECD's chief economist, has argued convincingly that the claim there has been a fundamental process of economic liberalization in the past fifteen or twenty years is much overdone. He believes that antiliberal forces have a new vigor in the new millennium, in the coalition of nongovernmental organizations and interest groups opposed to "globalization." In his view the Thatcher and Reagan "revolution" marked only a small tilt of the policy balance toward the liberal economic agenda, with their rolling back of government intervention in some areas countered increasingly by more intervention in areas such as environmental regulation, health and safety measures, and extensions of human rights–style legislation to the social and economic arena. The "new millennium collectivism" (as Henderson described it) is moreover winning widespread public assent for an interventionist approach, one that essentially sees government action or at least some form of regulation from above, not the impersonal forces of economics, as the source of material well-being. "Antiliberal views today are often associated, as in the days of Coleridge, Carlyle, and Ruskin, with hostility to economics and some of its characteristic ways of thinking," Henderson said in a lecture.[9]

Today's anticapitalist movement will, however, thoroughly doom itself if it does not recognize the benefits of technology-powered market forces. Now, as in 1968, it is the dynamic of capitalism itself that is creating the conditions for reform. The trends in the New Capitalism point to liberation from bureaucratic control, from traditional sources of authority, greater democracy, and wider choice. We are looking at the possibility of big improvements in prosperity thanks to the ending of the grip technocratic elites have held on political power in Western democracies since the Second World War. New technologies, especially the Internet, have had a direct impact on many formerly automatic sources of authority. What's more, the economic restructuring and growth stimulated by the wave of technologies are fatally burrowing into the deep and rotting roots of bureaucratic power wherever it clings on.

There is, therefore, a bitter paradox in the fact that the vigorous, Internet-organized opposition movement is focusing its attacks on the very forces that have created the conditions for fundamental political and economic change. Writing about the baby boom rebels of the late 1960s, Douglas Rushkoff notes that they "wanted to change the numbers on the dots so that the lines would be drawn in a different order and the picture would come out different," but they still sought to impose an underlying order, drawing their picture of reality.[10] The same is true of many critics of global capitalism now. They don't trust the people, and they are very sure that they are right. Oliver Cromwell was wary of the certainty of extremists when he pleaded with his own lieutenants: "I beseech you, in the bowels of Christ, think it possible you might be mistaken." It seems the moral is still hard for many idealists to accept.

> Today's anticapitalist movement will thoroughly doom itself if it does not recognize the benefits of technology-powered market forces. Now, as in 1968, it is the dynamic of capitalism itself that is creating the conditions for reform.

There is indeed an extraordinary reluctance amongst many people who consider themselves idealists or at least compassionate campaigners to feel at all optimistic about future prospects for well-being and democracy. Many varieties of pessimism abound. The most common is the breathless Chicken Licken catalogue of economic evils around the world, from desperate poverty in South Asia to shipyard redundancies in the rich West, starvation in debt-laden Africa to that vague sense of insecurity many of us feel about our own prospects. Relatively few of these get beyond the unhappy catalog to present much systematic evidence or rigorous analysis about how and why things are getting worse.

A more serious case was presented by Benjamin Barber, who projected his gloom onto the global canvas as *Jihad versus McWorld*.[11] His hypothesis was that American cultural imperialism manifested as globalism would clash with an alternative political future, tribalism; that alongside globalization we are seeing Balkanization, the disintegration of the nation-state into smaller but culturally homogeneous entities. "The planet is falling precipitately apart and coming reluctantly together at the very same moment." Would the parochial hatreds halt the universalizing markets? Clearly he felt they could: "The passing of communism has torn away the thin veneer of internationalism (workers of the world unite!) to reveal ethnic prejudices that are not only ugly and deep-seated but increasingly murderous." He wrote this at a time when in what used to be Yugoslavia, Communism had passed straight to ethnic murder, so pessimism was only natural. Almost a decade later the nasty ethnic wars are further away from the Anglo-Saxon and European world, in Africa, Indonesia, and Chechnya, so perhaps seem less ominous from our vantage point. Besides, Barber's conclusion was that globalism would eventually dominate: "The ethos of material 'civilization' has not yet encountered an obstacle it has been unable to thrust aside. . . . Jihad may be a last deep sigh before the eternal yawn of McWorld." However, this did not lead him to any sense of optimism; he argued that neither option led to democracy. Both represent antipolitics, the tribalism generally explicitly antidemocratic and centered around an authoritarian leader, the globalism technocratic, a rule by meritocratic elite—just as Marx predicted.

Other flavors of gloom also draw on Marx and especially his vision of capitalism as a global and imperialist force constantly in search of new markets to devour. The activists campaigning against globalization, and its institutional manifestation in bodies like the World Trade Organization, see a battle between the forces of evil, in the shape of big corporations and their friends in government who hop into the silk-lined pockets of business, and of good, in the form of "civil society" groups and allies in government who can resist the lure of champagne and caviar. They demonize markets, business, and indeed current institutions of government, but nevertheless have a bizarre faith that solutions to problems like poverty and inequality will still lie in Washington or Whitehall.

Indeed, although the opposition movement does include true rebels who, like the original punks, don't bother with bourgeois niceties, many of the campaigners actually have a vested interest in centralized governmental solutions. Their own jobs and organizations taxi on the back of the bureaucracy. For example, aid groups are often hired as consultants or technical experts in the field by officials responsible for international development, or they raise part of their funding in public sector grants or via tax relief for charitable donations. They have close personal and professional links with officials responsible for their area of interest, whether it is the environment, trade, or aid. There is some flow of personnel from the "civil society" groups into the bureaucracy, some overlap between campaigning and journalism or think tanks. In short, some of the activists belong to the same professional cadre as the technocrats whose policies they criticize. Their quarrel with the establishment is about the detail of policies, and their position makes them part of the problem rather than shapers of a solution.

A New Vision

There is nothing either radical or realistic in a political agenda that takes the form "the government should do X, not Y" when the people hold government in such contempt. The genuinely subversive course is not to hunt for an alternative big picture that will necessarily involve taming "turbo-capitalism" to a different set of ends, but instead to allow the newly dynamic market forces to uproot established elites. It is already possible for many people in the Western democracies to be radically independent in ways that were unthinkable a decade ago. For a select group in the professional classes, Robert Reich's "symbolic analysts,"[12] it is possible to avoid the conformism of a corporate career and shape a made-to-measure working life, and what's more, one that will be enjoyable because it involves creativity and initiative; to create a wider menu of choice by opting in and out of state-provided health and education; to find easily the information that makes it possible to challenge old priesthoods like the law and medicine; to travel freely around the world, select from a huge variety of goods and services, and so on. Although a minority, this class is sizable and growing. The aim should be to extend such freedoms to as many people as possible, something that will happen as the general level of prosperity, and with it the quality of jobs, increases. And even if this group of privileged workers never becomes anything like a majority, the impact on patterns of work through the entire economy will be the most dramatic since the Industrial Revolution ended the putting-out system and ushered in the factory era. The presumption has started to move against assembly-line hours and control even for the humblest jobs in most Western companies, with flexible and part-time patterns available in an increasing number of workplaces, and an emphasis on results rather than constant oversight as a means of monitoring performance.

> The genuinely subversive course is not to hunt for an alternative big picture that will necessarily involve taming "turbo-capitalism" to a different set of ends, but instead to allow the newly dynamic market forces to uproot established elites.

The dangerous radicals at the OECD have also spotted the opportunity for the overthrow of paternalism: "The firm, for example, has served for a long time as the economic and social crucible for the laws, customs and ancillary government programs of the industrial era," but now in sight are new patterns of employment and supply that will "explode the applicability of yesterday's legal and cultural frameworks."[13] This obviously poses a big challenge to many aspects of government. For example, for much of the twentieth century companies acted for governments as tax collectors and providers of pensions. In the absence of long-term relationships between breadwinners and corporations, that becomes an untenable pattern. Corporate paternalism has in the past tempered the need for direct government regulation of working conditions. It might well be that health and safety rules, minimum wages and conditions, and so on need to be rethought for companies that will look after their core workforce out of self-interest but might now be getting the offices cleaned by illegal immigrants working for a subcontractor.

Building a New Framework

How to reconcile new technologies with society is the principal challenge facing all of us today. Charles Babbage is regarded as one of the ancestors of the computer age. His designs for a Difference Engine and an Analytical Engine are commonly seen as forerunners of the programmable computer and ultimately the microprocessors, although his machines would only have been able to perform the one calculation for which they were hardwired, or rather hard-cogged. They never performed those calculations, however. Despite generous public funding and years of effort, Babbage never built them. There was no working Difference Engine until London's Science Museum built one in 1991. As the writer Francis Spufford explains, Victorian society ensured the machines remained ideas rather than inventions: "Babbage faced tangible and intangible obstacles, both problems with material and problems with ideas. Having conceived a machine some technical stages in advance of his era's power to manipulate metal, he lacked a whole set of supporting technologies for the Engine. . . . Likewise, he could not refer the intellectual endeavor represented by the Engines to any established context of ideas." There was no vocabulary or notation, no canon of procedures, to act as midwife to Babbage's designs, and they remained stillborn.

Every technological system is the offspring of a specific social and intellectual context. If the context is inappropriate, the technological innovation does not take place. It should hardly be necessary to spell this out, as many commentators from Karl Marx onward have made the point, but nevertheless it seems to bear repetition. Society both shapes the dominant technology and is in turn altered by it. The technologies of the industrial age—steam, rail, electricity—were thus intimately intertwined with mass production, the assembly line, and the bureaucratic organization. What, then, is the shape of the society being shaped by the new technologies, the ubiquitous microprocessor, fiber optics, biotech and genetic engineering, new materials, and nanotechnology?

The common response is that the economy and society are atomizing and polarizing. That in place of corporate structures we will see networks, free markets instead of planning, individualism instead of collectivism. These broad generalizations are sometimes challenged, anyway; but it is when the debate focuses on the details that the New Capitalism becomes controversial. And it is a misunderstanding of the implications that I believe makes many of the skeptics want to deny that it exists. For put as baldly as that, it sounds like believers in the "information revolution" also argue for the inevitability of an unappealing vision of the economy and society as no more than a collection of individuals. If governments and the corporation can no longer offer cradle-to-grave security (on the presumption that they once did), then individuals have to look out for number one. If there is no future for the nation-state, things don't look too good for the redistributive welfare state that protects the vulnerable, either. If free markets are better—that is, overwhelmingly more efficient economically—than planned economies, that seems to spell the end for any role for governments in economic management, a matter for regret to the many people who see the postwar era of Keynesian policies as a golden age of growth and stability. In short, the New Capitalism looks like a conservative, free-market political project racing toward a future where some of us will be encased in affluent cocoons of virtual reality with all the latest consumer gizmos, detached from the rest, who will live in an all too grim reality of poverty, violence, and alienation.

Yet this dismal fracturing of society is not inevitable, or even likely, despite the New Capitalism's roots in the neoconservatism of the 1980s. The technological motors of economic change are consistent with a variety of political outcomes. There is nothing ideologically determinate about the economy and society that will be shaped by technical change. I believe that the social and cultural context in which the technologies will come to full fruition, and be able to deliver vastly increased prosperity shared widely around the globe, is actually one in which connections among individuals are stronger, not weaker, than in the past. A fairer society will also prove to be a more prosperous society. But in order to achieve this vision it will be necessary, paradoxically, to shed the traditional center-left obsession with centralized government and paternalistic social engineering and embrace instead decentralization and market solutions. Markets are indeed potential tools of creative destruction, but if they are allowed to operate freely, what they destroy is established privileges and elites, and what they create is opportunity.

This argument goes against the grain of current progressive thinking, which is fundamentally hostile to technology-driven globalization. The global opposition movement for the most part can see many drawbacks and few benefits for everybody outside a narrow, privileged section of the most privileged societies. Neil Postman, Professor of Communications at New York University, set out a question to pose of every new technology, one that is widely cited: what is the problem to which it is a solution? He said in a widely quoted interview: "People who are very enthusiastic about technology are always telling us what it will do for us. They almost never address the question of what it will undo." Wendell Berry, the poet, farmer, and thinker who has had a profound influence on the environmental and anti-globalization movement, has a higher hurdle for assessing any technological innovation. It should "do work that is clearly and demonstrably better than the one it replaces."[14]

However, their challenges are relatively easy to answer. For example, information technology dissipates some, perhaps a lot, of the clouds of uncertainty that shroud business decisions, and will hence reduce costs, economize on the use of scarce resources, and improve customer satisfaction. The genetic revolution holds out the promise of staggering advances in health, longevity, and the quality of life. Like many technical advances in the past, they often answer problems that had not even been framed within the preceding realm of possibility; they are not direct replacements for work that was done before but address different work and satisfy new aims. A better challenge might be: what does this make possible that was not possible before?

> A fairer society will also prove to be a more prosperous society. But in order to achieve this vision it will be necessary, paradoxically, to shed the traditional center-left obsession with centralized government and paternalistic social engineering and embrace instead decentralization and market solutions.

The more interesting question still is the economist's or political scientist's supplementary: to whom does the new technology give wealth and power, and who loses? This is much harder to answer. Highly skilled globe-trotting professionals certainly look like winners, and less skilled manual workers rooted in depressed localities look like losers. At first glance, then, with income inequality as high as at any time in the past century in the most technophilic economies, there is no radical challenge to existing power relations. Nevertheless, the fact that the world economy is in a period of great turbulence that will overturn the existing structures and put power up for grabs, even though there is nothing inevitable about the outcome.

Dissent Has Never Been Easier

One reason for optimism about the real threat the New Capitalism poses to the rich and powerful is the direct impact of the Internet on the ability of anybody to say or broadcast anything. A Web newsletter, the Drudge Report, set in train the chain of events that almost saw Bill Clinton impeached over his affair with Monica Lewinsky. A free file-sharing program, Napster, has probably fatally weakened the business model of the huge music companies and will end their stranglehold on distribution. As detailed earlier, Napster lost in court but spawned many imitators—like the decentralized GNUtella, FreeNet, and OpenNap—before that defeat and, even more important, got the core music audience used to acquiring music in small, cheap packages instead of expensive multitrack CDs. Toppling the leader of the free world, bringing a powerful oligopoly to heel—that's not bad.

There is a growing concern amongst the traditionally libertarian Internet and hacker community about the growing determination of governments to police what had been a free-for-all. For example, there has been conflict over strong encryption, with governments demanding a key copy in order to monitor crime and terrorism. The British government's "RIP" legislation was bitterly condemned by campaigners for its authoritarian requirements on Internet service providers. A French court decided that Yahoo was subject to French law as far as its services to French citizens were concerned and required the company to censor sales of Nazi memorabilia on sites it hosted. The Chinese government has always imposed strict censorship rules on Chinese-language ISPs. So the simple view that the Net is a government-free zone and the ultimate democratic weapon is clearly no longer true, if it ever was.

Nevertheless, the Internet is a force for greater democratization. It is a tool the anticapitalist movement has used with great effectiveness to organize protests and advance debate. The rebellion in Mexico's Chiapas region and dissent in Slobodan Milosevic's Serbia used the Internet extremely effectively as an alternative media outlet, much as revolutionaries at the end of the nineteenth century used illegal printing presses or Soviet dissidents used samizdat literature. Except the Internet is an easier and more powerful weapon of democratic dissent. It's cheap, easy to hide, and taps into an instant global amplification system. Little local difficulties in faraway places are difficult to hide and can become major diplomatic embarrassments. Whereas Mexico's governing PRI might once upon a time have quietly isolated the Chiapas problem, meriting just the occasional short article in a few serious newspapers, the clever use of the Internet and TV by the pipe-smoking, balaclavad sub-commandant Marcos helped bring to an end its long period of rule and bring in a government that opened negotiations with the rebels. Moreover, an example set in one part of the world is widely seen and imitated elsewhere thanks to the globalization of mass media. After the peaceful overthrow of the Milosevic regime in Yugoslavia, Africans in Zimbabwe and the Ivory Coast were inspired to protest against their own undemocratic governments. The Internet and its convergence with television do not guarantee freedom but certainly make opposition more effective. Perhaps even more important, the Internet plants the idea of the possibility of opposition in the minds of the people.

Some people believe any optimism in this respect is naive when the corporate titans like Microsoft, NewsCorp, and TimeWarner are muscling onto the Internet like playground bullies.

The Internet is an easy and powerful weapon of democratic dissent.

Still, I agree with Douglas Rushkoff, who reckons the growth of new media has taken the entire networked media space beyond control and turned it into a natural system. He writes: "The media conglomerates are at the mercy of the market forces they used to stoke." The magnates only make money if they make people happy, and the people are not passive fools.

Building Social Assets

If old frameworks are, at last, being exploded, the urgent question is what new framework can be built in their place. The downfall of vested interests and self-serving elites is in itself a good reason for celebration, and for distrusting the pessimism of many well-meaning critics of current economic trends. But construction is harder than demolition. What sort of future is there to look forward to?

The global opposition movement is still glum about the failure of socialism in such a decisive way in 1989, and pessimistic about a future based on market forces and dynamic capitalism. It is proving very hard to overturn the equation that markets equals right wing, intervention equals left wing. My arguments so far about the irrelevance of conventional government might therefore seem marked out as right wing with the inevitability of algebra.

However, the traditional left- versus right-wing spectrum is indeed redundant. As I have argued in several separate contexts throughout this book, because what goes on inside people's heads is the raw material of the weightless economy, the quality of human relationships is crucial for economic progress, which must be encouraging to anybody, even old left-wingers, who is concerned about the prospects for the have-nots in our societies. The prosperity of the rich and also the merely comfortable is inextricably linked with that of the poor, the outsider, the powerless. Very few of us now have work that is not centered on interactions with other people. A growing proportion have work that demands creativity, communication, and the exchange of complex ideas. This puts a premium on face-to-face contact, on social skills, and on tacit forms of knowledge that cannot be written down and passed on easily. Grotesque urban poverty, a fear of strangers in the street, a run-down physical infrastructure—such conditions do not form the basis for long-term economic success. Diversity is a resource in itself, too, but it obviously puts greater demands on the social fabric, whether within a company or in the society at large. The very process of globalization cre-

The prosperity of the rich and also the merely comfortable is inextricably linked with that of the poor, the outsider, the powerless.

ates new sources of tension and conflict, which we have to find ways to manage.

The New Capitalism is, in short, a high-trust economy. Technological sophistication has to go hand in hand with more robust social relations. The social context of the market has always mattered for economic outcomes, but now it matters as never before. An accumulation of social capital is just as essential as a stock of physical or financial capital. Prime Minister Margaret Thatcher notoriously declared: "There is no such thing as society." On the contrary, society feeds directly into the bottom line, and one of the reasons Mrs. Thatcher's own economic reforms have not yet resulted in improved productivity and growth in the UK, where living standards remain below those in many other industrialized countries, is the neglect of social capital for two decades.

It did not take ardent free-market economists to overlook the importance of the social context of the markets. Here is one example of the way conventional economics has often skated over society. Reflecting on the gasoline protests in the autumn of 2000, when truckers' blockades of fuel depots brought Britain and other European countries to a halt, John Kay argued there was an informative contrast between the popular solution to shortages and the typical economist's reaction. An economist would see a higher price as the best rationing mechanism, any other means involving inefficiencies and arbitrary decisions; but petrol fuel companies were roundly condemned for raising pump prices. The people preferred rationing and prioritizing for health workers and other key staff. Kay concluded that the people were right. The capitalist system requires legitimacy if it is to deliver efficiency. Although individual incentives are important, so is social solidarity, and sometimes there is a better economic case for boosting social solidarity. "If you want a genuine smile on the face of the fast food server or the flight attendant, it has to come from a belief in the organization and its values rather than obedience to the company training manual," he wrote. Such social assets, part of the company's and community's stock of social capital, are in fact economic assets as well.

In one sense Mrs. Thatcher had every excuse for her foolish conclusion. The mainstream of the economics profession has for most of the postwar era been obsessed with the need to avoid politics, to avoid the analysis of institutions, to avoid psychology. This is a generalization—there are naturally very many honorable exceptions. Nevertheless, the typical jobbing economist will have had professional training in the core of the subject that involved no study of history or political economy. It will have been highly technical, often involving no basic practicalities like looking at data series or knowing the size of GDP. It was an eye-opener for me, starting work after specializing in econometrics (in other words, how to apply economic theory to real-world data) at graduate school, to discover that the first thing my experienced colleagues did in any assignment was to plot simple graphs of the figures they were studying. That would not only reveal normal data-entry errors but also show events. Political dramas, such as the miners strike, the Gulf War, a change of government, or a petrol crisis often manifest themselves forcefully in the economy.

New Capitalism is forcing politics and economics back into their traditional embrace because the potential spurt forward in economics growth and living standards is being driven by new technologies. As shown in the earlier chapters, the implementation of a new technology is no easy matter. It involves far-reaching reorganization of the working life of individuals, of the internal structures of companies, and of the framework of government. It requires additional investments, relocations, different skills and inputs. To make any predictions about the future of the economy therefore demands analysis of social and political trends.

In future the health of the economy will depend to an unprecedented degree on social solidarity and political maturity. An increasingly unequal and divisive or an authoritarian and elitist society cannot support a high-trust economy. The more sophisticated a technological system, the more sophisticated the society in which it is embedded. Often specific technologies exported to developing countries are described as appropriate, meaning they are simple enough to be used in a context in which workers are not highly skilled, perhaps not even literate, or perhaps where there is an erratic supply of power or other weaknesses in the infrastructure. The new wave of technologies are highly demanding in this sense. While some can substitute for mundane and repetitive work, the emerging technological system requires a very highly skilled workforce alongside the machines. It needs an advanced telecommunications infrastructure.

> New capitalism is forcing politics and economics back into their traditional embrace . . . In future the health of the economy will depend to an unprecedented degree on social solidarity and political maturity.

More subtly, it necessitates extremely high-trust relationships. As earlier chapters showed, the increasingly weightless nature of economic activity makes it next to impossible to do business on the basis of externally monitored written contracts. While a fair and effective legal framework is as important as ever in a market economy, most business and working relationships can only be sustained on the basis of one person's assessment of another. No contract can specify in detail the quality of a smile or escape the need for a subjective judgment about whether a piece of software or the design of a car is up to scratch. At one end of the high-tech spectrum, it is next to impossible to reach an absolute judgment about the quality of someone's work when the best ideas in industrial design or biological research might come when someone is chatting over a cappuccino. At the other, we all can tell the difference between the formulaic "have a nice day" greeting and a genuinely felt welcome in a restaurant, but could you write it down in such a way that an employer or customer could monitor the quality of service day in, day out? Relationships between employers and employees, between suppliers and customers, will in the future have to be based on reputation and mutual respect.

The point applies no matter what examples you look at. If a manufacturer in the United States or Europe wants to source products from one of the Asian countries, a decision made possible by modern communications, the executives making the choice will have to trust the supplier more than one close to home. It is a new and unfamiliar relationship, one the corporation probably would not risk at all without a compelling cost advantage. But if they do go ahead, it will involve them in a challenging process of understanding another culture and becoming familiar with the workforce and the wider society. What's more, in order to achieve the consistency and quality Western consumers require, there will be limits to the degree of exploitation involved. I would not want to push this point too far because there are certainly abuses; but many multinationals do provide better than local pay and conditions, not out of altruism, nor even the potential for embarrassment thanks to vigilant campaigners, but because the bottom line is that even cheap goods don't sell on price alone. There is more to making a profit in any Western market than piling goods high and selling them cheap. The silicon chips have to be fault free, and the sneakers can't fall apart if they are being sold for sixty dollars.

Take another example. In the United States and Europe alike predicted employment growth that falls into two broad camps. There will be big increases in demand for highly skilled professionals and for people to fill person-to-person service jobs such as nursing or serving in restaurants. The pattern has given rise to fears that the

> While a fair and effective legal framework is as important as ever in a market economy, most business and working relationships can only be sustained on the basis of one person's assessment of another.

workforce will polarize between the extremely well paid and highly educated on the one hand and the low-paid high school dropouts on the other. This fear overlooks the basic economic principle that what is in short supply will see its price rise, suggesting pay levels will eventually increase at the low-income end of the job market. But apart from that, it is not at all obvious that "low skill" jobs will stay that way. With an aging population and a chronic shortage of caring staff, caring is likely to be redefined as a skill. Our understanding of "skill" is fossilized by the needs of the Old Economy and what was in short supply there, which was brain as opposed to muscle. It isn't a matter of more of the same in the New Capitalism, now that we have gone well beyond mechanizing tasks requiring pure brawn. What's scarce now are qualities like creativity and imagination, compassion and warmth, insight and attention. If anything, pure academic intelligence, the IQ sort of skill, is in oversupply.

The human element tends to be overlooked by techno-enthusiasts. The most thoughtful certainly appreciate the importance of repeated relationships. For example, one of Kevin Kelly's ten "New Rules for the New Economy" is: "Start with technology, end with trust." He continues: "The central economic imperative of the New Economy is to amplify relationships."[15] However, few go on to make the point that nurturing individual economic relationships has a social spillover. Better individual relationships make for a better and more cohesive society, not an atomized and ruthless one. A network economy is defined not by the existence of lots of individual "nodes" but rather by the fact that they are connected to each other. If the connections fail, the whole economy suffers.

Another way of saying this is that social capital is an economic asset. Soci-

> Our understanding of "skill" is cemented by the needs of the Old Economy and what was in short supply there, which was brain as opposed to muscle. . . . What's scarce now are qualities like creativity and imagination, compassion and warmth, insight and attention.

eties that are peaceful, where the rule of law is both strong and accepted as fair, with little corruption and reasonably democratic government, are, on the whole, the most prosperous. The poorest countries are those with civil wars, corrupt dictators, and weak or nonexistent law of contract. Looking forward, future gains in prosperity will depend on investing in social capital. This is necessary at a pretty basic level in the very poor countries. In the advanced economies, building social capital will point us well away from the dog-eat-dog caricature of the New Capitalism painted by its critics. Although weightless trends seem to point to vastly greater inequalities of income and wealth, to growing polarization between neighbors, and a socially divisive awareness of greater unfairness thanks to the ubiquitous media, these are the transitional consequences of a failure to analyze the impact of new technologies. They are not the inevitable outcome.

In fact, just as the industrial economy based on mass production had to create mass consumption, the New Capitalism based on networks of supply and demand will have to shape its own consumer society. Henry Ford realized that assembly-line workers had to be paid enough to be able to afford his cars. There was no point being able to churn out automobiles more efficiently and cheaply if there was no market for them.

In his great blast against the moral poverty of consumerism, John Kenneth Galbraith makes the same point in a more jaundiced way: "Economic theory has managed to transfer the sense of urgency in meeting consumer need that once was felt in a world where more production meant more food for the hungry, more clothing for the cold, more houses for the homeless, to a world where increased output satisfies the craving for more elegant automobiles, more exotic food, more erotic clothing, more elaborate entertainment—indeed, for the entire modern range of sensuous, edifying and lethal desires."[16] The key element of economic theory, which has translated into our interpretation of increased production as economic progress, is the assumption that consumer wants are never sated.

In the advanced economies, building social capital will point us well away from the dog-eat-dog caricature of the New Capitalism painted by its critics.

Even if true, it is clear that they evolve, though. Since Galbraith published *The Affluent Society* in 1958, what consumers value has shifted from stuff to intangible qualities like design, image, ease of use, and quality of service. In other words, it is precisely what is not easily mass producible that adds most value now to a product or service. Customers want what has been customized.

Future productivity and growth will therefore depend on treating customers as individuals but in a way that strengthens relationships rather than atomizing them. This is why "customer relationship management" has become one of the new buzzwords amongst management gurus. To keep high-value customers you have to know more about them specifically. A great example is Amazon's list of suggested titles for repeat visitors to the site, based on their past purchases and on what other, similar customers have bought.

The companies that turn out, in a century's time, to have been the GM and Ford of the New Capitalism will have created the consumer base for the "mass customization" that is taking the place of mass production. As the term suggests, it will be a consumer base where affluence is widely spread, not confined to a small elite. And if consumers value wide choice, distinctiveness, and creative design, that's what they will get—and also what they will provide as members of the workforce serving other consumers. For they are the same people. Companies will be unable to meet the demands of the market without a workforce equipped with the necessary skills and attributes, and they will not be able to realize the full potential of all the new technologies unless demand and supply both become increasingly weightless.

One of the metaphors most used by apologists for the status quo is that a rising tide lifts all boats. In other words, it is fine to ignore concerns about inequality as long as there is economic growth, because everybody will gain and poverty will fall in absolute terms even if the poorest are doing worse compared to the richest in relative terms. The metaphor is misplaced, however. We are all in the same boat. And it will not travel as far as it might if those on one side are thriving to a far greater degree than those on the other side.

Go with the Tide

This analysis suggests a more powerfully radical philosophy than that of the global opposition movement, which the BBC's political editor Andrew Marr memorably described as "a ragged worldwide heckle against science-driven, free-trading consumerism." The philosophical battle has two frontiers, neither new. One is the Enlightenment clash of rationalism against romanticism. The hecklers represent the modern romantic movement, pessimistic about the potential of technology to improve the human lot, despite all the technological gains of the intervening century. They see the global turbo-economy of free markets and continuing growth as a true heir to Frankenstein's monster. The other frontline is the perpetual conflict between the power of established elites and the claims of the powerless.

The interests of the rich and powerful do not align neatly with the spread of new technologies. On the contrary, dramatic technical change alters the importance of different resources. So, just as the importance of physical and financial capital challenged the economic role of land in production and in the end fatally undermined the position of the landed aristocracy, the importance of human and social capital in the next century will rival finance and machines, and topple the technocratic and bureaucratic elite. The command- and-control structure of all economies, Communist and capitalist, in the era after the Second World War, infantilized the masses and thereby confirmed the members of the elite in their pessimism about popular attitudes and capabilities.

The highly individualist philosophy of the Thatcher and Reagan revolutions, intertwined with the economic vigor seeded by the new set of technologies, tapped into a deep vein of popular resentment with political, professional, and business leaders. Both leaders, although truly detested by their political opponents, were far more popular than subsequent governments. They changed the political climate with their attacks—no matter how hypocritical or narrowly focused—on big government and old hierarchies. Reagan crystallized a distrust of the elite within the Washington beltway, a distrust that had less to do with voters' judgments on tax and spending policies than their diminishing tolerance for being told what to do by official functionaries. Thatcher similarly tapped into the fact that people were fed up with officious intrusions into their lives, such as local councils instructing tenants what color to paint their front doors. No wonder her "right to buy" program of council house sales was popular. The masses really were revolting, in a quiet but persistent way.

The deregulation of the U.S. and to a lesser extent UK economies during the 1980s unleashed the technological forces that mean bureaucratic rule is over. The political impact of the New Capitalism ought to be welcome indeed to anybody who is a true democrat with faith in the ordinary people of this planet. It would be a mistake of the highest order to allow the old elites to hijack the new technologies to preserve their wealth and power, on the false assumption that economic trends are an obstacle rather than a weapon, or are nothing more than a manifestation of American imperialism.

So far the spurt of improved productivity and growth has been an entirely American phenomenon. That is unlikely to continue, however. A slowdown or even recession in the United States in the wake of collapsing high-tech share prices will go a long way toward eliminating smug expressions of manifest American economic superiority. Equally, it is one of the beneficial side effects of the 2000 presidential coup by George Bush and the Republican establishment that no longer will Americans be able to lecture other nations about how to do democracy without being greeted with derision. This creates an opening for other countries to find their own paths to the future.

It would be a mistake of the highest order to allow the old elites to hijack the new technologies to preserve their wealth and power, on the false assumption that economic trends are an obstacle rather than a weapon, or are nothing more than a manifestation of American imperialism.

The staggering technical advances will not come to a halt even if it does become much harder to raise finance for investment. The ups and downs of the business cycle will not eliminate the deep underlying trends. Nevertheless, the evolution of the economy will at last come to be seen as a more nuanced process, with complicated interactions among technology, society, and economy. The New Economy is not a steamroller flattening all countries into an inevitable uniformity any more than the Old Economy was. But just as the industrial era meant there were common features shared by all the capitalist countries and the planned economies as well, a new set of commonalities is emerging.

The time has come to finish off the job begun by radicals in the late 1960s. Their push for root and branch reform failed. The widespread social reforms like the women's and civil rights movements did amount to a genuine cultural revolution. They created in the Western democracies a personal liberalism that eventually undermined the respect for traditional paternalistic authorities, the old social order. For all their faults, Western societies are today more tolerant, fairer, and more diverse places than they used to be. The 1960s also opened the way to the radical right-wing economic deregulation that, however limited, gave the United States and UK a beachhead from which to attack corporatist and bureaucratic structures. The Reagan and Thatcher reforms were narrow in scope, but that has turned out to be enough in the long run. Although the traditional institutions of liberal democracy look frail, partly as a result of that narrowly focused economic liberalism, which has undermined social consensus and a sense of cohesion, the values of tolerance and fairness, of opportunity and aspiration, are far more deeply embedded than they were in 1968.

For a quarter century after the events of 1968, a powerful elite reaction against the radical rebellion locked the Western democracies in a social and economic ice age. It was disastrous. It caused mass unemployment, stagnant growth, high inflation; it led to fatal cracks in postwar structures like the Bretton Woods system, which resulted in a financial and banking crisis; it halted industrial restructuring and set innovation back a decade. The economic growth that did occur during the 1970s and early 1980s was destructive, wasteful of human and natural resources, and spending large amounts of existing social capital as whole communities and social groups were written off as expendable in order to preserve the old hierarchies of power. We have a second chance, and now is the time to grasp it.

Bibliography

AKERLOF, George. "Social Distance and Social Decisions." *Econometrica* 65 (1997):1005–1027.

ALESINA, Alberto, and R. Perotti. "The Political Economy of Growth: A Review of the Literature." *World Bank Economic Review* 8 (1994):4.

ATKINSON, A.B. "Equity Issues in a Globalizing World: The Experience of OECD Countries." Paper given at IMF Conference, 8-9 June 1998.

AUDRETSCH, David, and Maryann Feldman. "Spillovers and the Geography of Innovation and Production." *American Economic Review* 86, no. 3 (1996):630–640.

BARBER, Benjamin. "Jihad versus McWorld." *The Atlantic Monthly*, March 1992. Archived at http://www.theatlantic.com.

BARNETT, Anthony. "The Old Regime in a New Guise." *The Guardian* (London), 2 May 1988.

BAYLEY, Stephen. "The Power and the Glory." *The Independent* (London), 30 March 2000, review page 1.

BERMAN, Marshall. "Blue Jay Way." Available at http://www.dissent-magazine.org/archive/wi00/ berman.html.

BERRY, Wendell. *What are People For?* North Point Press, 1990.

BOLTHO, Andrea, and Gianni Toniolo. "The Twentieth Century." *Oxford Review of Economic Policy* 15, no. 4 (winter 1999).

BOSKIN, M., et al., "Consumer Prices, the Consumer Price Index, and the Cost of Living." *Journal of Economic Perspectives* 12 (winter 1998):3–26.

BOWLES, Samuel. "'Social Capital' and Community Governance." Working paper, University of Massachusetts. Available at http://www.unix.oit. umass.edu/~bowles/papers/.Socap.pdf.

BRAND, Stewart. *The Clock of the Long Now*: Weidenfeld and Nicolson, 1999.

BRESNAHAN, Timothy, Erik Brynjolfsson, and Lorin Hitt. "Information Technology, Workplace Organization, and the Demand for Skilled Labor: Firm Level Evidence." NBER working paper no. 7136, May 1999.

BRONSON, Po. *The Nudist on the Late Shift*: Random House/Secker & Warburg, 1999.

BROOKES, Martin, and Zaki Wahhaj. "The Shocking Economic Effect of B2B." Goldman Sachs Global Economics Paper, 3 February 2000.

——. "Is the Internet Better Than Electricity?" Goldman Sachs Global Economics Paper, 20 July 2000.

BRYNJOLFSSON, Erik, and Lorin Hitt. "Computing Productivity: Are Computers Pulling Their Weight?" Working paper, MIT Sloan School of Management, January 2000.

——. "Beyond Computation: Information Technology, Organizational Transformation, and Business Performance." *Journal of Economic Perspectives* 14, no. 4 (fall 2000):23–48.

CASSIDY, John. "The Next Thinker: The Return of Karl Marx." *The New Yorker*, 20–27 October 1997, 251.

CASTELLS, Manuel. *The Information Age*. Vols. I–III. Blackwell, 1996–98.

CLARKE, Arthur C. *2001: A Space Odyssey*. Reprint, Penguin, 2001.

COX, Michael, and Richard Alm. "The Right Stuff (But The Wrong National Statistics)." Annual Report, Federal Reserve Bank of Dallas, 1998.

COYLE, Diane. *The Weightless World*: Capstone, 1997.

——. *Governing the World Economy*: Polity Press, 2000.

CRAFTS, Nicholas. "Globalization and Growth in the 20th Century." IMF Working Paper WP/00/44, March 2000.

——. "Forging Ahead and Falling Behind: The Rise and Relative Decline of the First Industrial Nation." *Journal of Economic Perspectives* 12, no. 2 (spring 1998).

——. "The Human Development Index and Changes in Standards of Living: Some Historical Comparisons." *European Review of Economic History* I (1997): 299–322.

DAVID, Paul. "Computer and Dynamo: The Modern Productivity Paradox in a Not-too-distant Mirror." In Technology and Productivity, OECD 1991.

——. "Digital Technology and the Productivity Paradox: After Ten Years, What Has Been Learned?" Paper for U.S. Department of Commerce conference, 25–26 May 1999.

DAVID, Paul, and Gavin Wright. "Early 20th Century Productivity Dynamics: An Inquiry into the Economic History of Our Ignorance." Discussion Paper no. 33 in Economic and Social History, University of Oxford, October 1999.

DAVIS, Erik. *TechGnosis*. New York: Harmony Books, 1998.

DELONG, J. Bradford. "How Fast Is Modern Economic Growth?" Federal Reserve Bank of San Francisco Weekly Letter, 6 October 1998. Available at http://econ161.berkeley.edu/.

da SOTO, Hernando. *The Mystery of Capital: Why Capitalism Triumphs in the West and Fails Everywhere Else*: Bantam, 2000.

DIAMOND, Jared. *Guns, Germs, and Steel*: Jonathan Cape, 1997.

DICKENS, Charles. *Hard Times*. First published 1854.

DOLLAR, David, and Aart Kray. "Growth Is Good for the Poor." World Bank working paper, March 2000. Available at www.worldbank.org/research.

DORE, Ronald. *Stock Market Capitalism: Welfare Capitalism: Japan and Germany versus the Anglo-Saxons*: Oxford University Press, 2000.

DRAKULIC, Slavenka. *How We Survived Communism and Even Laughed*. 1988. Reprint: Hutchinson, 1992.

DRUCKER, Peter. *Management Challenges for the 21st Century*. Oxford/Woburn: Butterworth-Heinemann, 1999.

ECO. Umberto. *Travels in Hyper-reality*,

FAITH, Nicholas. *The World the Railways Made*: Bodley Head, 1990.

FUJITA, Paul Krugman, and Anthony Venables. *Spatial Economics*: MIT Press, 1999.

FEENBERG, Daniel, and James Poterba. "The Income and Tax Share of Very High Income Households 1960–95." *American Economic Review* 90, no. 2 (May 2000):264–270.

FOX, Robert. "The Dot-com Generation Won't Fight." *New Statesman*, 5 June 2000.

FRIEDMAN, Thomas. *The Lexus and the Olive Tree*. New York: Harper Collins, 2000.

FUKUYAMA, Francis. *Trust*. 1995.

——. "Social Capital and Civil Society." IMF Working Paper WP/00/74, April 2000.

FUSSELL, Paul. *The Great War and Modern Memory*. Oxford University Press, 1975.

GALBRAITH, J. K. *The Affluent Society*. First published 1958.

GERLERNTER, D. H. *Machine Beauty: Elegance and the Heart of Technology*: Basic Books, 1999.

GIDDENS, Anthony. *The Third Way*: Polity Press, 1998.

GLAESER, Edward, Hedi Kallal, Jose Scheinkman, and Andrei Schleifer. "Growth in Cities." *Journal of Political Economy* 100, no. 6 (December 1992):1126–52. GLAESER, Edward, Bruce Sacerdote, and Jose Scheinkman. "Crime and Social Interactions." *Quarterly Journal of Economics* 111, no.2 (1996):508–48.

GLAESER, Ed. "The Future of Urban Research." Working paper, Harvard University, September 1999.

GLAESER, Ed, Jed Kolko, and Albert Saiz. "Consumer City." Working paper no. 7790, National Bureau of Economic Research, July 2000.

GLEICK, James. *Faster*. New York: Little Brown, 1999.

GOLDIN, Claudia, and Lawrence Katz. "The Origins of Technology-Skill Complementarity." *Quarterly Journal of Economics* CXIII, no. 3 (August 1998):693–732.

GORDON, Robert. "U.S. Economic Growth since 1870: One Big Wave?" *American Economic Review Papers and Proceedings* 89, no. 2 (1999):123–28.

——. "Does the 'New Economy' Measure Up to the Great Inventions of the Past?" *Journal of Economic Perspectives* 14, no. 4 (fall 2000):49–74.

GRAHAM, Carol, and Stefano Pettinato. "Hardship and Happiness." *World Economics* I, no. 4 (October–December 2000):73–112.

GRAHAM, Gordon. *The Internet://A Philosophical Inquiry*: Routledge, 1999.

GREENSPAN, Alan. "Information, Productivity, and Capital Investment." Business Council, Boca Raton, Florida. Available at http://www.bog.frb.fed.us/BoardDocs/Speeches/1999/199910282.htm.

——. Speech to National Community Reinvestment Coalition, 22 March 2000. Available at http://www.bog.frb.fed.us/BoardDocs/Speeches/2000/20000322.htm

——. "Structural Change in the New Economy." National Governors' Association annual meeting, 11 July 2000. Available at http://www.federalreserve.gov/BoardDocs/Speeches/2000/20000711.htm.

HALL, Robert. "Struggling to Understand the Stock Market." 2001 Ely Lecture, American Economic Association.

————. "e-capital: The Link Between the Stock Market and the Labor Market in the 1990s." Brookings Papers on Economic Activity, 2001.

HALL, Robert, and Chad Jones. "Why Do Some Countries Produce So Much More Output per Worker Than Others?" National Bureau of Economic Research working paper 6564, March 1998.

HALTIWANGER, John, and Ron Jarmin. "Measuring the Digital Economy." Draft presented to Department of Commerce conference, May 1999.

HARBERGER, Arnold. "A Vision of the Growth Process." *American Economic Review* 88, no. 1 (March 1998):1–32.

HARDING, Jeremy. "The Uninvited: Refugees at the Rich Man's Gate." Profile Books and *London Review of Books*, 2000.

HART, Keith. *Money in an Unequal World: Keith Hart and His Memory Bank*: TEXERE, 2001.

HART, Oliver, and John Moore. "Property Rights and the Nature of the Firm." *Journal of Political Economy* 98, no. 6 (1990):1119–58.

HELD, David, David Goldblatt, and Jonathan Perraton. *Global Transformations*: Polity Press, 1999.

HELLER, Joseph. *Catch-22*. First published 1962.

HELPMAN, Elhanan, ed. *General Purpose Technologies and Economic Growth*: MIT Press, 1998.

HENDERSON, David. "Anti-Liberalism." Wincott Lecture 2000.

HOBSBAWM, Eric. *The Age of Capital*. First published 1975.

HOLMSTROM, Bengt, and John Roberts. "The Boundaries of the Firm Revisited." *Journal of Economic Perspectives* 12, no. 4 (fall 1998):73–94.

HONG, Lu, and Scott Page. "Diversity and Optimality." Working paper, October 1998. Available at Los Alamos Diversity Office Web site.

HORROBIN, David. "Innovation in the Pharmaceutical Industry." *Journal of the Royal Society of Medicine* 93 (July 2000):341–45.

HUXLEY, Aldous. *Brave New World*. First published 1932.

INTERNATIONAL LABOR ORGANIZATION. *Key Indicators of the Labor Market*. Geneva, 1999.

JAY, Mike, and Michael Neve, eds. *1900*: Penguin, 1999.

JORGENSON, Dale, and Kevin Stiroh. "Raising the Speed Limit: U.S. Economic Growth in the Information Age." Forthcoming Brookings Papers on Economic Activity.

————. "Information Technology and Growth." *American Economic Association Papers and Proceedings* 89, no. 2 (May 1999)

JOY, Bill. "Why the Future Doesn't Need Us. *Wired*, April 2000. Available at http://www.wired.com/wired/archive/8.04/joy_pr.html.

KAKU, Michio. *Visions*: Oxford University Press, 1998.

KANE, Pat. "Play for Today." *The Observer* (London), 22 October 2000.

KATZ, Lawrence. "Technological Change, Computerization, and the Wage Structure." Paper presented at Commerce Department Conference, 25–26 May 1999.

KEANE, John. *Reflections on Violence*. Verso, 1996.

KEILLER, Patrick. "To Change Life We Must First Change Space." *The Independent* (London), 6 March 2000, 19.

KELLY, Kevin. *Out of Control*: Addison Wesley, 1994.

———. *New Rules for the New Economy*. Fourth Estate, 1998.

KENNY, C. "Does Growth Cause Happiness, or Does Happiness Cause Growth?" *Kyklos* 52, no. I (1999):3–26.

KING, Mervyn. "The Tax System in the 21st Century." Bank of England working paper, September 1996.

KLEIN, Naomi. *No Logo*, 2000.

KREITZMAN, Leon. *The 24 Hour Society*: Profile Books, 1999.

KRUGMAN, Paul. *Geography and Trade*: MIT Press, 1991.

———. *Pop Internationalism*: MIT Press, 1996.

KURZWEIL, Ray. *The Age of Spiritual Machines*: Orion, 1999.

LaFEBER, Walter. *Michael Jordan and the New Global Capitalism*: W. W. Norton, 1999.

LANDES, David. *The Wealth and Poverty of Nations*: Little, Brown, 1998.

LA PORTA, Rafael, Florencio Lopez de Silanes, Andrei Shleifer, and Robert Vishny. "Trust in Large Organizations." *American Economic Association Papers and Proceedings* (May 1997):333–38.

LEADBEATER, Charles. *The Rise of the Social Entrepreneur*. Demos, 1997.

LESSIG, Lawrence. "Reclaiming a Commons." May 1999.

———. "Open Code and Open Societies." June 2000.

LEWIS, Michael. "Boom." *Business* 2.0, April 2000, 192–202.

MACKENZIE, Donald. *Knowing Machines*: MIT Press, 1996.

MARSHALL, Alfred. *Principles of Economics*. First published 1870.

MARTIN, John. "The Idea Is More Important Than the Experiment." *The Lancet* 356 (September 2000):934–37.

MARX, Karl. *The Eighteenth Brumaire of Louis Bonaparte*. First published 1869.

MATHIAS, Peter. *The First Industrial Nation: An Economic History of Britain 1700-1914*: Methuen, 1969, 1983.

MICHALSKI, Wolfgang. "The Challenges for Economic and Social Policy at the Turn of the 21st Century. "Unpublished working paper, October 1999.

NAUGHTON, John. *A Brief History of the Future*: Weidenfeld and Nicholson, 1999.

NETZ, Reviel. "Barbed Wire." *London Review of Books*, 20 July 2000, 30–35.

NEW YORK TIMES. The Downsizing of America, 1996.

NORDHAUS, W. "Do Real Output and Real Wage Measures Capture Reality?"In *The Economics of New Goods*, edited by T, Bresnahan and D. Raff, 26–69. Chicago: University of Chicago Press, 1997.

OECD. "A New Economy?: The Changing Role of Innovation and Information Technology in Growth." Background paper, June 2000.

——. "Information Technology Outlook." May 2000.

——. "Structural Factors Driving Industrial Growth." Background paper for Business and Industry Policy Forum, April 2000.

——. "Differences in Economic Growth Across the OECD in the 1990s: The Role of Innovation and Information Technologies." Background paper, February 2000.

OLINER, Stephen, and Daniel Sichel. "The Resurgence of Growth in the Late 1990s: Is Information Technology the Story." *Journal of Economic Perspectives* 14, no. 4 (fall 2000):3–22.

OLSON, Mancur. *The Rise and Decline of Nations: Economic Growth, Stagflation and Social Rigidities*. New Haven: Yale University Press, 1982.

ORMEROD, Paul. *Butterfly Economics*: Faber & Faber, 1998.

O'ROURKE, P. J. *Eat the Rich*: Picador, 1998.

OSWALD, Andrew. "Happiness and Economic Performance." *Economic Journal* 107 (November 1997):1815–31.

OURSLER, Tony. *Introjection*: Williams College Museum of Art, 1999.

PERRY BARLOW, John. "The Economy of Ideas." *Wired 2.03*, March 1994.

PROUDMAN, James, and Stephen Redding. "Openness and Growth." Bank of England, 1997.

PUTNAM, Robert. *Bowling Alone: The Collapse and Revival of American Community*: Simon & Schuster, 2000.

QUAH, Danny Tyson. "The Invisible Hand and the Weightless Economy." Lecture at Centre for Economic Performance, London School of Eco-

nomics, March 1996. Available at http://www.lse.ac.uk/~economics
/quahCHK.

——. "Policies for the Weightless Economy." Social Market Foundation,
April 1998.

REICH, Robert. *The Work of Nations*: Simon & Schuster, 1991.

RIFKIN, Jeremy. *The Age of Access*: Penguin, 2000.

ROMER, Paul. "Increasing Returns and Long Run Growth." *Journal of Political Economy* 94, no. 5 (October 1986):1002–37.

——. "Endogenous Technical Change." *Journal of Political Economy* 98,
no. 5, part 2 (October 1990):S71–102.

——. "The Origins of Endogenous Growth." *Journal of Economic Perspectives* 8, no. 1 (winter 1994):3–22.

RUSHKOFF, Douglas. *Children of Chaos*: HarperCollins, 1997.

SAKAIYA, Taichi. "The Knowledge Value Revolution." Paper presented at
OECD Forum 2000, Paris, 27 June 2000.

SCHNEIDER, Friedrich, and Dominik Enste. "Shadow Economies
Around the World: Sizes, Causes and Consequences." IMF Working
Paper 00/26, March 2000.

SCHOR, Juliet. *The Overworked American: The Unexpected Decline of
Leisure*: Basic, 1991.

SCHREYER, Paul. "The Contribution of Information and Communication Technology to Output Growth: A Study of the G7 Countries."
OECD STI working papers, February 2000. Available at http://www.
oecd.org/dsti/sti/prod/sti_wp.htm.

SCHUMPETER, Joseph. *Capitalism, Socialism and Democracy*.

SEELY BROWN, John, and Paul Duguid. *The Social Life of Information*.
Harvard Business School Press, 2000.

SEN, Amartya. "Economic Policy and Equity: An Overview." Paper presented at IMF Conference, 8–9 June 1998.

——. *Development as Freedom*: Oxford University Press, 2000.

SENNETT, Richard. *The Uses of Disorder: Personal Identity and City Life*:
Faber & Faber, 1996.

——. *The Corrosion of Character: The Personal Consequences of Work in
the New Capitalism*: W. W. Norton, 1999.

SHELLEY, Mary. *Frankenstein*. First published 1818.

SHORT, Sandra. "Time Use Data in the Household Satellite Account."
Economic Trends, October 2000, Office for National Statistics.

SHOWALTER, Elaine. *Hystories*. Columbia University Press, 1997.

SICHEL, Daniel. *The Computer Revolution: An Economic Perspective.* Washington, D.C.: Brookings Institute, 1997.

SIEGEL, D., and Zvi Griliches. "Purchased Services, Outsourcing, Computers, and Productivity." In *Output Measurement in the Service Sectors,* edited by Griliches: NBER and University of Chicago Press, 1994.

SIMON, Herbert. *Administrative Behavior.* 4th ed. Free Press, 1997.

SOROS, George. *The Crisis of Global Capitalism.* "Little, Brown, 1999.

SPUFFORD, Francis, and Jenny Uglow, eds. *Cultural Babbage: Technology, Time, and Invention.* Faber & Faber, 1996.

STANDAGE, Tom. *The Victorian Internet.* Phoenix, 1999.

STEPHENSON, Neal. *Cryptonomicon*: William Heinemann, 1999.

SWADE, Doron. *The Cogwheel Brain: Charles Babbage and the Quest to Build the First Computer*: Little, Brown, 2000.

TANZI, Vito. "The Changing Role of the State in the Economy: A Historical Perspective." IMF working paper no. 97/114, 1997.

TAYLOR, Matthew. "Blairite Blues." *Prospect,* May 2000, 40–42.

THOMPSON, E. P. *Time, Work-discipline, and Industrial Capitalism*: Pluto, 1967.

ULLMAN, Ellen. *Close to the Machine*: City Lights, 1997.

UNDP. Human Development Report, 1999.

U.S. DEPARTMENT OF COMMERCE, *Digital Economy 2000.* June 2000.

VARIAN, Hal. "How Much Information?" Available at http://www.sims.berkeley.edu/how-much-info/summary.html.

van ARK, B., and Crafts, N., eds. *Quantitative Aspects of Postwar European Growth*: CEPR and Cambridge University Press, 1996.

WEITZMAN, Martin. "Recombinant Growth." *Quarterly Journal of Economics* CXIII, no. 2 (May 1998):331–60.

WHEEN, Francis. *Karl Marx.* Fourth Estate, 1999.

WILLIAMSON, Oliver E. *The Economic Institutions of Capitalism.* Free Press, 1985.

WORLD BANK. "Attacking Poverty." World Development Report 2000/2001.

WORLD BANK. "High-Quality Growth." Washington, D.C., September 2000.

ZACHARY, G. *Pascal, The Global Me*: Nicholas Brealey, 2000.

Endnotes

Chapter One: The Growth Revolution

1. IMF working paper 00/74.
2. Gordon, 1999.
3. Boltho and Toniolo, 1999.
4. Landes, 1998.
5. Boskin, et al., 1998.
6. Nordhaus, 1997.
7. DeLong, 1998.
8. Cited in David and Wright, 1999.
9. *New York Times Review of Books*, 1987.
10. Crafts, IMF working paper 00/44, 2000.
11. Figures from OECD, 2000, Department of Commerce, 2000.
12. Brynjolfsson & Hitt, January 2000.
13. David, OECD, 1991.
14. John Kay, *How Markets Work*, forthcoming 2002.
15. Speech, 13 June 2000, available at http://www.federalreserve.gov/boarddocs/speeches/2000/20000613.htm
16. OECD, 1990.
17. Oliner and Sichel, 2000.
18. Jorgenson & Stiroh, 1999.
19. Gordon, "Does the New Economy Measure Up . . .," 2000.
20. Standage, 1999.
21. Crafts, 1998.

22. David, 2000.
23. Starting with Paul Romer, JPE 1990.
24. Schreyer, 2000.

Chapter Two: The Technological Recipe

1. David Gelernter
2. 11 July 2000 speech, available at http://www.federalreserve.gov/board-docs/speeches/2000/20000711.htm.
3. Data from OECD, June 2000.
4. David and Wright, 1999.
5. See Helpman, 1998.
6. Speech, 13 June 2000, available at http://www.federalreserve.gov/boarddocs/speeches/2000/20000613.htm.
7. June 2000, p. 71.
8. Kurzweil, 1999.
9. In Jay and Neve, 1999.
10. See Brookes and Wahhaj, February 2000.
11. See Helpman, 1998.
12. Reich, 1991.
13. *Business* 2.0, April 2000.
14. "The Future of the Global Economy: Towards a Long Boom?" OECD, 1999.
15. Ibid.

Chapter Three: The Gathering Clouds

1. "Make-up and other crucial questions." In Drakulic, 1988.
2. See Proudman and Redding, 1997.
3. Olson, 1982, p. 142.
4. "A New Map of the World," *The Economist*, 24 June 2000.
5. Dollar and Kraay, 2000.
6. UNDP Human Development Report, 1999.
7. See Sen, 1998.
8. See Feenberg and Poterba, 2000.
9. "Trade, jobs and wages" in Krugman, 1996.
10. See OECD Employment Outlook, 1999.
11. There is a lengthy discussion of this in my earlier book, *The Weightless World*.

12. Hosbawm, 1975, p. 258.
13. Davis, 1998.
14. Kurzweil, 1999.
15. See Castells, vol. I.
16. Leonard Cohen, *The Future*, Columbia Records, 1992.
17. Greenspan, "Structural Change in the New Economy," 2000. Available at http://www.federalreserve.gov/BoardDocs/Speeches/2000/20000711.htm
18. See *The Great Disruption*, chapter one.

Chapter Four: Vanishing Borders

1. LRB, 20 July 2000.
2. See Krugman, and Fujita, Krugman, and Venables, 1999.
3. In Drucker, 1999, p. 63.
4. Romer, 1990.
5. *Consilience*, p. 300.
6. Cited by Quah, 1998.
7. See Audretsch and Feldman, 1996.
8. In Seely Brown and Duguid, 2000, p. 161.
9. OECD, May 2000.
10. Vol. 1, p. 393ff.
11. See Glaeser, Sacerdote, and Scheinkman, 1996.
12. Da Soto, 2000, p. 67.
13. IMF WP 23/00.
14. Keith Hart, 2000, p. 107.
15. See World Development Report 2000/2001.
16. Figures from Held, Goldblatt, and Perraton, 1999, Fig 6.1.
17. Harding, 2000, p. 75.
18. In fact, the center took geographical inequality to an absurd extreme. Unable to tell the difference between inmates and visitors, the guards forced the former to sit on a different color of chair than the latter. The detainees became confined to an area no bigger than the seat of a chair.

Chapter Five: Time as Capital

1. Gleick, 1999, p. 230.
2. Kane, 2000.

3. Sennett, 1999.
4. Schor, 1991.
5. The figures are low because averaged over the entire adult population, including all those not working.
6. Interestingly, a separate 1997 survey for the Economic and Social Science Research Council found that while the average woman said she spent less than five hours a year making love, the average man claimed a day and a half.
7. The Futures Foundation, November 2000.
8. Quoted in Jay and Neve, 1999, p. 320.
19. Speech, 11 July 2000.
10. Naughton, 1999, p. 251.
11. Letter to I. McPherson, 13 August 1813.
12. *Deeper*, p. 216.
13. Text famously uses less storage space than images. It is in fact true in a digital sense that a picture is worth a thousand words.
14. Brand, 1999, p. 156.
15. In IMF WP/00/74.
16. Fukuyama, 1995. La Porta, et al., 1997.
17.
18. Bowles, "Social Capital and Community Governance."
19. Marx, 1869.
20. Keith Hart, 2000, p. 297.
21. Ibid, p. 16.
22. Ibid, p.age 259.
23. See chapter 13 of Naughton, 1999.
24. Rifkin, 2000, p. 112.

Chapter Six: Chaos, Control, and Culture in the Information Age

1. In Spufford and Uglow, 1996, p. 47.
2. Ibid, p. 277.
3. Davis, 1998, p. 302.
4. LaFeber, 1999, pp. 128–29.
5. *The Independent*, 2/8/00.
6. October 1999.
7. *The Great Disruption*, p. 12.
8. See Faith, 1990

9. *The Great Disruption*, p. 252.
10. Report by Sheila Jones, *Financial Times* (London), 1 August 2000.
11. Quoted in *The Independent on Sunday Review* (London), 5 November 2000.
12. See Bestor, *Foreign Policy*, November/December 2000.
13. See Vargas Llosa, *Foreign Policy*, January/February 2001.
14. See Rory Cellan-Jones, *Dot Bomb*, 2001.
15. Nigel Andrews, *Financial Times* (London), 31 March 2000.
16. Spufford and Uglow, 1996, p. 80.
17. Rushkoff, 1997, p. 43.
18. In Kelly, 1994.
19. For an introduction, see Ormerod, 1998.

Chapter Seven: The End of Bureaucracy

1. By Francis Wheen.
2. Castells, *The Information Age*, vol. II: *The Power of Identity*, p. 312, 349.
3. Also toilet paper and, bizarrely, deodorants.
4. Showalter, 1997, p. 5.
5. King, 1996.
6. Keith Hart, 2000, p. 310.
7. Henderson, 2000.
8. Kurzweil, 1999, p. 109.
9. *Wired*, http://www.wirednews.com/wired/5.05/netizen_pr.html.
10. Fussell, 1975, p. 7.
11. Keane, 1996, p. 23.
12. Ibid, p. 86.
14. *Hard Times*. It was in 1854 that Dickens mocked, a century and a half ahead of his time, Gradgrind's ideal that education should turn children into fact-processing machines.
15. Speech, 22 March 2000, to the Community Reinvestment Program annual conference.
16. *End of Millennium*, vol. 3, p. 256.
17. Ullman, 1997.
18. Krugman, *Pop Internationalism*, 1996.
19. See Katz, 1999, for survey of findings.
20. Bresnahan, Brynholfsson, and Hitt, 1999.

21. Seely Brown and Duguid, 2000, p. 217.
22. The Quality of Growth, September 2000.
23. Keith Hart, 2000, p. 310.

Chapter Eight: The Corporate Dinosaurs

1. *Journal of Economic Perspectives*, Fall 1998.
2. 8–9 December 2000.
3. Horrobin, 20004. Martin, September 2000.
5. Quoted in *The Observer* (London)"Life" supplement,10 December 2000, p. 56.
6. Quoted on Bloomberg, 9 December 2000.
7. http://www.actis-technology.com
8. *Analysis*, BBC Radio 4, 7 December 2000.
9. "Building a Commons," 20 May 1999.
10. Sennett, 1999, p. 99.

Chapter Nine: The New Politics

1. *The Unbound Prometheus*, p. 7.
2. Bresnahan, Brynholfsson, and Hitt, 1999.
3. Olsen, 1982, p. 145.
4. Speech at the London School of Economics, 2 February 2000.
5. Keith Hart, 2000, p. 66.
6. Putnam, 2000.
7. Taylor, 2000.
8. Barnett, 1988.
9. Henderson, October 2000.
10. Rushkoff, 1997, p. 43.
11. Barber, 1992.
12. *Work and the Wealth of Nations*.
13. 21st century dynamics, OECD.
14. Berry, 1990, p. 172.
15. Kelly, p. 118.
16. Galbraith, 1958, p. 117.

Index